JAMES E. BRASHER

11 DAYS ON THE COLORADO

THE PIVOTAL BATTLE UNFOUGHT

COVER PAINTING BY AMANDA DANNING

AUSTIN, TEXAS

This is Number 4 in the Watson Caufield and
Mary Maxwell Arnold Republic of Texas Series.

© 2024 Texas State Historical Association.
All rights reserved. Printed in the U.S.A.

LIBRARY OF CONGRESS CATALOGING-IN-PUBLICATION DATA

Names: Brasher, James E., author.
Title: Eleven Days on the Colorado: The Pivotal Battle Unfought / by James E. Brasher.
Description: Austin: Texas State Historical Association, [2024]
Includes bibliographical references.
Subjects: LCSH: Houston, Sam, 1793–1863—Military leadership. | Texas—History—Revolution, 1835–1836—Campaigns. | Colorado River (Tex.)—History, Military—19th century. | BISAC: BIOGRAPHY & AUTOBIOGRAPHY / Historical | HISTORY / North America
Classification: LCC F390 .B734 2024 | DDC 976.4/03—dc23/eng/20240824
LC record available at https://lccn.loc.gov/2024038048
Identifiers: LCCN 2024038048 | ISBN 9781625110770 (paperback) | ISBN 9781625110787 (ebook)

Interior and cover illustrations by Amanda Dunning
Maps and photographs by James E. Brasher (unless otherwise noted)
Interior design by Neil Ferguson

Texas State Historical Association
P.O. Box 5428
Austin, Texas 78763
(512) 471-2600
www.tshaonline.org

CONTENTS

Preface v

Introduction ix

1. Runaway Scrape Begins 1
2. To the Colorado–Day 1, March 16 19
3. Crossing at Burnam's Ferry–Day 2, March 17 ... 31
4. Crier's Creek–Day 3, March 18 47
5. On the Move–Day 4, March 19 63
6. Arriving at Beeson's–Day 5, March 20 75
7. Beeson's & Dewees'–Day 6, March 21 95
8. Beeson's & Dewees'–Day 7, March 22 113
9. Beeson's & Dewees'–Day 8, March 23 123
10. Beeson's & Dewees'–Day 9, March 24 133
11. Beeson's & Dewees'–Day 10, March 25 ... 141
12. Moving Eastward–Day 11, March 26 149
13. Toward the Brazos 171
14. Aftermath 191

Conclusion 195

Biographical Appendix 203

Notes 259

Bibliography 297

Index 309

PREFACE

THERE ARE SEVERAL HISTORICAL MARKERS along the Colorado River that acknowledge Sam Houston's actions during the Texas Revolution. However, there seems to be very little literature that put these actions into the broader context of the revolution. I took it upon myself to write something to fill that apparent void, and I thought could quickly complete that task. My naivety quickly became apparent as what I thought would take just months instead dragged on for years. I also found that thorough research of material and months of diligent writing requires the assistance of countless people.

I was fortunate that my base of operations was Columbus, Texas, home to the Nesbitt Memorial Library, which houses an extensive historical database. I spent countless hours in "The Bill Stein Texas Room," researching material that would seldom be available in typical small-town libraries. Special thanks go to Director Susan Chandler, who was of great assistance in helping me find the resources I needed. Many locals in Columbus are aware of the contributions made by Bill Stein, a long-time archivist and director of the Nesbitt Memorial Library. I only had the fortune to meet Bill once before his untimely passing, but his extensive historical research and written contributions to the history of Colorado County, often chronicled in the *Nesbitt Memorial Library Journal*, made my research considerably easier.

The Nesbitt Memorial Library Foundation provided generous support toward this project, and I hope this book delivers another valuable historical reference about the area that meets their expectations. Specifically, I would like to thank Tracey Wegenhoft and Jim Kearney for their part in helping to facilitate this project. I would also like to acknowledge Roger and Marilyn Wade for their feedback and encouragement.

I visited many libraries and archives and accessed countless other sources to further my research but wanted to particularly cite the help received from the Fayette Heritage Museum and Archives in La Grange and the Weimar Public Library.

Larry Burris generously allowed access to the cannonball found on his family's property and Curtiss Schonenberg helped facilitate the loan of this notable artifact. Travis Wegenhoft helped me gain entry to some important historical sites. Specifically, I want to show my appreciation to the Roy Wegenhoft Sr. family for allowing access to the Burnam/Holman cemetery and the site of Burnam's Ferry and to Douglas Potter for allowing access to the property where Beeson's Crossing was located.

I would like to thank Gregg Dimmick for his review and feedback on this project and for allowing access to his cache of translations of important Mexican documents. I also greatly appreciate Dr. Richard B. McCaslin of the Texas State Historical Association, who patiently and thoroughly edited the manuscript of this first-time author and helped shape the book into its final form.

My wife, Amanda Danning, has earned a national reputation as a forensic sculptor who can skillfully craft facial reconstructions of historical figures. Fortunately, her drawing skills are equally impressive. She adroitly brought to life some of the scenes described in this book and created superb portraits of some of the lesser-known participants of the Texas Revolution. I also want to acknowledge her essential help in navigating the computer program that helped me to generate the many maps that were critical to this book.

Lastly, for generations, my family has worked to ensure that present and future generations understand the unique history of the area along the Colorado River. As a direct descendant of one of Stephen F. Austin's original settlers, I want to share this book as a tribute to my son Christopher Brasher and my priceless grandchildren, Alexa, Cruz, and Niko.

James E. Brasher
Columbus, Texas

INTRODUCTION

Though Texas had not yet declared itself independent, the winds of revolution were blowing steadily by late 1835. The popular consensus was that Texians should fight to restore the more amendable federalist form of government presented in the Mexican Constitution of 1824. Some who were in favor of outright Texas independence probably conceded to this approach with the hope of garnering support from other rebellious Mexican states. Even stalwart Stephen F. Austin, who had for so long worked and advocated for Texas to remain a part of Mexico, had a change in attitude and seemed to acknowledge that an uprising was inevitable. A lengthy stay in a Mexican prison no doubt contributed to that attitude.

The spark for the rebellion occurred in Gonzales when, in October 1835, a Mexican regiment marched from San Antonio de Béxar to take possession of a small cannon that had previously been given to the village for protection against Indian attacks. The response to a call for help was quick and overwhelming, and it pointed to the general dissatisfaction of much of the Texas populace with the Mexican government. In short order, the Texians confronted and drove off the Mexican soldiers at Gonzales. Shortly after their victory at Gonzales, they successfully overwhelmed the severely undermanned garrison at the Presidio La Bahía in Goliad. By mid-October, the Texians had won two victories, albeit small ones, over the Mexican military.

Texian forces continued to grow, and the desire to drive the Mexican military out of Texas became pervasive. Austin was elected to lead the troops at Gonzales and immediately marched toward San Antonio.

After winning the Battle of Concepción, they laid siege to the town for six weeks. Then, after several days of street fighting, the Texians forced Mexican General Martín Perfecto de Cos to surrender. Under the terms he signed, his Mexican troops were paroled with the understanding that they would not fight against the Constitution of 1824, which at that time was still the impetus, if not the excuse, for taking up arms. After General Cos and his men had been forced out of Texas, most of the Texians returned home. Although most thought there would likely be a response to their actions, they were more concerned with preparing their homesteads for the winter season.

During the lull in military activity, a spotlight was shone on the ineptitude of the Texians' provisional government and military. A quarrel broke out between the governor and the general council about who had authority. It was at this time that Sam Houston was first appointed as the commander in chief of what was essentially a nonexistent "regular army."[1] His appointment did nothing to dissuade others from forming volunteer or militia groups to achieve more personal objectives. Houston found himself in the middle of a situation where different officers operated under conflicting orders from varying governmental entities. One of their questionable objectives was an ill-conceived expedition to Matamoros in support of other Mexican states that opposed the centralist government and were in the throes of rebellion. Houston thought the planned expedition was a bad idea and quickly moved to catch the group. He managed to successfully convince most of them to quit their campaign and halt at Refugio. The expedition leaders, however, continued their march.[2] The implication of this dysfunction was not lost on Houston and would substantially shape his future decisions.

Whatever confidence the Texians may have had after pushing the Mexican forces from Texas was short-lived. None other than General Antonio López de Santa Anna would step aside from his presidency and lead a substantial Mexican army hundreds of miles overland to punish and drive out the Anglo rebels. His ruthless measures were intended to serve as an example to the rest of the Mexican states to fall in line. Santa Anna had his sights set firmly on San Antonio, the political and economic center of Texas. He intended to eradicate the Texians fortified within the confines of the old mission popularly known as the Alamo. As the nascent Texas government was organizing a new government that would declare independence, Santa Anna was preparing to overwhelm the defenders of the Alamo. At the same time, General José de Urrea was moving along the coast of Texas, claiming military victories at the Battle of San Patricio and Battle of Agua Dulce.

It was in this setting that Houston took command of Texian forces. He realized that their earlier victories were essentially 'fool's gold' and that their discipline and command structure flaws, despite their victories, would ultimately lead to defeat if not corrected. The Texians were no longer battling remote outposts that were relatively undermanned. Instead, they were about to meet the full force of a Mexican army with accompanying artillery. A rag-tag militia, no matter their enthusiasm, could not compete with a large contingent of well-trained professional soldiers.

It is essential to understand Houston's mindset during this timeframe. Unlike earlier, when he was appointed commander in chief of only the regular land forces, Houston had to successfully gain complete control of all elements of the army, including volunteer companies. Recognition of his complete authority was essential to his task at hand.

So often, revolution is measured strictly by the battles waged. When Houston arrived to take command of forces in Gonzales in March 1836, he had not yet participated in any of the Texian battles. Houston knew independence must eventually be achieved on the battlefield, but he also was aware that success depended on the odds for victory to be shifted considerably more in favor of the Texians. Apart from the Goliad Massacre, the time between the Battle of the Alamo and the decisive Battle of San Jacinto is largely overlooked. Accounts of the Runaway Scrape are an exception. While more and more men mustered into the Texian army, left behind were their wives and families, most of whom would endure incredible hardships. The numerous compelling stories of what these people endured in the Runaway Scrape deserve review and should serve as a lesson, if not a tribute, to the fortitude of those pioneering families.

There is appreciably less review and discussion about the actions of the Texian military during this time frame. Most of the Anglo settlers lived east of the Colorado River—the very heart of Austin's first colony. The Texian army would ultimately spend eleven days encamped on the Colorado River. Upon arrival, the feeling of the troops was largely grief at the loss of their comrades in the Alamo and relief that they now had the natural defense of a major river to deter the pursuing Mexican army. By the eleventh day, however, the Texians were eager to engage their enemies.

Houston could ill afford to indulge in emotional whims. As commander in chief, he had to consider much wider circumstances and derive a strategy to achieve ultimate victory. Once the Mexican army arrived on the west bank of the Colorado, all signs pointed toward an impending battle. In fact, Houston made a proclamation declaring as much. The results of that looming engagement would have been crucial, perhaps deciding the fate of the young republic. Circumstances, however, would render this a battle unfought, and the future of the precarious republic would remain in doubt for weeks to come. Those circumstances and General Houston's decisions to delay battle are an important part of the story of the Texas Revolution.

1
RUNAWAY SCRAPE BEGINS

"Gen. Houston came down and ordered the horses to be got up, and the fires put out; after which, such a scramble and confusion commenced as I have never witnessed."[1]

WILLIAM J.E. HEARD

BY THE CLOSE OF 1835, spirits were high in Texas. Armed forces had defeated the Mexican troops at Gonzales, Goliad, and finally San Antonio de Béxar, sending them south in defeat. While giddy with the recent military success, any clear-thinking Texian knew that a response from the Mexican government would most assuredly come. Still, in the midst of a cold winter, there was no immediate concern that any reprisals would occur until well into the spring. This lack of concern would prove to be costly. Upon hearing of the debacle in Texas, the Mexican president and self-appointed commander in chief, Antonio López de Santa Anna, did not wait for better weather. Eager to quash the uprising of rebellious Americans in Texas, he force-marched his army toward San Antonio, commandeering provisions from the Mexican populace along the way. His arrival at San Antonio in late February 1836 caught the Texian leaders unprepared.

Sam Houston, recently appointed as commander in chief of all Texian forces by the interim government of the new Republic of Texas, arrived in Gonzales around 4:00 p.m. on March 11, 1836, to take command of the forces that had been gathering there in preparation to assist the men under siege at the Alamo. The troops here, loosely under the command of Colonel James C. Neill, consisted of mostly poorly trained volunteers with only a few members of the regular army of Texas. Among the companies present or soon-to-arrive in Gonzales were those led by Captain Moseley Baker from San Felipe de Austin, Captain Jesse Billingsley from Mina (present-day Bastrop), Captain William W. Hill from Washington, Captain Thomas J. Rabb from Egypt, and Colonel Sidney Sherman from Kentucky. In all, about 374 soldiers comprised the Texian forces at Gonzales.[2]

Within an hour or two of his arrival, Houston received some distressing news from two visitors. Andres Barcena and Anselmo Bergara were staying at the ranch of Barcena's father-in-law, Don José Flores, on Saturday night. One evening, a neighbor came with the tragic news that, after a horrific battle, all men in the Alamo had been put to the sword. He reported many details of the event, including his estimate that 500 Mexican soldiers had been killed in the attack and the same number injured. Barcena and Bergara arrived in Gonzales, and each gave a report. Afterward, Colonel George W. Hockley, Houston's chief of staff, noted inconsistencies between the men's stories. On that basis, the General had the two arrested as Mexican spies.[3]

Perhaps Houston thought the two men were Mexican spies sent to sow panic among the population. More likely, Houston surmised that they were telling the truth; however, during a military conflict, truth is not always the best medicine for a civilian population that contributed so many to the defense of Béxar. The General conveniently opted not to believe their statement and had the two men arrested and placed under guard.[4] Two weeks later, Houston would again employ this same tactic.

Whether the General believed the two men or not, he thought it prudent to deploy scouts to find the truth of the matter. On the morning of

Susanna Dickinson, holding her young daughter Angelina, and Joe, William B. Travis' slave, arrive in Gonzales to provide accounts of the events at the Alamo.

March 13, 1836, Houston sent Erastus "Deaf" Smith, Henry W. Karnes, and Robert E. Handy to determine the fate of the Alamo. Not more than twenty miles from Gonzales, the party met Susanna Dickinson, who was carrying her young daughter Angelina. Accompanying them was Joe, a slave to Colonel William B. Travis, and a free black named Ben who had been a cook for Mexican Colonel Juan N. Almonte and had been ordered by Santa Anna to accompany Dickinson to Gonzales.[5] Upon reaching Gonzales, the frightened and aggrieved widow quickly confirmed to Houston that the Alamo had indeed fallen, and all the defenders were dead. Among the slain was Susanna's husband, Almeron Dickinson, a Gonzales resident who fought in the Battle of Gonzales and the Siege of Béxar.

Dickinson delivered to Houston a letter dated March 7 and signed by Santa Anna. In it, Santa Anna angrily condemned the "parcel of audacious adventurers [who] dared to invade our territory." The Mexican commander pointedly related that, "It became necessary to check and chastise such enormous daring; and in consequence, some exemplary punishments have already taken place in San Patricio, Lipantitlan and this city." He added, "These ungrateful men must also necessarily suffer the just punishment that the laws and the public vengeance demand."[6] From the contents of the letter and the actions taken on several fields of battle, it was clear that Santa Anna would broker no compromise.

Second-hand reports about the status of the Alamo had startled the people of Gonzales, but Dickinson's first-hand account had a profound effect. Less than two weeks earlier, the citizens of Gonzales had sent thirty-two of their brothers and fathers to support Travis at the Alamo, and now, it was confirmed, they would never return.[7] After the initial shock, the harsh reality of the situation started to become apparent. The full force of the Mexican army was no more than sixty miles to the west and, as far as anyone knew, their arrival was imminent. Santa Anna would show no mercy to those in rebellion against the government of Mexico. The ragtag Texian army at Gonzales was in no condition to confront a trained military force with obviously superior manpower and supporting artillery. The time for grieving would have to wait.

Accounts from this time in Gonzales commonly portray two opposing perspectives. One was that the population in general was feeling a sense of panic. With rumors flying that the Mexican army was marching to Gonzales and expected at any hour, an understandable reaction was to flee. Jonathan H. Kuykendall's account indicated as much:

> A rumor became rife that two thousand of the enemy—the advance division of the Mexican army—might be hourly expected at Gonzales. As may be reasonably supposed this news produced intense excitement in our camp. In the little village of Gonzales the distress of the families was extreme.[8]

The men assembled at Gonzales had arrived with the intention of helping those trapped in the Alamo. An emotional Captain Baker, in a plea for help to the Standing Committee of San Felipe on March 8, reflected an alternative perspective for those in Gonzales:

> Our own situation is critical–too weak to advance, and insufficient to protect this place–and daily expecting two thousand cavalry to attack us. To retreat, however, would be the ruin of Texas; and we have all resolved to abide an attack, and to conquer or die. We are now busily engaged fortifying ourselves, with the hope that the people of Texas, en mass, are on the march to our assistance. Unless they are, the Alamo and our post must fall, and all, every man be destroyed. Not one of us will return to tell the dreadful tale–or to reproach those that remain for their supineness, or their cowardice. We have come here to repel the enemy, and my company will die beneath their standard sooner than the enemy shall advance, or they retreat.[9]

This 'fight or die' attitude may certainly be admirable in some situations.

For many in Gonzales, this mind-set morphed into one of vengeance. So it was that Houston found himself having to deal with some individuals who were panic-stricken and others who were bloodthirsty.

Regardless of the attitude of military or civilians, Houston was resolute. The only reasonable action was to withdraw from Gonzales. However, for those itching for a fight, that decision was unpopular. Some protested about Houston's leadership abilities, if not his courage. Robert M. Coleman, who later served on the General's staff through the Battle of San Jacinto, was blunt in his early criticism of the Texian leader:

> Now so much depended upon the energy and talent of the Commanding General, he clearly showed to the army his total unfitness to command…he became much agitated and showed every symptom of fear, he would sometimes rave like a madman, at others seemed much dejected. The troops were not long in discovering the condition of their General and became immediately disorganized. In a moment, we presume, of derangement, he ordered Gonzales to be burned.[10]

Of course, a leader's job is not to accept the demands of a vengeful army, but rather to make a measured assessment of the situation before deciding upon the correct course. To attack the Mexican army at San Antonio would have at the very best supplied a short-term moral victory. More likely, the decision would have resulted in the utter defeat of what was destined to be the last remaining Texian army. Those who later wrote critical memoirs and accounts condemning Houston's actions ignored the situation on the ground, were naive regarding military tactics and strategy, or had a personal vendetta against the General.

Although his military campaign was a priority, Houston was cognizant of the plight of the civilians. He donated several of his supply wagons to desperate citizens so that they could carry at least some of their belongings on the lengthy retreat.[11] While the grieving families may have laud-

Portrait of Robert M. Coleman, vocal critic of General Sam Houston and his decision to abandon Gonzales.

ed him for his compassion, the effect of this generosity hindered Houston's military retreat. With only one wagon and few draft animals to pull the artillery, there was no practical way to move the armaments located in Gonzales. The artillery consisted of two four-pound cannons, which had been mounted in Gonzales and taken to Houston's camp, and a third nine-pounder that was never mounted but rested on a wagon at a blacksmith shop. The General may have logically assumed that the interim government would supply artillery to his army when it reached the Colorado River. Alternatively, he may have expected that Colonel James W. Fannin would join him with artillery from Goliad. Either way, Houston reluctantly decided to sink the three cannons in the Guadalupe River rather than leave them for the advancing Mexican army's benefit.[12] By the time his retreat fully commenced from Gonzales, the supply and munitions train of the Texian army consisted of one partially loaded farm wagon. A week or so later, Houston may well have regretted that decision.

While the bulk of the Texian army in Gonzales was composed of volunteer units, Houston set about organizing a cohesive regiment of infantry. Colonel Edward Burleson, Lieutenant Colonel Sherman, and Major Alexander Somervell were selected to be the primary officers. When not under march, they were responsible for instilling discipline and order within the ranks.

As commander in chief of Texian forces, Houston had to consider not only the army camped at Gonzales, but also the overall strategic situation in Texas. Given the disorganized nature of the newly formed companies assembled in Gonzales, Houston must have considered the larger and more experienced forces posted at Goliad, located about fifty miles or so to the south, to be essential to his overall strategy. In short order, Houston sent a dispatch to Colonel Fannin, who commanded the Texian forces at Goliad, to fall back to Victoria.[13] Immediately prior to Houston's reinstatement as commander of all Texian military forces, Fannin had been at least nominally the senior officer in the field. Unfortunately, despite having military training, Fannin did not possess the decisiveness of a successful leader. Between his reluctance to fully embrace Houston's authority and his indecisiveness in retreat, the troops serving under Fannin would ultimately be of no assistance to Houston or the greater Texas cause except as martyrs.

Houston wasted little time after confirming that the Alamo had fallen. He ordered his troops to prepare for retreat with all possible haste. With no horses available to the infantry, baggage and provisions that could not be carried were thrown into the campfires. This included tents, clothing, coffee, and meal.[14] Lieutenant William J. E. Heard described the chaotic events as the retreat commenced:

> On the night of the 13th, about the time the men were preparing their night's repast, Gen. Houston came down and ordered the horses to be got up, and fires put out; after which, such a scramble and confusion commenced as I had never witnessed...As to guards, we had none; there was no order or regularity in the retreat from there to Peach Creek, 10 miles east.[15]

Just before midnight on March 13, the army commenced a slow march eastward. The night was pitch black, and the makeshift soldiers had to grope their way quietly along a seemingly invisible road.[16] Several miles to the east, they entered an extensive stand of post oak where the ground became very sandy, making the trek even more fatiguing. Adding to the misery, some soldiers were forced to march while afflicted with measles.[17]

The Texian retreat was so hasty that some pickets were not told about the evacuation.[18] Doubtless, it was unsettling to return from guard duty, having not been relieved as expected, to see not only your comrades absent, but the entire town mostly empty and ablaze.[19] There would be accusations that Houston made this mistake again at other stops, though that could be debated. Nevertheless, this was certainly a prominent sign of the colossal disorganization of the Texians.

Though some civilians managed to get out prior to the military evacuation, many families opted to travel with the protection of the army. Their motivation to pack was suddenly enhanced as their source of protection began to march out of town. Families could be seen through the windows desperately trying to gather whatever belongings they could, not knowing with any certainty whether they would ever return.[20] Thus began what would famously be called the Runaway Scrape.

Houston did not make it easy for the advancing Mexican army. The Texian commander correctly perceived that the Mexican supply chain would be stretched thin, and he was not about to accommodate the enemy by readily leaving valuable provisions. After his army departed, he ordered that Gonzales be destroyed.[21] John Sharp was one of the men left behind to perform the unfortunate act. He recalled:

> Captain Carnes [sic] then told us that the orders were to burn the Town, and that not a roof large enough to shelter a Mexican's head was to be left, with everything else that could be of any service to the enemy.[22]

After their hasty retreat from Gonzales, the Texian army's first stop came just before dawn at the plantation of Bartlett D. McClure on Peach Creek. Many of the soldiers, having gotten their first taste of a forced march, collapsed in exhaustion without even spreading a blanket.[23] The more energetic ones started campfires on which they brewed coffee and prepared a quick breakfast, unaware of what was happening behind them.

Not long after leaving their temporary encampment, soldiers and civilians alike noticed a pronounced orange glow emanating from the western horizon. The group sadly realized that they were witnessing the destruction of Gonzales. Sadness was quickly replaced with alarm however, when a succession of loud explosions shattered the silence. No doubt, the nervous population had visions of enemy artillery, only a few miles behind them, firing on the small town. The alarm was quelled when the

The families fleeing Gonzales are said to have listened to the General speak under what became known as the "Sam Houston Oak" located at the McClure Plantation on Peach Creek. This was the first rest stop for the Texian army after marching out of Gonzales. The restored house in the background was built by Sarah McClure's second husband, Charles Braches.

people were assured that the noise was the explosion of barrels of liquor that had been left behind. Other reports attributed the explosions to canisters of gunpowder that had been left in one of the burning houses.[24]

When the Texian army rested that night, so did many of the fleeing families that traveled with Houston's troops. Accounts indicate that twenty-seven women whose husbands were in the Alamo stopped at the McClure plantation, and there they learned about the massacre. Under the branches of a towering live oak, now popularly known as the "Sam Houston Oak," the General advised the settlers of the Peach Creek area to evacuate or "suffer the consequences."[25]

Perhaps cognizant of the impact the destruction of Gonzales had on his soldiers and the accompanying civilians, General Houston did not order the McClure plantation to be burned upon departure. However, the advancing Mexican army, under the command of General Joaquín Ramírez y Sesma, also camped at the McClure place and wreaked havoc on it themselves.[26]

The pause at Peach Creek served as a needed respite to Texians exhausted by marching for several hours over uncertain terrain through the pitch black of night. Houston, however, was also expecting to rendezvous at Peach Creek with his first reinforcements. He had dispatched messengers to relay the news of the fall of the Alamo. En route to Gonzales, Captain John Bird, in charge of roughly 125 mounted men organized in San Felipe met Houston's courier and was ordered to camp at Peach Creek to await the Texian army's arrival. The courier's arrival was fortuitous, since Bird was considering bypassing Gonzales and taking a more direct route to San Antonio. If he had, his company would likely have met the Mexican army head on.[27]

Houston's march resumed at daybreak and continued throughout March 14 with only a short beak at a spot known as "Big Hill," southwest of present-day Moulton. With the addition of Bird's company, the Texian army had grown to 470 men. Perhaps to give encouragement to his new troops, Houston inflated the size of his force to 800 while addressing his men.[28]

Shortly after sunset on March 14, the Texian army camped at Williamson Daniels' house on the Lavaca River. By this time, the soldiers had been marching for eighteen hours with only two short breaks at Peach Creek and Big Hill. They had covered about twenty-four miles; now, because they camped on the prairie and had no ready supply of wood for campfires, the soldiers were forced to make do with fence posts from around Daniels' homestead.[29]

A remnant of a trench can be seen today that runs approximately 380 feet in length, with about 120 feet parallel to and just north and east of the Lavaca River. This trench may have been dug on the night of March 14 as a defense against a sudden incursion by Mexican cavalry. Dirt was piled up behind the trench to provide protection for a second line of soldiers. The need for this trench would have been obvious considering this was the first night of the Texian army's retrograde movement and no one knew exactly where the advancing Mexicans were located.[30]

The campsite on Daniels' league was near a major crossroad called the La Bahía Road. About sixty-five miles south on that road lay the town of Goliad, where Colonel Fannin and his sizable army remained. A few miles to the north, the road curved northeast for about twenty-eight miles to Moore's Fort on the Colorado River (near modern La Grange) and then extended a further fifty-five or sixty miles to Washington, the new capital of the young Republic of Texas. Upon arrival, Houston made sure to help lagging civilians cross the Lavaca River. Considering the wet weather and resulting swollen rivers and creeks, crossing with carts, wagons, and livestock was no small feat. Some civilian refugees may have abandoned the Texian army's protection and headed northeast toward Washington and Nacogdoches. Houston, however, had no intention of traveling this route and moving toward the seat of the new government.

While camping at Daniels' place on the night of March 14, Houston

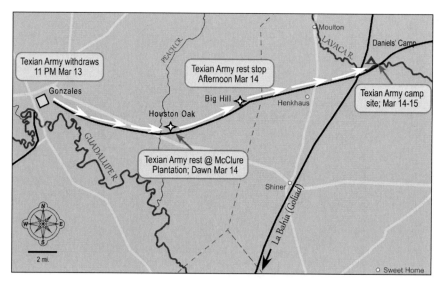

Projected route of the Texian army from Gonzales to their first campsite at Daniels' Camp near the Lavaca River close to the crossing of the La Bahía Road. Historic roads in black and modern roads in gray.

issued an order to his aide-de-camp, Major William T. Austin, to travel to the mouth of the Brazos River and "make a requisition upon Colonel John A. Wharton for six pieces of artillery."[31] Houston knew that there were several pieces of artillery at Velasco. His order further stated that the guns and ammunition were to be forwarded to "Head Quarters of the Army on the Colorado River near Burnam's."[32] What the General did not consider was that his priorities did not always coincide with those of others. When Austin met with Colonel Wharton on March 18, Houston's orders were set aside. Instead, Wharton ordered Austin to take command at Velasco and forward to Bell's Landing any weapons and provisions he could secure.[33] Houston would have to wait weeks for his artillery.

The Texians broke camp early on the morning of March 15. After a few hours' march of about ten miles or so, they reached Rocky Creek, a tributary of the Navidad River. An incident occurred here that shows Houston's concern for discipline, not to mention his purported frequent use of colorful language. John Rhodes, a member of Captain Robert McNutt's company, had been assigned guard duty on the night of March 14 (after the extended march through the night of March 13 and all the next day). There are two main duties of a night sentry: stay alert and warn the troops of any sign of trouble or danger. Rhodes failed at the former, which made him incapable of the latter, and the General was none too happy about it. Upon hearing of Rhodes' negligence, he immediately ordered the young man arrested. So it was as a prisoner that Rhodes was marching when they reached Rocky Creek. Deciding to quench his considerable thirst, the young man stopped to partake of the opportunity for a drink of water, causing a temporary halt to the army's progress, which in turn caused Houston to ask about the delay. Upon learning that Rhodes was the culprit, Sam Houston thundered, "Knock him down, God d—n him, knock him down–standing there and impeding the march of the whole army, G—d d—n him, knock him down!" Rhodes avoided a blow to the head by quickly resuming his march.[34]

Shortly after noon on March 15, Houston received his second reinforcements. Just before reaching the Navidad River, Captain Peyton Splane's mounted volunteers arrived. Unlike Bird's company, Splane's volunteers probably numbered no more than a couple of dozen. Nevertheless, Houston gladly welcomed them. Splane was already a veteran of service having participated in the Battle of Gonzales and the Siege of Béxar. He recruited and commanded troops from the lower Brazos River area.[35]

The Texian army and a considerable number of civilian refugees reached Houston's next campsite at about 1:00 on the afternoon of March 15.[36] Houston probably decided to make camp early rather than proceed, knowing he could not reach Burnam's Ferry before dark. Also, before departing the main road, he likely wanted to ensure that his rearguard was able to escort straggling civilians to the main camp. Moreover, by staying on the main road, additional reinforcements were much more likely to find him.

The march from Daniels' home to the new campsite on the Navidad River was about fifteen miles. The Texians' progress was considerably quicker than the previous day, as they traversed the distance in only six to seven hours. A full night's rest at Daniels' place and more open terrain likely contributed to the faster pace, but probably not as much as the fact that the march was in daylight and not in the pitch black of night. The projected site of Houston's campsite for the night of March 15 was a mile or two north of the present-day town of Oakland, just inside the present-day Colorado County line.

The Texian campsite, just east of the Navidad River, was likely on the property of William W. W. Thompson.[37] This arrival may have been more relaxed than the previous night. However, the night would prove to be anything but relaxing. A downpour soaked the unsheltered Texian soldiers, providing yet another test to the inexperienced army.[38] It would not be the last such test as rainy weather, muddy roads, and swollen rivers would be commonplace throughout their march eastward.

RUNAWAY SCRAPE BEGINS | 17

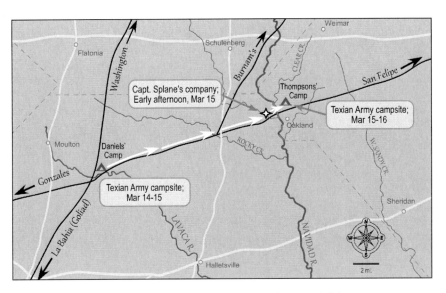

Projected route of the Texian army from Daniels' Camp to Thompson's Camp east of the Navidad River. Historic roads in black and modern roads in gray.

2
TO THE COLORADO
DAY 1, MARCH 16

"You crossed the Colorado fifteen miles above the great crossing at Beason's, taking a solitary and unusual route...What possible reason could you have for going to Burnham's crossing?"[1]

MOSELEY BAKER

BY MARCH 1836, THE ROAD from San Antonio de Béxar to Gonzales and San Felipe de Austin was well established. Logically, Sam Houston might have continued down this road to Beeson's Crossing on the Colorado, just south of the nascent town of Columbus and toward the most populated part of the colony. But Houston clearly had a different path in mind. In a letter dated March 14, 1836, Houston stipulated that any artillery and accompanying supplies should be forwarded to the "Head Quarters of the Army on the Colorado River near Burnham's."[2] This was the first mention of his plan to take his army to Burnam's Ferry.[3]

In a subsequent letter dated the next day and addressed to James T. Collinsworth, who as Chairman of the Military Committee would be a frequent recipient of Houston's correspondence directed to the government, the General also mentioned his intent to fall back to Burnam's on the Colorado River.⁴ These two communications suggested that Houston was committed to the idea of going to Burnam's Ferry and likely staying there some extended time.

Captain Moseley Baker, who became a vigorous and vocal opponent of Houston, asked in a later letter to him, "You crossed the Colorado fifteen miles above the great crossing at Beason's, taking a solitary and unusual route, one certainly which the enemy would not think of taking, and which they did not take… What possible reason could you have for going to Burnham's crossing?" He added, "No one that I have ever heard speak on the subject has been able to assign any."⁵

Baker was correct that Houston never really explained why he decided to travel to Burnam's instead of proceeding directly east to Beeson's. The crossing at Burnam's was not on a major route and seemingly had minimal strategic value. Despite occasional references on historical markers or in literature that Burnam's Ferry was on, or a cutoff from, the La Bahía Road, published maps of the time show virtually no reference or mapped route to this site.

Several maps were available. To fulfill promises to the Mexican government, Stephen F. Austin had surveyed and mapped the area around his newly established colony. One of the first maps that satisfied his pledge was dated 1829 and addressed to the president of Mexico.⁶ It did more than just show Austin's Colony; instead, it was a comprehensive map of the settled parts of Texas as well as Coahuila, Nuevo León, and Tamaulipas. Besides main roads, the map displayed rivers and tributaries, lakes, and topographic features. It also showed the locations of Indian sites, landscape, wildlife, and mines.

This detail from Austin's 1829 map shows the area between Green DeWitt's colony, headquartered in Gonzales, and Austin's colonial capital, designated on the map as "Austin" but which came to be known as San Felipe. The map shows the east-west road connecting the two colonial headquarters as well as the La Bahía Road, running north-south just east of Gonzales and then curving northeast as it crosses the Colorado River. The map also shows the Atascosito Road crossing the Colorado just below the Gonzales-San Felipe Road and proceeding northeast toward San Felipe. On the main Gonzales-San Felipe Road, the map shows a split of the road just east of Calavera Creek.[7] East of the Colorado River, the roads merge again. This is the earliest depiction of what would become known as Beeson's Crossing (to the south) and another crossing to the north. What this early map does not show is a road turning to the northeast toward Jesse Burnam's property, which lay just south of the creek designated as Williams.[8]

In 1833, Austin commenced another map that was focused more on his colonies. Surveyors for this map include John, Thomas, and Gail Borden. Austin, however, did not live to see the final version of this impressive map. Because he died in December 1836, completion of the map fell to his brother-in-law, James F. Perry.[9] This map has some important distinctions from Austin's earlier map. First, it includes the land grants that had been awarded to that point. The Atascosito Road, an important route in the early days of Texas, is not shown, supporting the notion that it had become largely obsolete. The map does show the location for Columbus, which had only recently been established. More importantly, this is one of the few maps that depicts the cutoff to Burnam's Ferry.

According to this map, the western cutoff to Burnam's was located at Lower Rocky Creek, presumably near where the previously mentioned incident with John Rhodes occurred and about five miles west of where the Texian army camped on the night of March 15. Houston's order, dated March 14 while at Williamson Daniels' home near the Lavaca, and his letter to Collinsworth, written on March 15 while in camp near the Navidad River, clearly show that Houston intended to march to Burnam's Ferry.[10] It is reasonable to wonder why he chose to bypass the road that would have led him there.

Little documentation exists explaining the reasons for Houston's deci-

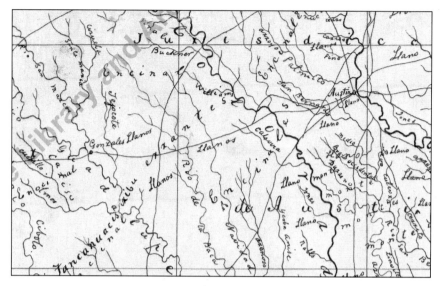

A portion of an early map, circa 1829, showing the roads, rivers, and features between Gonzales and Austin (San Felipe de). Courtesy of Texas State Library and Archives.

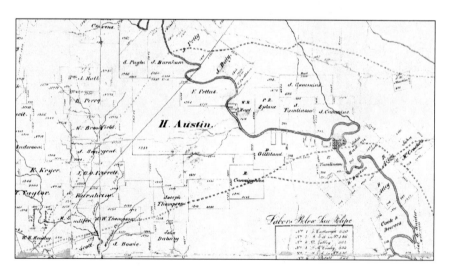

A portion of the 1833–1837 map of Austin's colony showing the two important Colorado River crossings (Dewees and Beeson's) near Columbus. It also is one of the very few maps that shows the road to Burnam's Ferry to the north. Courtesy of Texas State Library and Archives.

sion on the direction of his march, and he did not often hold council with subordinates. What was his rationale for taking a seemingly unexpected detour? Perhaps the answer lies within Baker's rant. It was a route that "the enemy would not think of taking."[11] Despite the criticisms of Baker and others, Houston was in no mood to engage the Mexican army at this time with ill-trained, poorly equipped troops. Burnam's Ferry was seemingly not on a primary route across Texas. Perhaps Houston was trying to dodge his pursuers by moving in an unexpected direction.[12] Once east of the Colorado, he could drill his untrained soldiers and instill some semblance of discipline while they waited for the requested supplies and volunteers.

Still, if Houston intended to go to Burnam's, why did he bypass the cutoff to that destination? Though it may seem unlikely, it may be that they simply missed the cutoff. In the modern world, signs and electronic devices point the way. In 1836, a cutoff to a seldom used road might not be too visible. Mexican Colonel Juan N. Almonte noted in his journal that "at the farms of the Navidad, the road to Washington branches off as was seen by the wagon tracks; it crosses the Colorado about 7 leagues higher up than where the division was."[13] According to maps of that time, there was no road to Washington at the location that Almonte described. If the Texian army moved north to Burnam's Ferry, just east of their previous camp on an unmarked route, then Almonte may have mistaken the tracks left by the Texians as the road to Burnam's place that, according to Austin's map of the time, was instead five miles behind them. This may support the idea that the cutoff to Burnam's was not obvious.

More probably, Houston knew exactly where he was leading the army. Avocational historians may be somewhat aware of the route taken by the Texian army during their retreat from Gonzales to the Colorado River. Considerably less well known was the route that Houston took from Washington on his way to Gonzales to take charge of the troops less than two weeks earlier. This trip may have played a part in Houston's decision on his route for a retreat.

Houston was designated as commander of the Texian army and dispatched by the newly formed government in Washington on March 6, 1836, to ride to Gonzales, gather men, and provide relief to the men at the Alamo.[14] The La Bahía Road was an old and well-traveled road that stretched from Goliad to Washington and beyond. It intersected the Gonzales-San Felipe Road near the Daniels' property, where Houston and his men camped on the night of March 14.

Captain John W. Smith, the last courier sent by Colonel William B. Travis from the Alamo, carried a message to the Texas government in Washington that described their perilous situation. Considering the urgency of his mission, it is likely that Smith chose the most efficient route. The route he traveled to Washington was what would be expected from the maps of the time–east to Gonzales, past Bartlett D. McClure's place on Peach Creek, up the La Bahía Road to Moore's Fort on the Colorado, and on to Washington.[15] This route (in reverse) was, however, not the one that Houston took from Washington to Gonzales. An 1830 map by surveyor Horatio Chriesman along Mill and Cummins Creek shows the Wilbarger and La Bahía Road.[16] This road is more clearly displayed on a commemorative map for the bicentennial of Austin's birthday.[17] Upon departing Washington, Houston likely went west down the La Bahía Road to Wilbarger and then south, along this lesser used road, toward Burnam's Ferry.

Though in a hurry to reach his troops in Gonzales, Houston made a point of traveling through Burnam's. The mystery of this unexpected detour was compounded by the fact that he stayed there for two nights. His actions demand further explanation. While staying at Burnam's home, Houston encountered William W. W. Thompson, who was a close friend of Burnam's and was living with him at the time. As might be expected, Thompson asked the General what was happening at the Alamo. Thompson's recollection of this conversation was nothing short of astounding, if not unbelievable. He reported that Houston held firm in the belief that there were no Mexicans at San Antonio and that the reports from Travis and James W. Fannin at Goliad were fabricated to enhance their own importance.[18] Thompson thus seemed to lend credence to the supposition that Houston was in no hurry to arrive in Gonzales.

More likely there were other explanations for Houston's actions. Thompson, though he may have had no ill will toward Houston at the time, eventually developed an intense dislike of him for reasons that will become clear later. Therefore, his recollections may have been colored by his hatred of the General. Considering Houston's passionate March 2 call to arms to the citizens of Texas and the clamor at the Convention in Washington after receiving Colonel Travis' plea for aid, it would almost defy belief that Houston would totally discount what was happening at the Alamo.[19] In a speech to the United States Senate in 1859, Houston claimed that his health was "infirm" during March 1836, which may account for his seemingly slower pace. Additionally, he reported that he met "fugitives" on his way to Gonzales and in fact already feared that the Alamo had fallen.[20]

So, what does any of this have to do with the fact that Houston's camp on the night of March 15 was on the Navidad River? Probably through no coincidence, the land on which the Texians encamped belonged to Thompson, the man that Houston had met at Burnam's on the way to Gonzales.[21] Being well acquainted with the area between his good friend Burnam's place and his own land grant on the Navidad, it may be that Thompson directed the General along a more direct route, where the Gonzales–San Felipe Road passed. Houston, by leading the retreat along the route that he chose, was simply leading the army back the way he had come from Burnam's to Thompson's property. Houston's previous acquaintance with Thompson and his subsequent directions were great influences on the General's 1836 route to Burnam's Ferry.

Knowing the Texian army's course, however, still does not explain why Houston chose that route. Though he later denied giving the command, he most certainly ordered Gonzales burned to keep provisions and shelter away from the advancing Mexicans. This may lead some to believe that Houston advocated a 'scorched earth' policy. Later testimony by William H. Smith tended to support that belief. On March 16, Houston promoted Smith to captain and gave him command of all mounted scouts.[22] Testifying in support of Burnam's claim to the Texas government in March 1874, Smith said that Houston "told me to keep before Cos's division and lay the Country in waste."[23] Smith was responsible for destroying some of Burnam's property on a land grant he had along the Navidad adjacent to Thompson's place.

The fact is, however, that Houston did not burn every structure he encountered. He was selective in what he destroyed. Colonel Almonte noted in his journal that houses were left abandoned and fully stocked.[24] More likely, Houston intended to burn places where significant provisions could be found or where there was a strategic reason to do so. When he traveled through Burnam's homestead on his way to Gonzales, he doubtless noted that Burnam was essentially operating a well-stocked supply depot. Houston likely thought a detour through Burnam's was necessary because of the abundance of provisions there. The destruction of this depot and the Colorado River ferry would deprive the Mexican army of a significant source of supplies and potentially help to impede their advance.[25]

Only a paucity of documentation exists regarding the Texians' March 16 trek from their camp at Thompson's to Burnam's Ferry.[26] Because of this lack of reporting, it can be reasonably presumed that no problems or unforeseen incidents occurred. With persistent rains resulting in swollen creeks and muddy ground, the Texian army, still leading a sizable civilian population, would have avoided low-lying areas as much as possible. Most probably, the route would have been northeast along the high ground just east of, but paralleling, Clear Creek. The march would have been about seven miles from Thompson's place to the present-day town of Weimar, with terrain that was open and only moderately hilly. Just north of Weimar, the Texian army would have entered present-day Fayette County. The march might have been a bit more arduous since the terrain was somewhat hillier. After about five miles, the Texians may have merged onto the original road to Burnam's that they had bypassed near Rocky Creek. They would have marched roughly parallel to modern FM 155 toward the present-day community of Holman and then east toward Burnam's Ferry. Houston's men reached their destination at about 4:30 p.m. on March 16, 1836.[27] Assuming they began at 8:00 a.m., the approximately sixteen-mile march took about eight and a half hours, a somewhat slower pace than the previous day.

Houston did not report whether he dispatched any scouts to determine the enemy positions during his march of the prior couple of days. If Smith's cavalry was responsible for "laying waste" to the countryside, they may have also been tasked with scouting the advancing Mexican army. Alternatively, Houston may simply have been relying on his rearguard to keep tabs. If that is true, there may have been a sense of unease among the ranks, marching with a significant civilian population and not knowing the location of the enemy. Major Alexander Somervell, one of the ranking officers of the army, expressed this in a letter to his friend Perry on March 16:

> We have retired to this place from Gonzales followed as we suppose by a large Mexican force, we have every reason to believe that Santa Anna at the head of a large army will make a descent upon the lower country and sweep the coast…I do not see any prospect of arresting his progress for some time to come…I would most earnestly recommend to you to abandon your place and move with all the property you can towards Sabine if it comes to the worst…no doubt asylum will be offered in the U States to all those who may be driven from this country…place your family in a place of safety

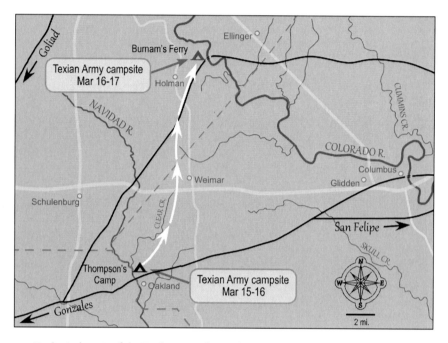

Projected route of the Texian army from Thompson's Camp to Burnam's Ferry on the Colorado River. Historic roads in black and modern roads in gray.

and take to the field for we all have to fight and desperately too or our all will be lost...show this to our immediate friends, do not cause any excitement.[28]

For all the bravado often expressed by members of the Texian army, this letter from one of their most prominent officers shows a leader expressing extreme caution if not outright pessimism. It is not hard to imagine that at least some in the ranks felt the same way and believed that victory was not guaranteed by any means.

Houston was cognizant of this underlying pessimism. One of his primary concerns during his time as commander was desertion. Immediately after learning that the Alamo had fallen, at least a couple dozen individuals deserted the ranks of the Texian army.[29] Though the impact on manpower was a cause for concern, Houston was most anxious as to what influence these men had in spreading fear among the population. Every defender of the Alamo had been slaughtered by an overwhelming force. Mexican armies were marching through Texas, to the north and south. Panicked civilians were desperately trying to drag what few belongings they could with them to escape the invaders. As a well-informed member of the Texian army, Major Somervell was right to urge his friend to "not cause any excitement." Perry's response to his worried friend was considerably more measured and positive. He answered, "I send you this, to Let you see our prospects which is pretty bad though I cannot think Santa Anna can take Texas with the force he now has."[30]

The approach of the Texian army toward the Colorado was a homecoming of sorts for some members of what would eventually become Company F of the First Regiment of Texas Volunteers. This unit, organized by Thomas J. Rabb upon hearing of Travis' situation at the Alamo, was composed of men who lived primarily along the Colorado. Among those that Rabb recruited from this area were William J. E. Heard (who later became commander of the unit), James Nelson, and Elijah and Eli

Mercer. Two notable members of the unit, John H. and William O. Burnam, were veterans of Texian military actions, having participated in the Grass Fight and the Siege of Béxar. The two oldest sons of Jesse Burnam arrived in Gonzales on March 6, 1836, the same day that the Alamo fell.[31] Ten days later, they arrived back at their homestead where they had started, now part of Houston's retreating Texian army.

CROSSING AT BURNAM'S FERRY
DAY 2, MARCH 17

> "By two or three o'clock, the last man was ferried over to the east bank of the Colorado, and the same evening the army marched down the river as far as Crier's."[1]
>
> JONATHAN H. KUYKENDALL

JESSE BURNAM WAS BORN in Kentucky in 1792, the youngest son of seven. His father died when he was young, and the family was always poor. When he was twenty, he was living in Tennessee and married an orphan girl named Temperance Nalle. He and his wife were just scraping by when he was called to serve in the War of 1812. During the war, he contracted a disease and was advised to seek a warmer climate, which provided the impetus to move to Texas.[2] There he became one of the "Old Three Hundred" who received a league of land on the west bank of the Colorado River in 1824. Some reports claim that Burnam's daughter, Nancy, was the first child born in Austin's Colony.[3]

For some time, Burnam was the northernmost settler on the Colorado and, as such, was exposed to frequent Indian attacks. To protect his family on this frontier, Burnam had to be proactive. He built a two-story blockhouse for defense against raids and frequently participated in expeditions against marauding Indians.[4] In May 1824, he was elected captain for the upper division of the Colorado.[5] For five years, Burnam served in this capacity, focusing on tracking down Indians who attacked settlements.[6] The time Burnam served in this unit earned him the moniker of "Captain Burnam" well after his time in the militia ended.

Burnam must have been the very model of the type of citizen that Stephen F. Austin envisioned for his colony. In short order, his place was well stocked with cows, pigs and chickens, a large garden and fields of corn and cotton. Noah Smithwick, who arrived in Texas in 1827, later wrote about Burnam's settlement: "Things looked more promising there than any place I had seen. The settlers were doing some farming, and all had milk, cows, poultry, etc."[7] Just as importantly, Burnam established a trading post and a ferry across the river. He also represented the Colorado District at the Convention of 1832 and the Convention of 1833, which met with the intent of working cooperatively within the framework of the Mexican government.

Burnam was successful in developing his property to its fullest and conscientious in helping the colony flourish. Nevertheless, life was hard in the new colony, and success did not make him immune to tragedy. In May 1833, his wife Temperance went on the ferry across the river to tend sick friends. While there, floodwaters prevented anyone from crossing the river for several days. When the river finally became passable, Burnam learned that his wife had died, a victim of cholera.[8] He was suddenly the single father of eight children.[9]

Burnam's Ferry is commonly, though erroneously, described as being on the La Bahía Road or a cutoff of the La Bahía Road.[10] As alluded to previously, it is difficult to find it on any of the maps of the time. Despite this, history shows that several notable characters made a point of detouring there. Why? Burnam had clearly established a reputation for hospitality and was a reliable source for essential supplies.

In 1835, for nearly two months, noted naturalist Gideon Lincecum made Burnam's Ferry his base of operations, whence he would go on expeditions studying the flora and fauna of the region as well as its suitability for emigration. Burnam made a deal that he could stay free of charge if he provided instruction to his son on bookkeeping.[11] Burnam and Lincecum became lifelong friends. Soon after meeting Burnam, Lincecum wrote, "he had the physiognomy of an honest, friendly man. Indeed, he made on me the impression of a familiar friend; and I very thankfully accepted his kind proposition to make his house my home." Later he noted, "Jesse Burnam...was as good a man as any country or situation could produce."[12] Lincecum likewise made a good impression on Burnam because years later, after remarrying, he gave his old friend the highest honor a man could bestow by naming one of his children after him.

In January 1836, Colonel James W. Fannin arrived. Fannin stayed for two weeks working with Burnam to solicit volunteers for the upcoming revolution and equip the men. Burnam was also generous in allowing the use of his horses. When it was time to depart, Colonel Fannin decided to leave his horse with the Burnam family. He had brought the horse with him from Georgia and did not want to see it come to any harm.[13] The military surgeon traveling with Fannin also decided to leave his medical books with Burnam.[14] Of course, the doomed leader would never return from his fateful assignment at Goliad, and the Burnam family cared for Fannin's horse for the rest of its natural life.

Shortly afterwards, another hero destined to die for the Texian cause, William B. Travis, stopped at Burnam's Ferry on his way west to become commander of the Alamo. Travis stocked up on provisions while there. He presented a claim in the amount of $143 against the Republic for money he spent equipping a company of soldiers. His list included articles such as blankets, coffee, corn, bread, twine, frying pans, tents, spurs, leggings, bridles, rope, and a flag.[15] Clearly, Burnam's Ferry was a common destination for those heading into battle and in need of supplies.

The winds of revolution were born in September 1835. Despite calls

Portrait of colonist Jesse Burnam.

Portrait of Burnam's close friend, naturalist Gideon Lincecum.

for volunteers to stop Mexican authorities from confiscating a cannon from the citizens of Gonzales, Burnam did not arrive until after the skirmish took place. Among the volunteers who arrived immediately after the Battle of Gonzales, there were conflicting opinions on who should be in command. Burnam was chosen to serve on a board to make a final selection.[16] Though by no means a military man, Austin was the unanimous choice to serve as commander.

Though not specifically recorded, Burnam likely continued for a while with the army on its march to San Antonio de Béxar. As military operations continued, a convention was planned with the purpose of helping to forward supplies and ammunition to the army and, as importantly, determine whether to support a state government under the Mexican Constitution of 1824 or move toward a full declaration of independence. Some members of the Texian army, including Burnam, were elected to attend what was called the Consultation of 1835.[17]

Austin, in a report on October 26, 1835, from Camp Salado mentioned that those members of the convention that were with the army, excepting him and his staff, were to leave that day so they could arrive in time for the convention, which was scheduled to begin on November 1.[18] It seems likely that Burnam left the army at that point, thus missing the Battle of Concepción and the Siege of Béxar. But the Texian army found him again in March 1836, when Houston led his troops to Burnam's Ferry.

The primary objective for the Texian army at Burnam's Ferry was to get everyone across the Colorado River, which would provide at least a temporary obstacle to the advancing enemy. Unfortunately, while the crossing was a gravel-bottom ford easily traversed when the river was down, recent rains caused the river to swell. As a result, the Texian troops had to employ the single ferry at the crossing, which proved to be a slow process.

While the Texian army reached the Colorado on March 16, 1836, many civilians did not. Houston's priority was his troops, but he could not help

Present site of Burnam's Ferry near Holman where the Texian army crossed the Colorado River on March 16 and 17, 1836.

but be concerned about the safety of the straggling refugees. To that end, he ordered his rear-guard, led by Captain Juan N. Seguín, to assist the civilians.[19] The General wrote to James T. Collinsworth about the situation: "I reached this point with about six hundred men, including my rear guard, which is a few miles behind with the families, which were not known to be on the route as the army marched, and for which the guard were sent back."[20] Houston had promised that civilians would have priority in crossing, but with a throng of refugees and then hundreds of soldiers all using a single ferry, the crossing took considerable time.[21] As the ferry made one trip after another, stragglers continued to wander in and were soon awaiting their turn to cross. It was not until 3:00 on the afternoon of March 17 that the last of Houston's forces finally traversed the Colorado.[22]

As mentioned earlier, Houston was set on destroying properties and supplies that could benefit the advancing Mexican army. He ordered the burning of those places that could provide a significant advantage to the enemy. Gonzales, a comparatively large community, certainly had significant supplies that could be used by the Mexican army. However, plenty of reports, by both Mexicans and Texians, indicate some houses along the path of his retreat were left intact. The Bartlett D. McClure home at Peach Creek, where the Texian army first rested, was not burned by Houston. Unfortunately, the Mexican army laid waste to most of the property. They drove off or killed all the livestock and filled the well with bricks scavenged from the kitchen. While they also torched several outbuildings, the main house miraculously escaped destruction.[23]

Sarah McClure was one of the lucky ones who came back to a house that was intact. When the opportunity arose, the advancing Mexican army was more than happy to plunder a property before destroying it. In a dispatch to Santa Anna, General Antonio Gaona reported that "his brigade had found the dwellings on the march to Nacogdoches so well supplied that neither the officers nor the soldiers had any more space in which to carry furniture and effects."[24]

Houston, having visited a week prior, knew about and planned to use the significant stores at Burnam's place, but he also made sure that the Mexicans did not do likewise. Colonel Edward Burleson signed an invoice for over $600 worth of provisions from Burnam, including corn, bacon, coffee, lard, salt, and live hogs as well as tools.[25] The supplies were obviously a boon to an army that had abandoned so much at Gonzales. However, just as he had done in Gonzales, Houston knew the goods left at Burnam's were too valuable to fall into Mexican hands and ordered the destruction of the depot, house, and outlying buildings, along with the ferry.

Burleson's receipt for supplies is directed to Burnam, but there is some uncertainty whether Burnam was present when his place was set ablaze. If he was indeed there, he must have known what had happened to Gonzales and realized that his place could be sacrificed as well. Even if he did not believe his fellow Texians would do anything to his place, he most certainly would have known that the Mexicans would enthusiastically loot it. He certainly would have taken steps to remove what he could.

In an affidavit in support of Burnam, once again, William W. W. Thompson was willing to supply incriminating testimony. In an 1840 affidavit, Thompson stated that as he and Burnam were returning to the latter's residence, they met Captain William Patton and simultaneously noticed smoke coming up from the outbuildings. Patton told Burnam and Thompson that he had set fire to the place under the orders of General Houston.[26] This would suggest that Burnam was totally unaware of plans to burn his place. As with Thompson's statement regarding Houston not believing the Alamo was in danger, it is likely that this testimony reflected his intense dislike for Houston. It is hard to envision that if Burnam had been present, his homeplace would have been destroyed without any warning.

In a petition to the Texas legislature in 1874 seeking compensation for his losses, Burnam mentioned that he was absent when his property was destroyed, which contradicted Thompson's testimony.[27] Most likely, after the Texian army had bought supplies from him, he would have been informed that the remainder of his property would have to be destroyed to prevent it being of benefit to the advancing Mexican army. Burnam would logically have supervised the removal of family members, workers, slaves, and whatever provisions he could reasonably transport and started east toward safety. Patton would not have started the fire until Burnam had departed.

Not surprisingly, Burnam was displeased with Houston's decision and increasingly bitter about receiving no compensation for his losses. In a plea for remuneration, he declared: "Under these considerations, your petitioner thinks that it is nothing but Justice to himself, for the government to pay him for loss he has sustained in this matter, as there was not the least reason, or sense of propriety, for the wanton distinction of his property at that time." He finished by stating, "There never did exist, for one moment, the least shadow of reason or sense of propriety, to justify the conduct of the officers, in this matter." Burnam's appeals to the Texas government continued through many years. In his 1874 petition he recalled, "On the retreat of the Army of Texas from the Colorado in 1836, his house and ferry was burned by order of the Commander of Texas forces...that he has borne all his losses this long with patience and resignation hoping that his Country would finally do him justice and pay for what he conceived, an act of unnecessary destruction, such remuneration as in your judgment he may be entitled to sustain him in his worn out old age."[28]

As painful as it was for Burnam to learn that his homestead went up in flames, it must have been every bit as traumatic for his two sons, who were serving in the army, to perhaps watch it. It cannot be often that an army in which you serve, and that allegedly exists to protect civilians, instead burns your home down. To the young Burnam men's credit though, records indicate that both continued to serve and participated honorably in the Battle of San Jacinto.[29]

Though Burnam may have felt that Houston's orders were somehow personal, similar directives were consistently applied to others as well. William P. Zuber described the scene as they proceeded from Moore's Fort down the river toward Burnam's place. "Captain [Joseph L.] Bennett received a dispatch from General Houston, ordering us to proceed down the river. We marched down to [James] Ross's farm. Here, of course, the place was desolate. The barn and its contents were in ashes, said to have been burned by General Houston's men to prevent the enemy from using them."[30]

Despite Houston's correspondence indicating that he was setting up his headquarters at Burnam's Ferry, he instead decided to move the army immediately downriver. Perhaps he was cognizant of the impact the smoldering ashes from the Burnam place might have on his troops. Alternatively, he may have realized that once the supply depot and ferry had been destroyed, Burnam's held no strategic value. Regardless of the reason, as soon as his men crossed the river, they wasted little time moving south along the east side of the Colorado. The army only made it about five miles downriver before the evening light began to fail. They camped close to the home of John Crier, whose house was located near the edge of, but within, the Joseph Duty Survey, inside present-day Colorado County. It was here that Andrew Crier, John's sixteen-year-old son, joined the army.[31] A nearby creek, which feeds the Colorado, would later come to be known as Crier Creek.

Toward the end of the day, General Houston sent out communications. One was to Colonel Fannin, whom he mistakenly believed had evacuated Goliad. He certainly would have been appalled to learn that Fannin was still in Presidio La Bahía.[32] Instead, he ordered him to "take a position on the bay of Lavaca, or any other point best calculated for the protection of provisions, ammunition, &c., at Coxe's point and Dimitt's landing." He continued, "The army now near Burnham's, on the Colorado, will remain for a time, and, according to circumstances, fall down the

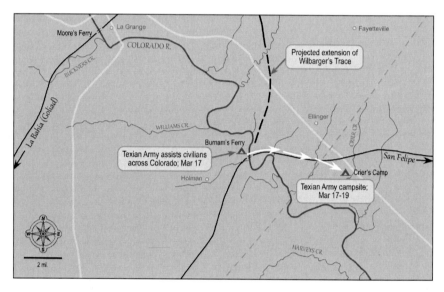

Projected route of the Texian army from Burnam's Ferry to Crier's Camp.

river. Colonel Fannin will therefore hold himself in constant readiness to join the commander in chief."[33]

Another letter went to Collinsworth at Washington.[34] This was part status report, part orders (or perhaps suggestions). Besides apprising him of his situation, he urged Collinsworth to "keep the navy busy." He made clear his concern about deserters and the impact they had on morale. He wrote, "It pains my heart that such consternation should have been spread by the deserters from camp." He also relayed his low opinion of the Mexican forces: "I am assured that the mules and horses of their army are miserably poor; and that there are several hundred women and children with the army, with a view to colonize Texas."

Houston's remark about women and children is worthy of comment. His notation of "several hundred women and children" may have been low; instead, there were thousands. Whether they were present to help colonize Texas was problematic. More likely they were camp followers. General Vicente Filisola, second-in-command of the Mexican forces in Texas, described this phenomenon as follows:

> Here then is one of the serious inconveniences of the ill-advised custom practiced by our army that tolerates the company of families, women and boys who also tag along with them. We see that the worst of it is not the discomfort and scarcity they cause within the Divisions, but there are other more injurious consequences that trespass morality and good behavior. If these men happen to have young women in tow, or have daughters of a certain age, squalor and circumstances drives them to prostitute themselves. From this comes not only desertion, but also corruption, disease, so common among our troops, altercations and even murder.[35]

Lieutenant Colonel José Enrique de la Peña of the Mexican army was even more blunt in his opinion:

> At least three-fifths or one-half the number of our soldiers were squadrons composed of women, mule drivers, wagon-train drivers, boys, and sutlers; a family much like locusts that destroy everything in their path, these people perpetrated excesses difficult to remedy.[36]

Most of the camp followers probably stayed with the bulk of the army and were less likely to be in the forward commands. Nevertheless, even those soldiers in forward positions were likely somewhat distracted by the knowledge that they were behind them.

Houston continued in his letter to Collinsworth at Washington concerning his estimate of the condition of his opponent:

> "Do let it be known that, on close examination, and upon reflection, the force of Santa Anna has been greatly overrated. He must have lost one thousand, or perhaps more, at the Alamo. It is said the officers have to whip and slash the soldiers on the march. And, if they should advance to the Colorado, it will be some time, as there is such scanty subsistence for animals."

He assured Collinsworth that the Texians were ready to engage the enemy and win. "Our own people, if they would act, are enough to expel every Mexican from Texas... Let them entertain no fears for the present. We can raise three thousand men in Texas, and fifteen hundred can defeat all that Santa Anna can send to the Colorado. We would fight on our own ground, and the enemy would lose all confidence from our annoyance. Let the men from the east of the Trinity rush to us! Let all the disposable force of Texas fly to arms! If the United States intend to aid us, let them do it now!"[37] Houston's determination provided a stark contrast to the pessimism of Texians like Somervell.

One of the concerns of the Texian army leadership was the lack of discipline among the troops. There was an incident within the ranks, however, that showed someone was working on the problem. General Houston, having occasion to travel beyond the lines, was hailed by a sentinel who demanded his pass. The General asked the guard if he did not know that he had a right to pass without being challenged. The sentinel, not swayed by the title of the unexpected interloper, told him that the officer of the day had instructed him that no man should pass the lines without written permission. "Well, my friend," Houston replied, "if such were your orders, you are right." He sat down on a stump and waited until the officer of the day came to rescue him.[38] The inconvenience to Houston was well worth it. This was a sign of a soldier taking orders and following them to the letter. He would need this kind of adherence to discipline if he had any chance to defeat the enemy.

In a letter to Secretary of War Thomas J. Rusk a few days later, Colonel George W. Hockley of Houston's staff stated, "Our army are in very fine spirits, and good health, not having one on our sick list. They are eager to meet the enemy—to check their impetuosity is all that will be required."[39] Indeed, Hockley skillfully gave a positive spin to Rusk. Reveille was beaten on the drum, often by Houston himself, an hour before dawn. Periodically each day, the General would roam the camp to visit every company for inspection, with each soldier expected to be aligned at attention. The same formality occurred in the evening, when tattoo was drummed.[40] Over the course of his time on the Colorado, Houston worked hard to instill discipline and order among his soldiers. Circumstances often made this necessity a challenge, but at least some of his officers, such as Hockley, were beginning to see some improvement.

4

CRIER'S CREEK
DAY 3, MARCH 18

"I shall raise a company of spies...to range the country from this to Gonzales."[1]

SAM HOUSTON

SINCE TAKING COMMAND of the Texian army, March 18, 1836, must have been the first day that Sam Houston could figuratively 'catch his breath.' Although he had a rear-guard, until the General crossed the Colorado, there must have been some lingering concern that the Mexican army might surprise the vulnerable Texians. While Houston could at least temporarily breathe a little easier, he still had to begin implementing two priorities. One was to continue training his army, the vast majority of which had no military experience. The second was to learn more about the strength and location of the enemy. For this, he relied heavily on two individuals—Erastus "Deaf" Smith and Henry W. Karnes.

Deaf Smith is well known in lore from his heroics as a scout and spy for the Texian cause. Lesser known but just as indispensable was Karnes. Unlike Smith, who was approaching forty-nine years of age, Karnes was only twenty-three. Despite his young age, however, Karnes was a well-respected captain in the Texian army because of to his experiences in early battles of the Texas Revolution. In a letter to James T. Collinsworth dated March 17, 1836, from Burnam's Ferry, Houston wrote, "I shall raise a company of spies to-morrow, to range the country from this to Gonzales."[2] He tasked Karnes with leading an expedition to determine the location of the Mexican troops and find out all he could regarding their plans. Karnes left the Texian camp with his command and headed across the Colorado by way of Burnam's Ferry.[3]

General Houston had good reason to hold Karnes in high regard. The young trooper, along with Deaf Smith and Robert Handy, had been dispatched by Houston from Gonzales to find out the disposition of the Alamo defenders. But Karnes' excellent reputation was largely earned a few months earlier at the Battle of Concepción and the Siege of Béxar. On December 7, 1835, during the final days of the latter engagement, Karnes was standing next to Benjamin R. Milam when he was unexpectedly struck down by a Mexican sniper. The popular leader's death enraged the Texians, who soon cleared the tree line of enemy riflemen. Although successful in this, the Texians were still under constant fire from Mexican artillery. They brought up their own artillery and a two-way barrage ensued. Mexican *soldados* took position on the roof of a large stone house, pinning down the Texians with relentless fire. Karnes, a short, stocky man who stood out mostly because of his bright red hair, had enough. He boldly told his comrades to cover him while he ran across the road and broke into that house. His fellow soldiers thought him crazy and implored him to remain, but Karnes sprang over the barricades, heading for a door. Quickly reaching it, he frantically began trying to pry it open with a crowbar. Fortunately, his position relative to the Mexicans above was such that he was somewhat protected. After a short while, he managed to force his way into the house. By this time, inspired by Karnes, others joined him. The unexpected entry by the Texians prompted a hasty attempt to exit by the Mexicans. While some escaped, several were taken prisoner. Karnes' heroic actions won him the respect of his compatriots.[4]

A call was made for volunteers to reconnoiter westward toward Gonzales and search for the location of the Mexican army. In a letter to Secretary of War Thomas J. Rusk, Colonel George W. Hockley, the ranking officer in Houston's staff, mentioned the spy company led by Karnes and reported that he was accompanied by five men.[5] Some sources report that six men were involved in this mission; however, an account of the expedition by one of the members, John Sharp, indicated that there were nine members.[6] Deaf Smith and Washington Secrest were part of Karnes' company. Sharp, Robert Handy, and Benjamin C. Franklin were from Captain Robert J. Calder's company. There are indications that James Owen was also present from Calder's troops. Another member was Clark Harmon, who belonged to Captain William Patton's company. Sharp identified another man as Murphy, but there is no record of anyone by that name. Most likely, he was remembering David Murphree, who had joined Patton a couple of days earlier.[7]

The group met at Burnam's place on the west side of the Colorado River on the afternoon of March 18, 1836. After acquiring provisions and corn for the horses, they set out. In Sharp's account, he states that "we were to go back the way we had come" to find the enemy. If this is the case, the group retraced the unusual route that Houston had led only two days prior. Upon reaching the Gonzales-San Felipe Road, the first thing to do was look for evidence that a large army had passed. If they found this, the Texians would have ridden east toward the Colorado. Clearly, they saw no such evidence and chose to go west. About an hour before nightfall, they stopped at the Navidad River and had supper before riding on to find a safe place to sleep. They settled under a large post oak on a prairie some distance from the main road, where they camped without a fire to avoid the attention of Indians or Mexican troops.[8] That night's rest would prove fortunate for them, because the next day they encountered the enemy.

Most of the population of Texas was enthusiastically supportive of the military when the battle was to the west in Gonzales or San Antonio

Portrait of renowned spy Erastus "Deaf" Smith.

Smith's scout Washington Secrest.

de Béxar. In a few days, however, the Texian army had withdrawn to the very doorstep of Stephen F. Austin's colony. The war was suddenly very close, and many of those men who had moved quickly to support the Texian cause now found themselves in an army camped near their own homesteads. As a result, the focus for many men became the safety of their family rather than the advancing Mexican army.

Houston was sympathetic to the situation. He was willing to allow furloughs if done in an official manner. Better this than desertions. In a letter dated March 17, Captain Moseley Baker, with approval from Colonel Edward Burleson, granted permission to Franklin J. Starr to return home so long as he agreed to return as soon as he made a "suitable disposition of his family."[9] Starr had arrived in Texas with his new bride late in 1835 and settled in San Felipe, where he became a law partner with William B. Travis. During March 1836, he relocated his family to Nacogdoches, where his wife gave birth.[10] He did not return from his furlough before the Battle of San Jacinto, but he did complete military service afterward. There were likely a few other furloughs granted at this time. Little did Houston realize that, in about a week's time, requests for furloughs would explode.

The Texian army under the command of Houston reached the Colorado with every intention of making a stand. It was logical for the Texians to guard the main roads that crossed the river. Houston had destroyed the ferry at Burnam's with the goal of moving down the river to Beeson's Crossing near Columbus. To the north of Burnam's place lay the La Bahía Road, which crossed the Colorado at Colonel John H. Moore's home near present-day La Grange. Here, the crossing was guarded on the east bank of the river by a company led by Joseph L. Bennett. Organized in Washington just a few days earlier, the company was on the way to Gonzales when news came of the defeat at the Alamo.[11]

One of the members of Bennett's company was fifteen-year-old William P. Zuber, who lived with his family in the eastern portion of present-day Grimes County. Zuber was meticulous in later documenting the events of the Texas Revolution and is regarded by some as the last living veteran of that conflict. The Moore family and others in the area had evacuated, and Zuber recounted the flow of refugees along the La Bahía Road: "A number of families in flight from Gonzales encamped near us. I saw old Mr. Martin, the father of Capt. Albert Martin who fell at the Alamo. He was sitting on the bank of the river, gazing into the flowing stream. He shed not a tear, but his whole body was convulsed in grief. His son had been in command of the thirty-two citizens of Gonzales who had entered the fort on the night of March 1."[12]

The refugees Zuber described likely included some that had parted with Houston at Williamson Daniels' place, choosing to head northwest along the La Bahía Road rather than continuing with the bulk of the Texian army due east. Some of the refugees fleeing Gonzales chose the La Bahía Road as an escape, but others decided to follow the Texian army to Burnam's Ferry. The civilian population would have been able to see firsthand whether the Texians could stop the advancing Mexicans and allow for a timely return for the families to their respective homesteads. A few other families may have opted not to follow the Texian army but to keep proceeding down the main road toward San Felipe and the heart of Austin's Colony.

After Captain Bennett's company had taken the time to fortify their position against possible enemy transgressions, Zuber described how guard duty was assigned:

> It was composed of three sergeants and six privates and divided into three reliefs, one sergeant and two privates to each relief. These reliefs were to stand on post alternatively, each two hours at a time. Their duty was to watch the river and, if they should see any man or body of men trying to cross from the west side, to hail them. Should they prove to be enemies, they should give an alarm

by firing upon them, then run into the encampment and join their comrades in defense or in retreat if such should be necessary... William Kennard and I were on this first guard. Neither of us having served previously, we were broken in by being placed on the first relief. We stood during the first tour and were also on post at midnight and at daybreak.[13]

Although the crossing on the La Bahía Road at Moore's Fort, as the site was known, could be considered potentially strategic, information obtained by Houston would change the priorities. Captain Bennett's time there soon came to an end. The owner of the property, however, was certainly a man relevant to the history of Texas.

Born in 1800, Moore had emigrated to Texas from Tennessee as a young man in 1821 and was one of Stephen F. Austin's "Old Three Hundred." Being single, he did as several others in Austin's Colony did by developing a partnership to maximize their potential land grant. He partnered with Thomas Gray and received title to a league west of the San Bernard River in what would become Brazoria County and a labor of land just northwest of present-day Glidden, bordering the Colorado.[14]

Moore earned an additional half league because of his marriage in 1827 to Eliza Cummins, the eighteen-year-old daughter of Judge James Cummins. This land was located on the Colorado at the crossing of the La Bahía Road. From there, the road extended to the northeast toward Washington and then onto Nacogdoches. To the south and west, it crossed the Gonzales-San Felipe Road near the Lavaca River and continued to Goliad. Shortly after receiving title to this land in 1831, Moore prioritized two things. First, he built a sturdy defensive structure for protection against attacks. Second, he applied to the Mina *ayuntamiento* for permission to establish a ferry at the site.[15] This crossing was a boon for Moore because it was on a road that connected the frontier settlements in the west with Austin's Colony and older communities such as Nacogdoches.

Portrait of John Henry Moore, commander of Texian forces at the Battle of Gonzales and owner of Moore's Crossing, located on the La Bahía Road on the Colorado River and located at the present site of La Grange.

After his marriage to Eliza, Moore started a family. His first son, William Bowen, was born in 1828, the year after his marriage and before he had moved onto his new property at what would become La Grange. Within three years, another boy, Armstead Adam, was born, but he tragically died in infancy. The next year, the couple welcomed their first girl, Tabitha. They lived in several buildings on the Moore property, including the blockhouse built to defend against an attacking enemy. It was described in detail by Zuber:

> At Colonel Moore's place I saw specimens of the old "blockhouses," built for fortification against assaults by Indians. It was a log cabin with the ground for the first floor and built as other log cabins to a height of about eight feet. A round of strong logs jutted out on each side and end, and probably twenty inches beyond the wall below. On these were placed two rounds of logs, one immediately above the wall below, the other six or eight inches farther out, making an opening through which a man could shoot down upon an enemy approaching the wall. The inner-side logs served as sills, or plates, upon which to place joists, and a puncheon floor extended about three feet inward from the side, all around the house. This served as a platform upon which a defender could stand or walk from point to point, as occasion might demand. Then a second story was built upon the outer rounds of logs and finished as other log cabins. At the proper height in the upper story, portholes were made in the walls, through which a defender could shoot an enemy before he could advance to the wall. I have never heard that Indians attacked a blockhouse, but, besides having a good defense, it was an excellent scarecrow to frighten them away.[16]

Blockhouses similar to that which Zuber described could be found at the homesteads of Burnam and Zadock Woods, as well as Moore.[17]

The oldest structure in Fayette County is purportedly located in

Blockhouse at Fort Parker, similar to the one present at Moore's Fort.

Classic dog-trot style house built in 1831, originally built at John Henry Moore's homestead and later restored and moved to Round Top.

present-day Round Top. A historical marker in La Grange, near the site of the building, refers to it as a "twin blockhouse" relocated from the property of Moore.[18] In reality, the building is a typical dogtrot, built with two enclosed areas with an open breezeway in between. There is precedent for such a building with a cannon positioned in the open passageway being referred to as a fort.[19] However, given Zuber's description, which is consistent with the distinctive cantilevered overhang that was typical of blockhouses, it is hard to call the Round Top structure a blockhouse. The dogtrot design was considerably more comfortable to live in, while the blockhouse described by Zuber would have been preferable during an attack. Moore, and others, likely had multiple houses. The dogtrot house in Round Top fortunately survived the widespread destruction of the Texas Revolution, especially during the Runaway Scrape, to serve as a tangible reminder of their stories.

In the early days of Austin's Colony, Indian depredations were common, and Moore was quick to volunteer to help in expeditions to quash that problem. In 1823, he was involved as a scout in an expedition against Karankawas at Skull Creek—possibly the first documented fight in Austin's Colony. Over the years, as his experience grew, Moore assumed more of a leadership role. In 1834, after reports of attacks along the upper Colorado, he sent calls to settlements on the Guadalupe, Colorado, Brazos, and Trinity rivers for reinforcements. He took charge of seventy-five men with Robert M. Williamson ("Three-legged Willie") as his second-in-command. During the next twenty-one days, they doggedly pursued a group of Indians. Finally, in a surprise attack, Moore's group routed the Indians, killing eleven of their foes and recovering several horses and cattle. One Texian was killed in the engagement.[20]

In 1835, Moore was involved in a peculiar and tragic event involving his brother-in-law, James Ross. Like Moore, Ross could be relied upon to join the militia when there were Indian depredations against colonists. Over time, however, he became increasingly friendly with some

Tonkawas, who often camped near his property. Ross purportedly had them gather his crops in exchange for whiskey. More disturbing, Ross encouraged them to raid Comanches for horses. Sabrina Townsend provided context when she recalled that: "Although they [the Tonkawas] were friendly with us, they were constantly plundering unfriendly Indians, causing them to follow the Tonkawas into the settlements when they would kill our people and steal our horses."[21] Ross benefitted greatly from the additional horseflesh, but his neighbors were understandably irritated.

The colonists had enough and demanded that Ross disassociate himself from the Tonkawas, which he refused to do. Moore was tasked with helping to rid the colonists of the nuisance of the Tonkawas. On January 14, 1835, Moore, accompanied by John Rabb and James Lester, rode for the Tonkawa encampment. As they were passing Ross' home, Ross yelled "halt, you have gone far enough." He then raised a gun and fired. Moore, Lester, and Rabb returned fire, killing Ross.[22] Moore thus bore part of the blame for killing the husband of his wife's sister.

Although 'Indian fighter' is the sobriquet most often used for Moore, he played a significant role in the Texas Revolution. It began in the village of Gonzales where in late September 1835, a Mexican officer was ordered to retrieve a cannon from the residents there. Mexican forces were positioned on the west side of the Guadalupe, unable to cross because of high water and lack of access to a ferry, which was safely sequestered on the east side. While the citizens of Gonzales were stalling Mexican officials who had come to retrieve the cannon in question, Texians from the Guadalupe to the Brazos were rushing to heed the call for aid. Upon arrival, the group elected Moore to lead their group, with the rank of colonel. Joseph W. E. Wallace was elected to be second-in-command with the rank of lieutenant colonel.[23]

The Mexican officer was informed that they would not give up the cannon without a fight. As a show of defiance, Williamson, a major in

Moore's command, and others drew the cannon out into the view of the helpless Mexicans. Above it flew a flag that boldly proclaimed, "Come and Take It!"[24] The Mexicans responded by moving their camp upriver several miles to find another crossing.

On the morning of October 1, 1835, Moore called a council of war. The impatient Texians decided that they had ridden too far to just go home without a fight. The council unanimously declared that "we will hoist the flag of liberty and attack the Mexican in their encampment on to-morrow morning at daybreak."[25] That night, the Texians, led by Moore, crossed to the west bank of the Guadalupe and moved upriver toward the Mexican encampment with their small cannon in tow. During a foggy morning, the Texians crept closer. Once they were in position, Moore ordered the cavalry to attack, then fall back. A small group of Mexican troopers pursued the retreating Texian horsemen and was greeted by fire from the disputed cannon.[26]

Lieutenant Francisco Casteñeda, who had been ordered to retrieve the cannon without inciting hostilities, called for a parlay. Moore and Casteñeda met within sight of the two camps and, after conversing for some time, departed with no resolution to the situation. Just as Moore crossed the lines, Lieutenant Colonel Wallace ordered the Texians to open fire. The Mexicans immediately withdrew, and the encounter ended. The first conflict of the Texas Revolution resulted in but a single Mexican casualty.[27]

In a letter dated October 6, Moore reported that the volunteers at Gonzales had ballooned to three hundred. A request was submitted that Austin come immediately to Gonzales to assume command of the forces there. While they waited, the many factions of the volunteers could not agree on who should be in command. Fortunately, Austin arrived and unified the forces, being elected commander unanimously.[28]

After Austin's arrival, elections were held once again to establish the officers and, once again, Moore was elected as a colonel.[29] However, with

Austin clearly in charge, Moore's duties as primary decision-maker were over. The last date for orders issued to Moore was October 26, when Austin ordered him to organize a unit of cavalry "formed by those who have double barrel shot guns and pistols."[30] The Battle of Concepción raged while Moore was on patrol. Maybe sensing that his duties had been usurped or deciding that he had other priorities, Moore resigned his commission on November 6. Perhaps not coincidentally, Travis, who was performing similar duties as Moore, resigned his commission as "Captain of Cavalry" on the same day.[31] Austin wrote in accepting Moore's resignation, "He is therefore discharged from service by request. I have to add that he has faithfully and diligently discharged his duty as a patriot and a friend to the cause."[32]

By the time Texian forces under Houston had reached Burnam's, Moore had already moved his family from their homestead near present-day La Grange.[33] As Texian forces were crossing the river at Burnam's, Moore was in Washington helping to recruit and organize a company for the town's defense. This company, known as the "Washington Guards," filled its ranks by April 7, 1836. Moore did not take charge of the recruits; instead, command went to Captain Joseph B. Chance and Major Williamson.[34] Though Moore participated in no other battles of the Texas Revolution, he continued to lead men in expeditions and remain an important asset to the new Republic going forward.

5

ON THE MOVE
DAY 4, MARCH 19

"They had taken one prisoner, who, poor devil, was so busily engaged pleading for his life, that we could get little out of him, for some time."[1]

JOHN SHARP

UNTIL THE TEXIAN ARMY CROSSED the Colorado River, desperate civilians trying to escape the Mexican advance impeded its movement. After crossing, some civilians may have moved north along the Wilbarger Road and on to Washington and Nacogdoches. Other families may have remained with the army. Regardless, crossing the Colorado helped create a barrier from the pursuing Mexican army and lifted, at least somewhat, the burden of the Texian army for overseeing the passage of the civilian population.

Though Sam Houston may have originally intended to stay at Burnam's Ferry for a period, he clearly revised those plans, as evidenced by the fact that he instructed Henry W. Karnes to meet them at Beeson's Crossing after his scouting expedition. After the Texian army crossed the Colorado, Houston immediately moved south a few miles to John Crier's homestead.

His stay at Crier's was brief. On the morning of departure, Quartermaster Benjamin F. Smith purchased two cows, one steer and forty bushels of corn from Crier. David Kornegay, a recent recruit from the area for the Texian army, also signed some of the official invoices for supplies.[2] After buying provisions from Jesse Burnam, the Texians had destroyed his homestead. Did the same happen at Crier's? No record was found that indicated Crier asked the government to compensate him for the destruction of his property. Burnam's place was located at a significant river crossing and had been a refuge where nearby settlers would escape when there were Indian depredations in the area. Perhaps the size and scale of Crier's property was too small and too far off the beaten track for Houston to think it held much value for the Mexicans.

Alternatively, it may be that Houston set fire to Crier's home as well. William P. Zuber noted that the barn and its contents at James Ross' former homestead, located across from and slightly upriver of Burnam's, had been burned.[3] This, along with Houston's future actions, would suggest that Crier's place may have met the same fate as the others. If so, sixteen-year-old Andrew Crier, who had joined the army the previous day, may have watched his home go up in flames, just as John H. and William Burnam had.[4] Unfortunately, over the coming days, other army members would have to endure the same trauma while watching their homes destroyed.

On the morning of March 19, General Houston and the Texian soldiers commenced the arduous march toward the major Colorado crossings on the Gonzales-San Felipe Road. This was the same road that they had left shortly after leaving Thompson's place on the morning of March 16, 1836. This road split a few miles west of the Colorado River. The south road led to Beeson's Crossing. The northern road led to what sometimes was called Moseley's Crossing, but it later became more closely associated with a low-water ford at William B. Dewees' homestead.[5] The distance to traverse from Crier's to Beeson's was about fifteen miles.

Unlike their trip from Thompson's home to Burnam's Ferry, during which the Texians stayed mostly on high ground and traveled over open areas, the route roughly paralleling the Colorado, and present-day Highway 71, would force them to cross at least five creeks and travel through more heavily wooded areas. Today, the average person does not think twice when riding in a car along a paved road as they cross numerous, often unnoticed creeks. However, every one of those small creeks was an obstacle that had to be navigated, and with the persistent rain during this time, crossing was often no small matter.[6] Though most maps of this time give no evidence of a road in this area, Stephen F. Austin's 1829 map does show a road paralleling the Colorado's east bank. There were several land grants along the river, so perhaps Austin's depiction of a road should not be surprising. One of the grant recipients along the way was Captain Peyton Splane, whose company had joined Houston's retreat only a few days prior. He may have provided some directions for the General.

Some uncertainty remains about exactly where the Texians camped on the night of March 19. Few accounts of what was happening in Houston's army during this interval exist. One came from Zuber, who stayed with Captain Joseph L. Bennett's company as it trailed behind the main Texian army from Burnam's. Zuber stated that his company "marched during all the night of the nineteenth, and just at daybreak on the morning of the twentieth we arrived at the encampment." He noted that a detachment under Captains William Patton and William Ware was already there when they arrived.[7] If this account is accurate, it might suggest that the Texian army arrived at Dewees' Ford on March 19 from Crier's. Another account by Jonathan H. Kuykendall, who was with the main army, reported that, "On the 19th, we marched a few miles farther down [from Crier's] and camped early in the day in the post oak woods." He further noted that "on the 20th, the army moved a few miles farther down the river and encamped nearly opposite Beason's." If he is correct, the army did not arrive until March 20 at Dewees' and Beeson's homesteads.[8]

Both accounts were recorded several years after the fact, but since Kuykendall was traveling with the main army, the assumption will be that the bulk of the Texian army arrived at Beeson's homesite early on March 20.[9] If so, the most logical campsite for the army on the night of March 19 might have been on the banks of Cummins Creek, named after James Cummins, who had leagues of land on that waterway awarded to him. Cummins, the largest of five creeks in this area that the Texian army would have to navigate, was also the closest waterway to their final destination.[10]

When Cummins Creek was swollen, it could be quite formidable to cross. The incised creek bed had steep banks on either side that, with a rapid flow of water, made any crossing treacherous. Not often is routine travel recorded in historical accounts, but one incident does show the significance of Cummins Creek as a barrier. James T. Ross, the son of James Ross, was a young boy when he was sent to acquire refreshments for a ball that his father was planning. The Ross place was located on the eastern side of the Colorado, upriver from where Houston had encamped at Crier's. Young Ross was sent to San Felipe to get the required refreshments. The trip was not without incident: "Cummins Creek was very high, and my father thought I might not cross it. When I arrived at the creek, it was booming. I was thinking of going home." Ultimately, the young boy made it across with the help of a Coushatta Indian. As he arrived home from his errand, he remembered, "The whole gallery [was] filled with people. I saw them waving their handkerchiefs, but I did not know what it meant until I reached the house. They had been betting with my father on my not getting over Cummins Creek."[11]

Perhaps Houston knew that it was going to take some time for his army to safely cross and did not want to be in a position of only having half of his troops cross before dark. He may have decided just to camp there and traverse the stream early the next morning. This delay may not have seemed significant at the time, but considering the Mexican army's location, it could have been a significant miscalculation. Fortunately for the Texians, the scouts that Houston dispatched had an impact on the Mexican army.

Cummins Creek at FM 109, north of Columbus, and near the point where the Texian army likely camped the night of March 19, 1836. High water and steep banks would have made a crossing challenging.

On the morning of March 19, 1836, Karnes' small party left their make-shift camp and worked their way back to the main Gonzales-San Felipe Road near the Navidad River.[12] Shortly afterward, as they approached Rocky Creek, they found fresh tracks.[13] Erastus "Deaf" Smith, being the most experienced tracker, examined these and determined that ten to twelve horses had passed within the hour.[14] Knowing the enemy was close at hand, the men checked their firearms to ensure they were ready and proceeded at a brisk pace to follow the tracks westward.

It did not take long for the Texians to find what they were looking for. Two or three hundred yards off the road, they saw six Mexican soldiers on horseback leisurely leading several other horses.[15] While Karnes was tasked with seeking out the whereabouts of Mexican troops, the latter evidently wanted no part of an encounter with the Texians. Instead, after seeing the Texians approach, they scattered in different directions, spurring their mounts to depart as quickly as their abilities would allow. Unattended horses were left to fend for themselves. The Texian party pursued vigorously, firing their pistols. The Mexicans managed to stay ahead of their pursuers until Robert Handy shot one of their horses. The Mexican soldier recovered from his fall and fired a shot at Karnes as he rode past, still pursuing the others. Washington Secrest dealt with the threat by shooting the Mexican in the torso. When the soldier still showed some fight, Secrest finished the job by shooting him through the head.[16] Meanwhile, the rest of the Texians continued their pursuit of the Mexicans on horseback.

While being chased on horseback, one must assess the tactical situation on the fly. If you are outpacing your pursuer, then just keep riding and increase the distance. But if your pursuers are closing the gap at an unacceptable rate, it becomes necessary to take stock of the situation and adjust your tactics. Some of the fleeing Mexican soldiers did just that. They rode for the thick brush of the Navidad River bottom, where pursuit by horseback was virtually impossible. Abandoning their horses, they dove into the dense thickets. Karnes and his men, one hundred yards behind, did the same, continuing their pursuit on foot.[17]

John Sharp, diligently in pursuit, jumped into Rocky Creek and began to wade across. With his focus on the enemy ahead, it must have come as quite the surprise when he was suddenly knocked over by a flying horse who, frightened by the activity, decided that he was following his rider rather than waiting out in the open prairie. Sharp found himself and his gun submerged, yielding both temporarily useless. Fortunately, he was uninjured and was able to find dry gunpowder to refill his gun.

Meanwhile, Karnes, Smith, and Daniel Murphree had better luck in their pursuit. The three had managed to capture one of the fleeing Mexican scouts. The Texians were interested in learning from their new prisoner the disposition of the enemy. The captive Mexican's priority was decidedly different. He spent time begging for his life. Perhaps he had reason to be worried since later it was determined that one of the Mexican horses captured by the Texian scouts had saddlebags containing clothing that was identified as belonging to an Alamo defender.[18]

Three Texian pursuers had lost their horses after having dismounted to enter the heavy brush. Karnes, however, managed to capture a Mexican horse. The group tied the prisoner's hands behind him and, led by Smith, started the walk back along their original line of pursuit. Along the way, they found two lances, a wallet of provisions and a pair of hats and cloaks. Eventually, Karnes, Smith and Murphree made their way back to where Secrest was waiting for them next to the body of the Mexican soldier. The Texians gathered his weapons and checked his horse who, unfortunately, was too lame to ride. They then started toward the main road.

Their progress east was slow, having to travel on foot. They crossed the Navidad at Thompson's home near where the Texian army had camped on the night of March 15. There, they stopped for their first meal of the day and to check the Mexican wallets that they had appropriated earlier. Most importantly, they started to question their prisoner. With

While pursuing a fleeing Mexican soldier, John Sharp is surprised when his horse decides to unexpectedly join him.

Deaf Smith as translator, they learned that the Mexican army, led by General Joaquín Ramírez y Sesma, was 600 to 800 men strong with two pieces of artillery and 60 to 70 cavalrymen. More importantly, this army had camped at Daniels' place the night before and was scheduled to continue its move eastward to the Colorado that day.[19] For the Texian scouts who, at present, were on foot, this information no doubt inspired them to a more rapid pace.

When the Texian army had departed from Thompson's place on the morning of March 16, they left his home intact. This time, in keeping with Houston's precedent, Karnes' group made the difficult decision to burn Thompson's homestead.[20] They then headed east along the main road toward Beeson's Crossing on the Colorado. The distance was about twenty-two miles and, with Murphree, Sharp, and the prisoner on foot, it proved to be a slow journey. Fortunately for the Texians, not long after their departure, Karnes and Secrest joined them with two horses, one with nothing but a rope around its neck and the other fully saddled.

After some time, they finally discovered some of the remaining members of their group: Benjamin C. Franklin, Clark Harmon, and James Owen. Prisoner transport was assigned to Franklin, and the frightened Mexican soldier, with his hands still bound behind him, was put on the back of his horse. With the possibility that the Mexicans would send more cavalry on patrol, it was in the Texians' best interest to make themselves scarce. The additional horses made the distance to travel seem considerably easier. Unfortunately, luck would not stay on their side. The horse that Sharp was riding had been abandoned by the Mexicans. It was so "completely broken down" that it was deemed to be unrideable, and Sharp was again relegated to traveling by foot, although others in the group did take turns sharing their mounts with him.[21]

By nightfall, the group finally arrived at Beeson's Crossing, just south of present-day Columbus, where they encountered a guard posted by Captain Wyly Martin's company. Owen was assigned the task of escort-

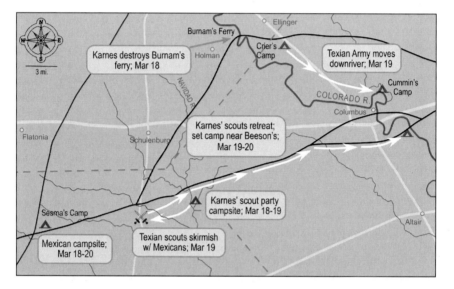

Projected route of Henry W. Karnes' scout party from the campsite on the Navidad River to the site of the skirmish with Mexican soldiers and then to the Colorado River at Beeson's Crossing. Map also shows the site of the Mexican army encampment and the projected route of the Texian army from Crier's Camp to Cummins Creek. Historic roads in black and modern roads in gray.

ing the prisoner across the river to Houston and the rest of the army. Since Houston had not reached Beeson's yet, Owen would have a bit further to travel in the darkness to deliver his prisoner. Doubtless exhausted by a long day and comfortable that they were out of reach of the enemy, the others camped on the western side of the Colorado.[22]

6

ARRIVING AT BEESON'S
DAY 5, MARCH 20

> "On arriving at the Colorado, a detachment of some one hundred and fifty or two hundred men were left at Dewees'…, and the main army encamped…on the east side of the Colorado, about a mile from the river, and opposite Beason's."[1]
>
> ROBERT J. CALDER

AFTER HAVING RECEIVED the report from the recently captured Mexican prisoner, Sam Houston probably moved his army out before dawn on March 20, 1836, to have time to set up a defensive position at his chosen sites along the east bank of the Colorado River. As noted earlier, two crossings near modern Columbus were commonly used. The one near William B. Dewees' home was a low-water ford where no ferry operated. When the river was high, as it was during this period, crossing would have been difficult and possibly dangerous. The southern crossing was located near Benjamin Beeson's house. Unlike Dewees' Ford, this location did employ a ferry when the river was high.

Regardless of the likelihood of Dewees' Ford as a potential crossing site for the Mexican army, it was only prudent for Houston to guard it. As a result, he split his army for the first time. After his troops crossed Cummins Creek and rounded the big loop in the river, Houston sent Lieutenant Colonel Sidney Sherman and Captain William Patton's company toward Dewees' Ford with orders to guard that crossing. When Sherman arrived at Dewees', he found a small company of volunteers already there. Captain William Ware had organized his company a week earlier in the San Bernard River area. Most of his men, about eighteen in number, were from present-day Montgomery County.[2] Ware had come to Texas in 1831 and settled near present-day Willis. He was a commander during the Siege of Béxar, in which he was slightly wounded.[3]

After Sherman's new command departed, Houston led the remainder of his army southeast another three miles or so to the crossing that he considered more strategic: Beeson's Crossing. Like Sherman, Houston was met by reinforcements already there. A company of thirty men under the command of Captain Wyly Martin awaited the arrival of the Texian army.[4] Martin was one of Stephen F. Austin's Old Three Hundred and, at the age of sixty, one of the oldest in the Texian army. He was an important and influential member of Austin's Colony, having served as an *alcalde* and a delegate representing San Felipe in the conventions of 1832, 1833 and 1835.[5] Like Austin, Martin was reluctant to join the early calls for independence. After the recent massacre at the Alamo, he quickly changed his mind and raised his company from around San Felipe and along the Brazos. Unlike many others, Martin had military experience, having been an officer in the War of 1812 under William Henry Harrison and Andrew Jackson.[6]

Houston issued no dispatches or written orders on March 20, 1836. The day must have been chaotic, to say the least. The Texians had just arrived at the two key crossings on the Colorado. While they had to prepare for the impending arrival of the Mexican army, they also had to deal with a notable influx of manpower. While it was certainly good that volunteers heeded the call to arms, it must have been particularly hectic trying to organize a defensive position while absorbing additional companies into the command.

DAY 5: ARRIVING *at* BEESON'S | 77

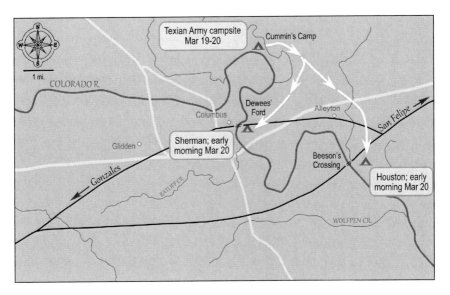

Projected route of the Texian army from Cummins Creek and the split of the army to Dewees' Ford and Beeson's Crossing on the Colorado River. Historic roads in black and modern roads in gray.

New recruits poured into both encampments. Besides the arrival of Captain Martin's company on March 19, three other companies joined Houston's encampment at Beeson's. The largest contingent was Captain William M. Logan's Liberty Volunteers. Logan, an early and active resident of Austin's Colony and a veteran of the Siege of Béxar, began recruiting the company in early March when word of William B. Travis' appeal for help reached Liberty.[7] Others helped to fill the ranks. Benjamin Harper recruited twenty-eight men in Beaumont. Benjamin F. Hardin mustered an additional twenty volunteers north of Liberty. The company elected Logan as captain and Harper and Hardin as lieutenants.[8] Before they reached the Colorado, their ranks had swelled to nearly eighty, significantly enhancing Houston's army.[9]

One of the notable members of the Liberty Volunteers was Nicholas D. Labadie. A French Canadian who had settled in Texas in 1831, Labadie had previously served as surgeon for a military outpost in Anahuac. His medical expertise proved useful to the fledgling army. On the march to Beeson's, Labadie reported regularly treating "cramps, colics and diarrhea" among those in his company.[10] He was also a good chronicler of the events of the Texas Revolution.

Not all the volunteers at Beeson's came from Liberty. Captain Thomas McIntire, a recent arrival to Texas in February, recruited heavily around Washington Municipality. Although new to the area, McIntire was able to recruit several veterans of the Siege of Béxar. His company numbered about forty.[11] Another company of men, recruited from the Fort Bend area under the command of Captain Daniel Perry, arrived around March 20. Lieutenant Ebenezer Hale bought supplies while the small company was passing through San Felipe on March 18. This date would be consistent with the company arriving about March 20, shortly after the main Texian army.[12]

Reinforcements were arriving at Dewees' Ford as well. A company under the command of Captain Joseph L. Bennett had been guarding the

La Bahía Road crossing at Moore's Fort near present-day La Grange when he received orders to march down the river to join forces with Houston. Bennett, a veteran of both the Battle of Concepción and Siege of Béxar, recruited men from the area that now comprises Montgomery, Walker, and Grimes counties.[13] Among them was William P. Zuber, whose recollections became a popular source for the history of Texas.

Captain Stephen Townsend's company of rangers formed on February 1, 1836, in response to Indian attacks along the Colorado. The men were stationed at the head of Mill Creek, near present-day Burton. The company included three of Townsend's younger brothers and a nephew, in addition to a few neighbors who were veterans of the Siege of Béxar.[14] Answering the call to arms, Townsend's rangers rode to Burnam's Ferry, where they met Captain Bennett's company moving south to join Houston's forces. The two companies marched together all night, arriving at Dewees' Ford in the early morning hours of March 20, probably not long after Sherman and Patton had arrived.[15]

Later in the same day, a company of regulars arrived at Dewees'. The company, formed in Nacogdoches under the command of Lieutenant Henry Teal, was composed mostly of men who had recently arrived in Texas.[16] This company marched to Washington, where on March 15, 1836, Teal was officially made captain in command of the company and invited to attend the proceedings of the Convention for the day.[17] Teal's company would not stay long at Dewees' Ford. Two days later, the company of about forty men moved downriver to support Houston at Beeson's Crossing.

Based on the information gleaned from the prisoner captured by Henry W. Karnes' scouting expedition, Houston learned who commanded the approaching Mexican forces, the approximate number of his cavalry and infantry, their morale and condition, the nature of their artillery, and their anticipated arrival time, not to mention information on the overall strategy of his opponent, Antonio López de Santa Anna. Houston's priority, of course, was to prepare for the arrival of the enemy. This preparation included multiple elements.

First, both Texian campsites needed to fortify their positions. Trenches were dug and breastworks built to protect against enemy fire. In a letter to Secretary of War Thomas J. Rusk, Colonel George W. Hockley described conditions at Sherman's encampment: "A detachment of two hundred men are now at Mosely's (Dewees') crossing. The camp will be reformed in a thick wood on the bank of the river, and in a position highly favorable for observation and defense, its present flanks and front being well protected by felled trees, brush, and timber." Sherman was initially dug in only a few yards away and within the sand deposits of the Colorado.[18]

The main encampment of the Texian army is described in correspondence as "Camp near Beason's." Because they were across the river from Benjamin Beeson's homestead, they were indeed only "near Beason's." In reality, they were some distance away from the river and ferry within the timberline of post oaks near the homestead of Rhoda Hunt.[19] Perhaps by keeping Sherman's encampment more visible and Houston's more hidden, the Mexican army would be less certain as to where the bulk of the Texians might be.

Houston's next task was to ensure an adequate supply of provisions. Fortunately for his army, numerous settlers had stockpiled abundant provisions along this section of the Colorado. Accumulating these on the east side of the river would not only provide for the needs of the Texians but would also serve to deprive the Mexican army.

One of the nearby sources of provisions was Hunt, who later claimed that she provided the Texian army with 2,000 pounds of bacon, 300 pounds of lard, and twenty hogs. Additionally, Hunt alleged that Houston's men used all her household and kitchen furniture after she departed. Joseph W. E. Wallace happened to live with the Hunts and had a store on the premises.[20] Wallace was a lieutenant colonel and second in command

Approximate site of Dewees' Ford (also known as Moseley's) near present-day Columbus and near where Lieutenant Colonel Sidney Sherman's command encamped.

at the Battle of Gonzales.²¹ Provisions signed for by Captain Patton for the benefit of Sherman's troops at Dewees' Ford included coffee, sugar, whiskey, and several types of fabrics. Captain William Wood signed for provisions for Houston's encampment near Beeson's Crossing, although some axes were evidently delivered to Martin's company. Wallace also made note of provisions lost after his store was abandoned.²²

Throughout the Texian's sojourn on the Colorado, they repeatedly tried to drive livestock across the river, presumably to not only provide for the Texian army, but to keep them from the Mexicans. Houston specifically directed in his March 17 orders that "Stock of all descriptions will be driven to the east side of the Colorado."²³ Soon after he arrived, Robert H. Hunter of Captain John Bird's company noted an unsuccessful attempt to drive a sheep herd across the river near Beeson's.²⁴ Likewise, there was an early attempt to drive a herd of cattle over the river as the Mexican army approached.²⁵ Even Colonel Juan N. Almonte of the Mexican army, who did not arrive at the Colorado until several days after General Joaquín Ramírez y Sesma, wrote in his journal that "about 50 cavalry of the enemy started off in small parties, and carried with them about 50 cattle that were grazing in the plain, within sight."²⁶

Sherman camped across from the nascent town of Columbus. Though the town might have been surveyed, no lots had been sold and no construction commenced. Nevertheless, some lived in the immediate area, including Martha Hill Bostick, James Wright, Robert Moseley, and, of course, Dewees.²⁷ The deed for the Elizabeth Tumlinson league, when it was divided among her children in 1833, had used a schoolhouse as a point of reference.²⁸ Some of that family may still have resided in the immediate area. It appears there were several houses and structures in the immediate vicinity of Dewees' on both sides of the river. One of the more bizarre orders from the Texians was to physically move the Bostick home from its location inside the bend of the Colorado. According to Wallace, this was done by Juan N. Seguín and members of his company for "the purpose of shelter during the difficulties of the time."²⁹

Despite Dewees' best efforts, the area around Beeson's was at this point still the primary river crossing and population center. With a gin, sawmill, and boardinghouse, not to mention their home and any slave quarters, there were plenty of buildings around Beeson's property. Additionally, other residents that had occupations such as tanners, blacksmiths, and tailors, among others, may well have lived in the immediate vicinity.

Despite the approach of the Mexican army, reconnaissance was not necessarily a priority. Houston already had reliable information about the oncoming enemy. The final element of preparation would be a proactive one. As much as possible, he wanted to dictate where the Mexicans encamped. Certainly, one of the worst scenarios would be for the Mexican army, with its superior artillery, to settle within and behind the structures across the river. To that end, rather than committing a simple scouting party to track the Mexican army position, Houston decided instead to commit a larger contingent across the river shortly after his arrival on March 20. If the Mexicans approached, they would meet resistance, which would hopefully slow their advance to the river. The companies of Captains Peyton Splane and Captain Robert J. Calder were therefore ordered to camp at Beeson's during the evening and night of March 21, 1836. Major Benjamin F. Smith, appointed by Houston to be his acting Quartermaster General and Adjutant General, was given command of these units.³⁰ Houston had plans for Smith to help ensure the Mexican army encampment would be pushed further from the river.

On New Year's Day of 1823, while he was still in Mexico, Austin wrote to his brother, "give my respects to Baron Bastrop...He must come and live with me on the Colorado when I get comfortably fixed there."³¹ It was another eight months before Austin arrived back in his colony, bringing with him the news that the newly installed Mexican government had approved his grant and that the settlers would soon be receiving titles to their land. His first stop upon his arrival was at the settlements along the Colorado.³²

Present site of Beeson's Crossing south of present-day Columbus and near where General Sam Houston's command encamped.

The site Austin favored was downriver from James Cummins' home, which he described as being "very well watered with the best of springs."[33] Dewees claimed to have accompanied Austin on his reconnaissance of the area. "He [Austin] was on this river with a surveyor, having lots laid off from a tract of land that he had just located for the purpose of building a town."[34] The surveyor that Dewees referenced was most likely Rawson Alley, an early settler on the Colorado in Austin's Colony. Alley surveyed many of the grants in this vicinity, including the Elizabeth Tumlinson survey where Austin was presumably looking to build his headquarters.[35] Austin's enthusiasm for the site, however, was diminished when he realized the frequency of Indian incursions into the area. He eventually selected a site on the Brazos River for his home. But other colonists took notice of Austin's interest, including Beeson and Dewees.

Early lawlessness in the area was of concern to the settlers along the Colorado. Baron de Bastrop encouraged settlers there to form a local government with a militia to combat Indian depredations and other acts of crime. The colonists elected John J. Tumlinson as *alcalde* and Robert H. Kuykendall as captain of the militia.[36]

Austin included a map in his application for an empresario grant to the Mexican government. This early map showed three roads that extended through the area of Texas that interested him. The three roads were essentially equivalent to the San Antonio Road, the La Bahía Road and the Atascosito Road.[37] Other early maps by Austin had the same three roads, often with different names. The San Antonio Road represented the northern boundary of Austin's original colony, crossing the Colorado at Mina (now Bastrop). The La Bahía Road crossed the Colorado near present-day La Grange. The Atascosito Road crossed the Colorado about eight miles south of present-day Columbus. In a later map, Austin labeled this crossing as Montezuma, named by the Spaniards for an old Indian campsite that was evidently present there.[38]

As more colonists began to arrive, Tumlinson encouraged Thomas

Rogers to offer a ferry service at Montezuma along the Atascosito Road. Rogers agreed, and by December 1822 he had built a cabin and was operating a ferry. Within weeks, however, Rogers and another visitor were brutally murdered. A witness claimed the murderers were four Spanish men who had visited Rogers earlier.[39] Colonists were understandably horrified by this news. The murder and the remoteness of the site relative to other settlements meant that no one was clamoring to replace Rogers. This may have in part contributed to the demise of the Atascosito Road as a primary thoroughfare.

It was important to establish another river crossing and the settler with the most fortuitous location for this crossing was Beeson. As part of Austin's Old Three Hundred, Benjamin and Elizabeth Beeson had received title to their land on August 7, 1824.[40] Their property was only about three miles north of the Atascosito Crossing and thirty miles south of the crossing at La Bahía, and it was more or less on a direct line between Austin's headquarters at San Felipe to the east and San Antonio de Béxar to the west.

As fortuitous as Beeson's location may have seemed, he faced a lot of adversity. Shortly after arriving, his family was abducted by Wacos. The Indians had also taken some residents of Béxar and fortunately, being more familiar with their ways, the San Antonio residents managed to negotiate their release.[41] Nevertheless, it was more than understandable that the Beesons were reluctant to move from the John Hadden grant on the east side of the river, where they originally settled, to their grant on the west side. However, the laws of Austin Colony stated that Beeson needed to reside upon (or cultivate) his land or else forfeit it.[42] By the time Beeson moved to his new residence west of the Colorado, he had a family with a wife and six children, a hired hand, and seven slaves who provided some degree of security against Indian attacks.[43]

Beeson made the most of his advantageous location. He quickly established a ferry service near the southern end of his grant. He built an inn to accommodate travelers, which his wife Elizabeth, known as Betsy, managed. With hard work, they garnered success and happiness. From 1827 through 1829, Manuel de Mier y Terán led an expedition in Texas commissioned ostensibly for scientific purposes and to determine the United States-Mexico boundary. In 1828, Terán passed through the Beeson property and came away suitably impressed:

> He is quite urbane, his family very honorable. Their services were very helpful to us.... This settler enjoys more comforts than all those at the Guadalupe: a nice dwelling, a large field, 60 to 80 head of cattle, and a greater number of pigs and hens. They have begun to grow garden plants, having already served us lettuce and onions. They cultivate corn, from which they make a bread... Madame speaks Spanish well enough to be understood in conversation, as does a daughter aged sixteen...Madame says they have 1,200 pesos in savings. They have been on this land for five years, and they speak with great satisfaction of its fertility and good climate. In a word, they seem happy.[44]

Jean Louis Berlandier, a naturalist and anthropologist accompanying Mier y Terán on the same trip, made similar observations:

> Today, aside from a capital of two thousand piastres, they number their livestock by the hundreds and have quite a comfortable house and several cleared and sown fields. Their industry is wholly rural: they raise pigs, oxen, cows, and some horses, and cultivate corn and camotes. The land there grows cotton, tobacco, and beans, and in dry years wheat has prospered.[45]

Just like the Burnam clan upriver, the Beeson family seemed to be thriving. From 1825 to 1836, Beeson's became an increasingly popular way station for travelers crossing Texas.

Austin was generally not in favor of single men in his colony, preferring established family men such as Burnam or Beeson. The original allocation was that a household (husband and wife) would receive a labor (about 177 acres) of land if they were farmers and a full league of land (about 4,428 acres) if they raised livestock. Single men felt disadvantaged by this rule. Through negotiation and compromise, the rule was modified so that eventually two or more men could partner together and receive the same benefit as a household.[46] Eventually, Austin awarded grants to thirty-two partnerships of this type.

Dewees was a single man when he arrived in Austin's Colony in 1822. He partnered with James Cook and in August 1824, Austin awarded them a league of land about five miles below Beeson's property. Dewees later married Lydia Beeson, the daughter of Benjamin and his wife Elizabeth. Because Dewees' status had changed and he was part of a household, he was awarded an augmentation property–an additional half league located to the north of where the Colorado River turned west.[47]

Dewees took a keen interest in Austin's reconnoitering activities in 1823. His enthusiasm for the area Austin surveyed did not diminish, even when Austin chose to place his capital on the Brazos. Indeed, Dewees was motivated from an early time to acquire and develop acreage near the big, distinctive loop in the Colorado River. Although the augmentation property he received after his marriage was near the area Austin had surveyed, the land that he seemed to covet most was granted to the Tumlinson family. He spent the better part of a decade trying to acquire this prime real estate.

John J. and Elizabeth Tumlinson arrived with their family of six children from North Carolina in 1821. John quickly became a leader within the colony. Appointed the district's first *alcalde*, he was credited, in part, with forming what would eventually become the forerunner of the Texas Rangers. Unfortunately, he was also the first in that organization to lose his life when he was killed in July 1823 by Wacos or Tawakonis while on his way to San Antonio.[48] The death of her husband put Elizabeth in a difficult position. She had not yet been granted a deed to the land that they settled. However, because John had been such an asset to the colony and several of their children were of or near adult age, Austin did the right thing and gave the widow a league and labor in 1824.[49]

Tumlinson and her family did what they could to meet the necessary requirements for the league of land. No doubt, Austin and her neighbors were sympathetic, but the situation only worsened when, in 1829, Elizabeth died, adding considerable uncertainty as to what would happen to the desirable property she possessed. To show a presence on the land and perhaps more importantly, provide an income, the Tumlinson plantation was put up for rent. In 1830, notices appeared in area newspapers advertising rental of "The Plantation, formerly occupied by Mrs. E. Tumlinson, Colorado."[50] It may well be that Moseley saw the advertisements and responded; however, though he clearly became a resident of the area, it seems that Moseley settled on the east side of the river, on the Hadden survey, rather than on the Tumlinson grant.

Bill Stein, a historian well versed in the events of this area, wrote that Moseley rented and lived on the Tumlinson property on the west side of the river.[51] Travis, future commander at the Alamo but then a lawyer from San Felipe, conducted business with a client while at Moseley's place. In an April 26, 1834, diary entry, he wrote, "Left Mosely's—swam creek—& arrived in San Felipe—to supper…" This might suggest that upon leaving Moseley's residence, he swam the Colorado to go to San Felipe, further suggesting that Moseley lived west of the river.[52] Alternatively, it might have been the San Bernard River or some other creek that Travis swam. Almonte, in his journal, specifically mentions crossing to the eastern side of the Colorado and traveling to Moseley's house.[53] Regardless of the exact location, Moseley's residence became associated with the crossing during its early usage. On October 8, 1835, Austin, on his way from San Felipe to take command of the Texian forces at Gonzales, wrote a letter addressed from "Mosley's" [sic].[54]

The first time the site was referenced with the Dewees' name was by Benjamin Lundy in August 1834.[55] Dewees was clearly living on the site but must have been renting from the Tumlinsons at that point. In 1829, he had continued to acquire acreage in this area by buying property from Zadack Woods that had originally belonged to James Cummins.[56] Unlike most of Cummins' other properties that were full leagues, this labor was located on the southern side of the river and surrounded by the Elizabeth Tumlinson grant. Then, during February 1830, the *ayuntamiento* ordered persons interested in *labors* on the Colorado that adjoined the Elizabeth Tumlinson league to appear before it on March 2.[57] Dewees was quick to claim the *labors*. It should be noted that besides the property he had purchased from Woods, Dewees did own most of the property just west of the Tumlinson league and was probably the closest of any settler not named Tumlinson to the *labors* under review. He would be disappointed, however, when the *ayuntamiento* disallowed his claim and declared the *labors* vacant.[58]

By 1833, it was decided that the Tumlinson property would be divided between the children. A surveyor and three commissioners, one of whom was Dewees, set about to determine how best to accomplish the task. Ultimately, it was decided that each heir would randomly draw a lot that corresponded to an assigned portion of the land. The event took place on December 19, 1833. John J. Tumlinson Jr. drew Lot 2, which was clearly the one that Dewees thought was the most desirable. Less than a year later, Dewees contracted to buy half of the property owned by Tumlinson Jr. for the handsome price of $112.[59] After a decade of scouting and negotiating, he owned a portion of the property he had coveted for so long.

Dewees would get to work trying to develop the area. Access from the east was made easy by the presence of a suitable low water crossing. This crossing was very near where the river took a jog to the east (ironically very near the location of where Beason's Park is now) and very near where Dewees and Moseley lived opposite one another. When the river

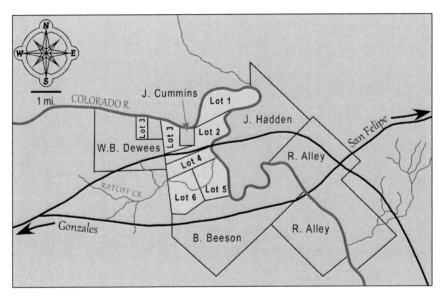

Modified map depicting the lot assignments to be randomly drawn by the heirs of Ellizabeth Tumlinson. Historic roads in black.

was low, this crossing was just as popular as the crossing at Beeson's. Dewees' efforts were boosted when, in December 1835, a petition to the Provisional Government asked for a new municipality to be carved from the Municipality of Austin, to be designated the Municipality of Colorado. The petition declared that 1,500 people lived in the proposed new municipality, which included all of present-day Colorado County and roughly the southeastern half of Fayette County, the northern part of Wharton County, and a large portion of northeastern Lavaca County. The petition further stated that a town had been laid out to be the seat of government, and that it would be called Columbus. Fifty-four men signed the petition, including Beeson, Crier, Moseley, Burnam and, at the very top, Dewees.[60]

There is considerable uncertainty as to how Columbus derived its name. It is often assumed that Dewees' suggested the name after spending time in Kentucky and Arkansas. Stein believes instead that it was the popularity of Washington Irving's 1828 work *A History of the Life and Voyages of Christopher Columbus*, which enhanced the explorer's reputation and gave Dewees the idea for Columbus as a name.[61] There was, however, a recent visitor who hailed from a town called Columbus-Gideon Lincecum. As one of the founders and most prominent citizens of Columbus, Mississippi, Lincecum was sent on an expedition to Texas at the behest of the citizens of that area to explore emigration possibilities. Considering that Burnam had guided Lincecum to other nearby settlements, it may well be that others had met the naturalist and wanted to encourage his project.[62] Perhaps it is a coincidence that the naming of the town and Lincecum's visit coincided so closely, but it is something to consider.

On January 8, 1836, the General Council of the Provisional Government passed the law approving the new municipality. The next day, William Menefee and William Lacey were elected the municipality's first and second judges.[63] These two individuals also represented the Municipality of Colorado at the March convention in Washington and ultimately signed the Texas Declaration of Independence.

Although the town of Columbus was officially authorized by the time the Texian army reached the area on March 20, 1836, there was no reference to it in any official documents. In correspondence from Colonel Hockley, the crossing where Sherman's command encamped was known as Moseley's. Ironically, Captain Moseley Baker, in his call to arms that appeared in the March 24, 1836 issue of the *Telegraph and Texas Register*, referenced the Colorado crossing at Dewees' home.[64] His drive to establish Columbus as a settlement may have been admirable, but Dewees' timing could not have been worse. The Texians would need to win a revolution before the infant town would truly be recognized.

7

BEESON'S & DEWEES' DAY 6, MARCH 21

"Four miles farther down the river was the Atascocito [sic] crossing, which was unguarded. This circumstance, probably, did not occur to the general until late in the evening, about dusk."[1]

JONATHAN H. KUYKENDALL

THE TEXIAN ARMY was a hodgepodge of volunteer, militia, and regular army companies. In the volunteer companies, a man merely needed to have enough influence to be elected an officer. Volunteers often tended to come and go as they deemed necessary, and if they did not like the decisions of military leaders, they would simply leave. One of the conditions upon accepting the job as commander in chief that Sam Houston asked of the delegates convened in Washington was that he would have authority over not only the regular army, but the volunteers and militia as well. Houston wanted there to be no doubt that he was in charge. There would be no situation like the Alamo, where there were co-commanders–one in charge of regulars and the other in charge of volunteers.[2] Also, desertion would not be tolerated, and those that tried would be held accountable.

At the suggestion that his army should have engaged the Mexicans at Gonzales, Houston responded, "as we were, without supplies for the men in camp, of either provisions, ammunition, or artillery, and remote from succor, it would have been madness to hazard a contest." He added, "they had not been taught the first principles of the drill."[3] However, since he had taken charge of the Texian forces at Gonzales, they had been constantly on the move. Now that they had made camp and intended to stay for some time, it was prudent to start establishing order and discipline. The troops must have spent this day and much of the next few going through the drills that Houston considered so essential.

While the Texian forces had increased substantially the previous day, volunteers continued to arrive. Captain William Sadler's company joined Lieutenant Colonel Sydney Sherman at Dewees' on March 21. Sadler had come to Texas from Georgia in 1835, accompanied for part of the trip by fellow Georgian Mirabeau B. Lamar, future hero of San Jacinto and president of the Republic of Texas.[4] In November 1835, the provisional Texas government created a ranger battalion.[5] Sadler became one of the first ranger commanders in East Texas. Helping with the construction of Fort Houston near present day Palestine, he disbanded his unit when word came that the Alamo had fallen. Sadler, along with seven remaining rangers, immediately rode to join the Texian army with Houston.[6] His small company would soon merge with the Nacogdoches Volunteers, who arrived a few days later.

Based on the information provided by the prisoner captured by Henry W. Karnes' scouts, Houston knew that the Mexican army would arrive soon. It was in his best interest to find out exactly where the Mexicans were and what they were doing. This required a reconnaissance. Since the enemy might appear on the banks of the Colorado River at any time, a relatively large force was ordered across the waterway rather than the small scouting parties previously used. Colonel George W. Hockley, in a letter to Secretary of War Thomas J. Rusk, reported that "a detachment of one hundred men are now crossing the river to meet the enemy's advance–and every confidence may be placed in their entire success."[7] The same day, Houston, in his written orders, declared that he "sent a force of near two hundred men on the west side of the river."[8] It may well be that the actual number was somewhere in between the two reports.

Despite Hockley's confidence, the success of this mission would not be measured by victory in battle. Instead, Houston wanted a 'reconnaissance in force.'[9] The idea was to send a sizable, yet not overwhelming, force to engage the enemy to gauge their numbers, formations, and armaments. Though perhaps riskier than sending a simple scouting party, this tactical operation could provide substantially more information.

Major Benjamin F. Smith was given command of the expedition.[10] The mission required both infantry and cavalry. The twenty-five or so mounted scouts led by Karnes and Captain William H. Smith were not sufficient for the mission, so detachments from Captain William M. Logan's Liberty Volunteers and the companies commanded by Captain Robert J. Calder, and Captain Peyton Splane were recruited to bring the number of mounted men to sixty-four. Captain John Bird's company supplied the infantry.[11] That night, with rations for two days, the mixed expedition crossed the river and camped near Benjamin Beeson's homestead, waiting to begin their mission the next day.

As noted earlier, before the establishment of the Austin Colony, there were three primary roads through the southeastern part of Texas. One was the San Antonio Road, from San Antonio de Béxar to Nacogdoches, a second was the La Bahía Road, which stretched from Goliad to Nacogdoches, and the third was the Atascosito Road, established as a military highway from a Spanish outpost called Atascosito on the Trinity River south and west to Goliad. The eastern extent of the latter road was also known as the Opelousas Road.

With the influx of Austin's colonists, the map of Texas changed appreciably from the days of Spanish rule, when the area between San Antonio de Béxar and Nacogdoches was largely vacant of settlers. New communities developed, as did roads to connect them. When Stephen F. Austin founded San Felipe as his colony headquarters, it was logical for a road to be established between San Felipe and the provincial capital of Texas in San Antonio. The road would naturally also extend through Green DeWitt's colony headquarters in Gonzales, located almost on a direct line between San Felipe and San Antonio.

As Austin's Colony developed, the roads blazed by his colonists became better known. However, to the advancing Mexican army, the more established La Bahía and Atascosito roads may have been more familiar, or at least were more likely to appear on their maps. So, while Beeson's Crossing and Dewees' Ford may have been common crossing points for colonists, it may well have been the Atascosito Road crossing over the Colorado that was more familiar to Mexican army leaders.

The Colorado was a natural defensive barrier for the Texians against the Mexican army, and Houston intended to use it to his strategic advantage. If the Mexicans wished to cross, he would not make it easy for them. Hence, he destroyed the ferries at Burnam's and Beeson's homesites. Whether he realized it on his own, or some of the locals pointed it out, is not known, but on the evening of March 21, Houston suddenly became aware, perhaps with chagrin, that the Atascosito Crossing, located only about three miles downriver, was completely unguarded. Though largely unused by the colonists, the crossing was certainly known to the Mexicans. The thought that his army could suddenly be flanked to the south by the enemy must have been alarming to Houston.

Houston solicited volunteers who could proceed immediately to the crossing that night and report any movement by the enemy there. Ultimately, four soldiers undertook this task. From Captain Robert McNutt's company, Felix Wright, David Lawrence, and Jonathan H. Kuykendall volunteered.[12] John Ingram, of Captain Phillip Coe's company that had joined the Texian army only the day before, also volunteered.[13] Being familiar with the area, Ingram was assigned with the task of leading his fellow privates to the designated crossing. Ingram had been an orphan at the age of fourteen when he made his first journey into Texas from Arkansas in 1821. After returning to Arkansas for a brief time, he returned to Texas for good in 1823, accompanying two other settlers, William Rabb and James Gilleland. From the earliest days, Ingram was quick to volunteer to aid frontier settlers attacked by raiding Indians. It was during the Texas Revolution that he particularly distinguished himself in the Battle of Gonzales and the Siege of Béxar.[14]

In the volunteers' briefing with Houston, the General suggested that, because it was so dark, the four men should proceed on foot to the Atascosito Crossing rather than travel by horseback. They were told to remain there on watch until the next morning, at which time they would be relieved. Should they see any sign of the enemy, Houston ordered them to report to headquarters as speedily as possible.[15] The men arrived at the crossing and stood watch through the night. Fortunately for the small group, they saw no sign of the Mexican army, and they were indeed relieved the next morning.

Interestingly, the Atascosito Crossing was on a land grant issued to Rawson Alley but subsequently owned by his brother Abraham, commonly called Abram.[16] The latter was upset that Houston wanted him to help with citizen evacuations when he instead wanted to join the army.[17] Nonetheless, he enlisted in Captain William Walker's company, whose responsibility it was to ensure the safe removal of civilians to the east, away from the advancing Mexicans. His family likely moved eastward with him and Walker's company. Alley's cabin was reduced to ashes. Whether it was Ingram's group, the subsequent relief company, or the Mexican army that burned Alley's home may never be known. Family lore reports that it was Alley himself that burned it before his departure.[18]

The burning of Alley's home, however, was not the only tragedy that befell his family. In 1798, Moses Austin had moved into the Ste. Genevieve district of Upper Louisiana. Versed in mining operations, he secured a concession from Spanish officials there.[19] About the same time, Thomas Alley and his partner, Abraham Baker, moved to the Ste. Genevieve district and quickly discovered ore, opening what became known as the "Alley mines."[20] Owing to the proximity to one another and their common vocation, the Austin and Alley families became friends. Thomas Alley's son by his first marriage was Rawson; he later married Catherine Baker and had five more children, including Thomas V., John C., William A., Abraham, and Cynthia.[21] When Moses Austin's eldest son, Stephen, brought colonists to Texas, the Alley brothers came with him. Rawson migrated with Austin to Texas in 1821. The following spring, Thomas, John, and Abram arrived.[22] William immigrated in 1824.

Tragedy began soon after the Alley brothers arrived in Texas. In the winter of 1823, John and two others made a trip down the Colorado to the coast to purchase corn and other supplies.[23] On their return trip, loaded with provisions in their canoe, a band of Karankawas attacked at the mouth of Skull Creek. The Indians killed John and another young man and severely wounded a third, who managed to escape.[24] Shortly thereafter, the same band severely wounded a settler near his residence close to Beeson's Crossing. Over the next few days, colonists led by Captain Robert H. Kuykendall tracked down the attackers.[25] It was likely that some or all the Alley brothers were part of this expedition, but they never recovered John's body.

Thomas Alley became a leader in the development of Austin's Colony; for example, in March 1823 he became the first constable of Texas.[26] In 1826, Austin, in response to repeated Indian attacks, ordered a force of two hundred men, led by Aylett C. Buckner, to deal with the offenders. One of the captains of this force was Rawson Alley, and two of his company were his brothers Abram and Thomas. As the contingent of volunteers from the Colorado rode to the rendezvous point for the expedition, tragedy struck. While fording the Brazos, the horse carrying Thomas fell, dislodging its rider. Alley, injured and staggering, waded a few feet in the river, but was soon pulled under by the current. Abram and Rawson watched helplessly as their brother was carried down river. After a time, Thomas' body was recovered, and he was interred nearby. In a letter dated June 15, 1826, to their sister Emily in Missouri, Austin and his brother reported the unfortunate death of Thomas Alley.[27]

Rawson was the next Alley brother to die in Texas. Austin trusted him to survey his initial choice for his colony headquarters near the site of what would become Columbus. As one of the six original surveyors for Austin, he surveyed many of the land grants on the Colorado.[28] On August 3, 1824, he got his own grant for 1½ leagues of land located on both sides of the river.[29] In 1825, Rawson was considered for the position of *alcalde* for the Colorado District but was defeated by James Cummins in the election.[30] He subsequently served as a militia captain and, in 1828, became a *sindico procurador*, a position to which he was elected again in 1832.[31] Chosen to be a delegate to the Convention of 1833, he could not attend because he was ill.[32] Rawson succumbed to his ailment as heavy rains pushed the Colorado out of its banks in May 1833 and floodwaters surrounded his house. The remaining brothers could do nothing but wait until the water finally receded before they could provide a muddy burial for their brother.[33] The attorney that handled Rawson Alley's estate was Travis, the future commander of the Alamo during the Mexican attack.[34]

By the time Abram Alley's home was burned, only two of the five Alley brothers still survived in Texas. The last to arrive, William, received title to a league of land in what would become Brazoria County on July 29, 1824.[35] Like his brothers, William was a farmer and quick to accompany any expedition against raiding Indians as needed. Abram received a grant to land immediately to the east of Rawson's tract on the Colorado. In 1835, he married Nancy Millar, daughter of John and Elizabeth Millar, who had settled on the western side of the river at the Atascosito Crossing.[36] Abram built a cabin for his new bride on the eastern side of the river, on higher ground near where Rawson had previously met his untimely death. This homestead was reduced to ashes during the Runaway Scrape.

While the Texians gathered on the Colorado, General Antonio López de Santa Anna, after his victory at the Alamo, essentially considered the Texas conflict to be over and prepared to depart for Mexico City. His staff vehemently argued otherwise and finally convinced him to continue his campaign. San Antonio de Béxar became a temporary staging area for Mexican operations in Texas. On March 8, 1836, General Antonio Gaona arrived with the remainder of the First Infantry Brigade. The next day, General Vicente Filisola, second in command to Santa Anna, arrived. The following day, General Juan José Andrade arrived with a cavalry brigade. On March 11, General Eugenio Tolsa arrived with the Second Infantry Brigade.[37] Santa Anna did not waste time deploying the recent arrivals. To "teach the ungrateful rebels a lesson," he launched a three-pronged attack upon the Texians, showing no mercy to the population.[38] General José de Urrea, recently victorious at San Patricio, marched to Goliad to confront the Texians there. Afterwards, he was to proceed to Victoria and along the Texas coast. Colonel Juan Morales went to Goliad with the San Luis and Jimenez Battalions to support Urrea.[39] For the northern drive, Santa Anna ordered Gaona to lead about 725 men of the Morelos Battalion and Guanajuato Auxiliaries to Mina (now Bastrop) and then to Nacogdoches by way of the San Antonio Road.[40] The center thrust was spearheaded by General Joaquín Ramírez y Sesma, in command of seven hundred infantry from the Aldama, Matamoros and Toluca Battalions. His orders were to proceed through Gonzales, cross the Colorado at Beeson's, and push to San Felipe de Austin. There, Santa Anna, who for the time being remained in Béxar, would establish his headquarters. About one hundred cavalry troopers from the Dolores and Tampico regiments accompanied Sesma, along with two six-pounders and their crews. Adrián Woll, Quartermaster General for the Mexican army, was with Sesma as well.[41]

The selection of General Ramírez y Sesma to lead the central thrust was a curious one. His battalions had borne the brunt of the casualties at

Portrait of General Joaquín Ramírez y Sesma, commander of the Mexican forces pursuing the Texian army to the Colorado River.

the Alamo.⁴² Additionally, in the Mexican army, as with many across the world, leadership positions were assigned not necessarily by talent, but were often based on money, power, influence, or nepotism. Urrea, leading the southern thrust across Texas, was a well-respected leader. Conversely, Sesma was perceived by some in a considerably dimmer light.

Like the Texian army, Sesma's troops traveled slowly, owing to the poor weather and subsequently muddy roads. Creeks and rivers were swollen by rain, and the destruction of transport across these rivers by the retreating Texians made the attempted crossings all the more harrowing. Sesma, in a letter to Santa Anna dated March 15, complained that the "barbarians" set fire to everything, including the barges and canoes on the river. He further noted in the same correspondence that ditches had been dug on either side of the ford across the Guadalupe River, which inhibited his ability to cross with artillery, supplies, and cavalry.⁴³

Sesma's army proceeded through the burned ruins of Gonzales, down the road toward San Felipe, and camped on the night of March 18 at Williamson Daniels' place, the same site where the Texians had camped only four days prior. The next day, the Mexicans reported an encounter with the enemy. Scouts from Sesma's army were surprised by "Americans," resulting in two Mexicans killed and one wounded.⁴⁴ Of course, what they did not realize was that one of those they assumed was dead had instead been captured by Captain Karnes' scouting expedition and provided invaluable information to the Texian army.

Karnes' encounter with the Mexican scouts seems to have caught Sesma off-guard. Upon finding that his men had been attacked, rather than try to pursue the attackers, Sesma made the unusual decision to remain encamped at Daniels' for another night. This would turn out to be a fortuitous development for Houston. Having no indications of other Texian incursions, Sesma resumed his advance on March 20. Assuming his pace was similar to that of the Texians, his army made it to the Navidad River by the next evening. Presumably, Sesma would have seen

DAY 6: BEESON'S & DEWEES' | 105

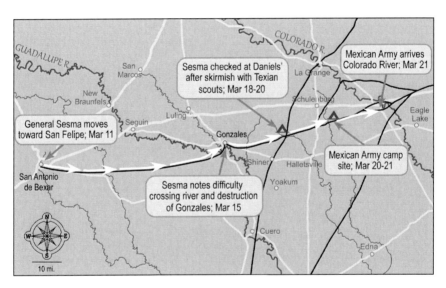

Projected route of the Mexican army under command of General Joaquín Ramirez y Sesma from San Antonio de Béxar to the Colorado River. Historic roads in black and modern roads in gray.

evidence there that the Texian army had moved north toward Burnam's Ferry. His orders, of course, were not to pursue them, but rather to reach San Felipe. Having camped somewhere around the Navidad on the night of March 20, the Mexican army would have stayed on the main road toward Beeson's and San Felipe.

Sesma's Mexican army arrived at the west bank of the Colorado to find the Texian army guarding the two primary crossings in the area. Finding the Texians divided, it became necessary for Sesma's forces to camp in a strategic position so they could observe both Texian groups. The question is, where exactly did the Mexican army camp?

About six miles west of the Colorado, the Gonzales-San Felipe Road split. The northern fork led to Dewees' Ford and the southern to Beeson's Crossing.[45] To determine more accurately where Sesma's campsite was located, it is necessary to reference relevant sources and employ simple logic. First, considering the heavy rain in the area, the Mexicans would require a ferry to cross the river. The north fork of the road led to Dewees', which was a shallow-water ford across the river that did not employ a ferry. The southern route to Beeson's, however, did have a ferry.

Second, with the Texians divided, the Mexicans would logically want to be able to observe at least the approach from both camps. If the Mexican army had proceeded along the northern route, they would likely have continued to high ground located on modern-day Highway 90, where the current Columbus High School stands overlooking the municipal golf course. There is in fact, a historical marker near there, designating the place where Sesma camped. The problem with this site, however, is that while it was almost directly across from Sherman at Dewees' Ford, it was more than five miles from the bulk of the Texian army at Beeson's Crossing. The Mexicans would have no reason to sequester themselves at this site, with the bulk of the Texian troops remaining almost invisible to them.[46]

Jonathan H. Kuykendall, posted at Beeson's, wrote that "on the morning of the 21st, our scouts came in and reported that a considerable force of the enemy was encamped on the west side of the Colorado within three miles of headquarters, and within less than two of Sherman's position." Shortly afterwards, as he was about to leave for Sherman's camp, he noted that "a strong division of the enemy were encamped within two miles, and in sight of Col. Sherman's position." William P. Zuber, stationed with Sherman, also recalled that "the Mexican general Sesma, with about eight hundred men, was encamped on the west side, midway between our two encampments, about one-and-a-half miles from each."[47] Captain David Kokernot, a well-traveled Dutchman, said the Mexicans "encamped on Matletts Creek, about one and a half miles from Columbus." While there is no Matletts Creek, there is a Ratliff Creek that flows to the west, opposite and between the two Texian encampments.[48] The recollection of "Matletts Creek" by Kokernot may have been due to the passing years and was likely a result of English not being his native language. Colonel Juan N. Almonte, in his journal, noted that his troops "arrived at our camp on the Colorado, passing by the farm of Los Nogales, the streams of the Alamo and San Antoñito, which is lined with a thick wood." The streams mentioned are likely Skull and Ratliff Creek respectively. This additionally confirms the location of the Mexican army.[49]

Lastly, it would seem reasonable that the Mexican army would want to be in an elevated position to have as clear a view as possible toward both divisions of the Texian army. Nicholas D. Labadie noted that "Gen. Sezma [sic] had pitched his camp on the opposite or west bank, about one mile from the river."[50] This is consistent with modern topographic maps of the area that show that higher ground is one to two miles from the Colorado. Notably, however, the immediate area near the river has been greatly affected by decades of open-pit sand and gravel mining. 'Cutbacks' in the contour lines seem to correspond with the presence of old gravel pits. This might suggest that the mining has changed the topography of the area which in turn might alter the interpretation of where the Mexican encampment was located.

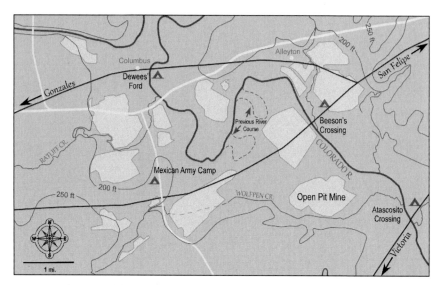

Topographic map showing contour elevations and the location of open pit sand and gravel mines along the Colorado River from Dewees' Ford to the Atascosito Crossing.

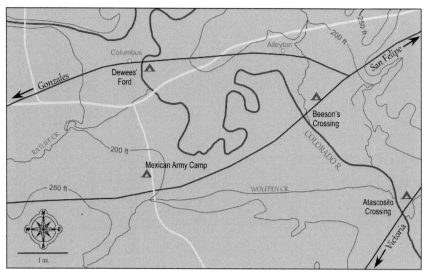

Map showing presumed watercourse and elevation without the effects of mining in 1836. Historic roads in black and modern roads in gray.

This map shows the projected elevation without the effect of mining, as it might have appeared in 1836.[51] Based on the evidence, the most logical campsite for the Mexican forces under the command of Sesma would be at the highest elevation near a site where the Colorado bends. The next chapter will show more evidence in support of this site.

It might be valid to question whether General Houston made a wise choice to lead the Texian army to Burnam's Ferry. He was encumbered with having to accompany a considerable civilian population desperately fleeing from the approaching Mexican army and dependent upon the Texian army's protection. The pace of movement may have been slower than it might have been otherwise. Houston was aware that the Mexicans were following and, though he could not be sure where they were, it would have been prudent to assume they were fast approaching. By diverting to Burnam's, Houston could have given Sesma the opportunity to cross at Beeson's before he had a chance to move down the eastern side of the river in opposition. In fact, Houston was extremely fortunate that this did not happen.

Burnam's place may have been an important, perhaps essential, destination considering the abundant stores and supplies there, and the fact that there was an established ferry crossing. If Houston's purpose was to deny these supplies to the Mexican army and destroy the ferry, why did he not simply send a company of men to perform this task? Instead, he diverted his entire army toward that destination and gave Sesma a chance to cross the Colorado below, making his flank vulnerable.

Sesma was not the most talented nor astute of the Mexican command. Colonel José de la Peña certainly had no kind words for the commander. He wrote, "General Ramírez y Sesma is a timid and irresolute commander, dilatory in his judgment and apathetic in his movements, and since within this poor attitude he worries about every possible difficulty, his plans are always exaggerated." De la Peña added,

> We have already noted that our soldiers were able to see the flames at Gonzales. The enemy had retreated shortly before carrying this out; his march had been slow and cumbersome, as he took with him a great number of covered wagons, which carried all the families in the village and their possessions. Since Sesma had 700 infantry, two field pieces, and 100 horsemen, he could easily have dispersed his enemy, who was inferior both in numbers and discipline. He should have pursued him between the Guadalupe and the Colorado to prevent his joining reinforcements on the left bank of the later stream; it was a great mistake not to have done so.

De la Peña was not alone in criticizing Sesma, recalling that "General Woll, who was under General Ramírez y Sesma's command, realized the importance of such a maneuver and requested the use of the choice companies and the cavalry to carry out this scheme, but he was refused."[52]

Sesma's perspective, of course, was considerably different. He claimed in his report to Santa Anna, written while passing through Gonzales, that his cavalry only brought "28 tired horses to the crossing," and he cited this as the reason for not pursuing the slow-moving Texian forces.[53] But De la Peña's assessment that Sesma was not as quick to pursue Houston as he might have been seems to be fair. Sesma's reaction to Karnes' encounter with his scouts on March 19 is a good example of this. In a letter to Secretary of War Rusk dated March 23, Hockley wrote, "They [the Mexican Army] are evidently checked by the skirmish with our spies. The prisoners say that General Sesma halted the next day to rest." Considering that the Mexicans reached the Colorado late on March 21, despite their slow pace and a day's delay from the encounter with Karnes, they could have certainly been at the Colorado by March 19, before Houston arrived. Perhaps Captain Wyly Martin's company, who had arrived earlier and was waiting to join Houston at Beeson's place, could have temporarily dissuaded Sesma from crossing the Colorado, but there is no guarantee of this. If not, Houston could have suddenly faced an equal force of the enemy, with artillery, east of the Colorado. If this had happened, the course of the entire 1836 campaign might have been dramatically different.

BEESON'S & DEWEES'
DAY 7, MARCH 22

"Major Smith left our encampment at Beason's with about
one hundred men, to skirmish with the enemy."[1]

ROBERT J. CALDER

CAPTAIN MOSELEY BAKER was a colorful if not controversial figure during (and after) the Texas Revolution. Not shy about voicing his opinion, Baker wrote an open letter dated March 22, 1836, to the residents of the young republic, which was published two days later in the *Telegraph and Texas Register* in San Felipe, one of the few newspapers in Texas at this time. The editors took the liberty of quoting Captain Baker at times and paraphrasing him at others:

> The enemy had at last appeared in sight, and were attempting to cross the river at Dewees's, and the battle was then raging.[2] Mr. Baker entertains no doubt that the enemy will be repelled and calls earnestly and solemnly on the people of Texas to turn out. Our army consists of 800 men, and the enemy cannot exceed 1200, while their whole number in Texas is not more than 3000 or 4000.[3] Our army have made a stand at the Colorado, where they intend

that victory shall be theirs, and win Texas: as to defeat, it does not enter into their contemplation. Mr. Baker thinks there is no reason for moving the families, and tells his fair countrywomen to lay, in this hour of trouble, the heroines of Texas; to act well their parts, and drive from their presence fathers, brother and friends; to permit no man to stay at home, but to bid them go where duty and honor calls them; to participate in the dangers as well as the benefits of Texas, and then only to return to their smiles. A postscript says that the firing heard was between the spies of our army and those of the enemy; that they had taken three prisoners, and the enemy were not far off, and would probably be whipped by to-day.[4]

The letter gave the impression of inevitable victory, which would encourage volunteers to flock to the army. The direct appeal to the women of Texas seems to be an attempt to shame any man for not enlisting. It is hard to say if Baker's letter had any direct impact on enlistment, but a steady stream of volunteers certainly joined the Texian ranks on the Colorado River.

Captain Henry Teal's regulars, who had previously arrived at Lieutenant Colonel Sydney Sherman's camp at Dewees' place, were re-assigned to join General Sam Houston at Beeson's Crossing. Unlike many of the others who joined the Texians on the Colorado, Teal commanded regulars who had some semblance of military order and discipline. Houston certainly hoped that the presence of regular troops would set an example to the less disciplined volunteers that made up a majority of his forces. Teal's regulars likely brought more military process to the army. Included in his company were a pair of musicians, Frederick Lemsky and Martin Flores, who greatly facilitated playing tattoo in the morning and reveille at night.[5]

Though there was a constant flux of Texian troops positioned along the Colorado at this time, one deployment was not documented, yet it is nevertheless important. The previous night, Houston had realized that no Texians guarded the Atascosito Crossing to the south. Though it had been essentially abandoned by the colonists, the old Atascosito Road was still on many maps of the period and was a potential place for the Mexican army to cross the Colorado. Houston deployed a handful of men, familiar with the area, to make their way downriver and guard the crossing through the night, at which time they would be relieved. One of the members of this small band of men, Jonathan H. Kuykendall, mentioned that "after sunrise the next morning without seeing or hearing aught of the enemy" they had "already started back to camp when we met a relief guard of mounted men."[6]

The importance of this crossing was highlighted by the fact that, in his letter to Secretary of War Thomas J. Rusk several days later, Colonel George W. Hockley specifically reported that the army "still maintains the position at this place [Beeson's], commanding the crossing of the Colorado at Mosely's [also known as Dewees'] above Beason's and *Atascosito* below."[7] What was never recorded was the identity of the riders who relieved Kuykendall and his comrades on the morning of March 22. The fact that the Texians were mounted might suggest that they came from one of the cavalry companies, of which there were few. The problem, of course, is that two Texas cavalry companies, led by captains Henry W. Karnes and William H. Smith, were with the expedition led by Major Benjamin F. Smith across the Colorado, which will be discussed later in this chapter. In fact, additional troopers from several other companies were solicited to go on this mission.

There is, however, no mention of the cavalry unit under the command of Captain Juan N. Seguín. They had been tasked as a rear-guard for the Texian army during their eastward trek from Gonzales. The assignment at the Atascocito Crossing would not require a full company, but rather only a few individuals that could quickly report if there was movement by the Mexicans from across the river. If not Seguín's company, another alternative might be the small ranger company that had recently arrived led by William Sadler. Though possible, this seems less likely since Sadler's company was stationed at Dewees' Ford with Sherman and would not have been as accessible to Houston. Perhaps a rotation had been made for guarding this crossing. Whether this is the case or not will likely never be known.

Houston's plan for the reconnaissance was for the mounted members of the Smith expedition, led by Karnes, to probe the Mexican lines to provoke a response. As the cavalrymen fell back, Captain Bird's company, in position at the edge of the tree line, would provide covering fire. One of Stephen F. Austin's early maps of this area marked the area between Calavira (Skull) Creek and the Colorado with *"encinales,"* meaning oak groves.[8] Additionally, most waterways were lined with trees and brush. With the understanding that creeks may have been differently located than their present beds, the Texians may have used the tree-lined ravine through which Wolfpen Creek flows to make their way toward the Mexican position.

The Mexican army spotted the Texian cavalry as they emerged from the cover of trees and, as expected, their sudden appearance caused quite a stir. Nicholas D. Labadie, a member of the small group of horsemen near the front of the action, recalled what happened:

> We were about to wheel to the right, expecting to make a dash in full gallop to take the enemy's cannon, but at the last moment Carnes [sic] rides up to the orderly, and gives the order: 'Wheel to the left, to the left!' Just as he spoke, the whistle of a ball from the cannon, passing over our heads, was heard, and the report had scarcely subsided, before another, and then another followed, causing our line to break in three or four places, as our horses became almost unmanageable. The balls struck the ground at some distance beyond us, throwing up clouds of dust.[9]

DAY 7: BEESON'S & DEWEES' | 117

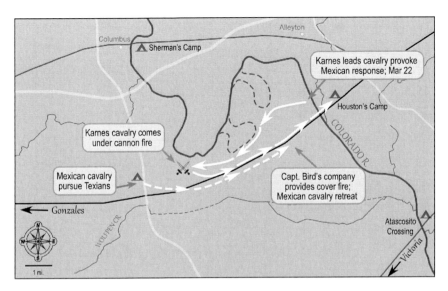

Projected route of the Texian cavalry across the Colorado River at Beeson's Crossing to the site of the skirmish with the Mexican army and then back across the river. Location of found cannonball near skirmish emblem.

Captain Henry W. Karnes and the Texian cavalry beat a hasty retreat once Mexican cannons open fire.

With this sudden bombardment, the Texians, realizing their precarious situation, hastily retired.

Interestingly, there may well be physical evidence of this encounter. The Burris family, longtime landowners in the area south of Columbus, later discovered bronze cannonballs on their property while cultivating their land. These are consistent with the type of ammunition that would have been used for a six-pound cannon, which Sesma's command reportedly possessed.[10]

There is no way to conclusively determine that the pictured cannonball was used in this fight, but it does seem plausible. During the Mexican retreat in April, much of the Mexican munitions had already been discarded, thereby making it an unlikely source of this cannonball. Also, the line of retreat would have been toward Victoria along the Atascosito Road, rather than any movement toward the north.[11] The location of this cannonball discovery is more evidence of the site of the Mexican encampment as depicted and the track likely taken by the Texian cavalrymen.

As the attacking troops began their retreat, something unusual occurred. Whether under orders or on their own initiative, two young Texians, mounted on white horses and wearing handkerchiefs around their heads, rode full gallop toward some Mexican cavalry who may have been a scouting party. The mounted Mexicans quickly retreated as the two riders advanced until they were out of sight. Shortly afterwards, some cattle in the area started running as if frightened, suggesting that an impending counterattack was imminent. Seconds later, the same two young men who had ridden by earlier were seen driving a herd of Mexican horses and mules that, in all the confusion, they had managed to take from the enemy.[12]

During this time, the Mexicans did not sit idle. The enemy mounted their horses and chased the retreating Texians. Fortunately for the latter, Captain Bird's infantry, as planned, was hidden at the edge of the tree line, and provided cover for the retreating cavalry. The riders stripped

DAY 7: BEESON'S & DEWEES' | 119

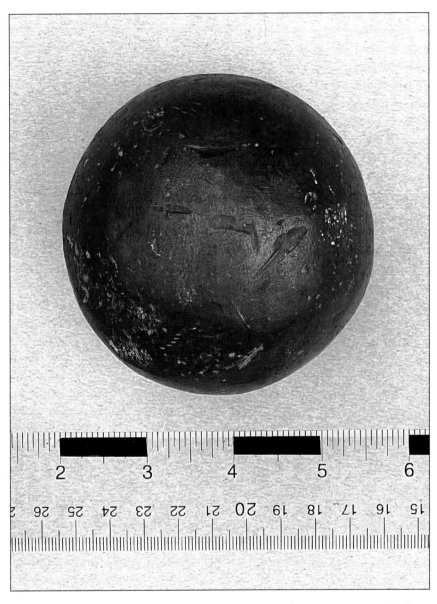

A brass Mexican cannonball discovered on the Burris family property south of Columbus. Cannonball diameter is 3.55 inches and weight is 7.16 pounds.

their horses, threw their saddles and blankets into the ferryboat, and guided their horses to swim the river. They then took cover along the bank of the river and awaited the attack they expected. Perhaps sensing the Texians were waiting for them or maybe not wanting to venture too far from their own lines, the Mexican cavalrymen stopped their pursuit before coming within range of the Texian rifles. Thus, the anticipated battle never happened. By the time the Texians re-crossed the Colorado, it was almost dark. They had trouble recovering their horses, and evidently many of their provisions were lost.[13]

The soldiers of Sherman's detachment camped at Dewees' Ford were not involved in Smith's reconnaissance mission. However, Sherman had other important tasks. Captain David Kokernot was sent by Houston to Sherman's camp in order "to collect all the provisions which could be procured and store them in Mosley's gin house."[14] Kokernot was a trusted friend and had received a captain's commission by Houston in the regular army only two weeks earlier.

Once Kokernot moved provisions to Moseley's place, Sherman gave him another vital mission:

> Opposite Gen. Sherman's camp stood a large double log house belonging to W. B. Deweese [sic], which could have afforded the enemy a good fortification for their cannon and enabled them to drive us out of the bottom. Gen. Sherman ordered the house to be burned. Not expecting any danger, another man and myself got into a small dugout, crossed the river and set fire to the house and some corn and cotton pens. We had just pulled off on our return when about one hundred Mexican muskets were let loose at us, riddling the boat with holes, but we escaped unhurt, with a tight squeeze, the bushes being alive with the enemy.[15]

For Sherman, the burning of Dewees' cabin was not necessarily a matter of keeping the enemy from obtaining a place for shelter and comfort, but rather a defensive necessity that potentially precluded a future bombardment by Mexican artillery.

Houston had sent Major Smith across the Colorado with orders to engage the enemy, but without details of the assignment, it is difficult to ascertain the success or failure of his units. Captain Bird and his infantry were part of this expedition and were, at least in part, assigned the responsibility of providing cover for the cavalry. While on the expedition, however, some of Bird's company may have had different responsibilities because they clearly were not providing cover for Karnes. According to Robert H. Hunter of Bird's company, "Capt Bird & Capt Easin or Easlens Company was trying to cross a large hird of sheep across the river." The reference to "Capt Easin" was most likely William M. Eastland, a lieutenant in Captain Thomas J. Rabb's company. It may have been that some men were ordered to try to round up as much livestock as possible and drive or even coax them across the river. This endeavor was evidently a failure.

While Bird and part of his company were busy providing cover for Karnes and others were rounding up sheep and other livestock, there were evidently some with other priorities to attend on the west side of the river. Just downriver from their position was Benjamin Beeson's homestead. One building that seemed to receive an inordinate amount of attention there was his smokehouse. Five men managed to find the smokehouse, but upon entering they found a soldier assigned to the place. When the men inquired of the individual what he was doing there, he told them that General Houston had given orders to guard the place. When the group then asked if he was the only guard, he responded that he was one of ten, but that the others had gone out back, behind the hill, to fight the Mexicans that had come to harass the Texian army.[16]

The presence of the Mexican soldiers in the immediate vicinity was evidently secondary to this group's mission. They informed the guard that they wanted bacon and meant to have it. Realizing that he was in no position to stop them, the guard made it clear that he had no intention of trying to deter the miscreants. The five intruders broke down the door to the smokehouse and helped themselves. Each acquired a moderate size slab of bacon, which they promptly cut in half and then tied together to load onto their horses more easily. Just as the bandits were about to abscond with their porcine prize, they were startled by a ruckus from the area where they had just come. They were surprised when the afore-mentioned guards came running at full speed toward them, with Mexican soldiers in hot pursuit. The unexpected appearance of the Mexicans quickly changed the men's priority. Realizing that they were cut off from the ferry, they had to retreat about a quarter mile upriver to a more fordable point on the river. Although Mexican pursuers followed them past Beeson's house, the Texians managed to escape without further incident. Evidently, the planned skirmish with the Mexican army was underway, and these Texians were unintended participants. But their close encounter did not seem to upset them too much. The next morning, the same five men ventured back across the river to nab more bacon. To their great dismay, however, they found Beeson's smokehouse and the surrounding buildings all burned down, the smoke still swirling.[17]

9

BEESON'S & DEWEES' DAY 8, MARCH 23

"The force of the enemy in this quarter is less than I had heard. Let the Mexican force be what it may, if the country will turn out, we can beat them."[1]

SAM HOUSTON

ONE OF THE CONDITIONS of Sam Houston's appointment as commander in chief was that he would command all military personnel, regular and volunteer. While leading the Texian forces, Houston left no doubt who was in charge. He held no councils of war and did not ask for a vote on a course of action. The final word on each course of action lay with him. Despite his solitary style, however, any competent commander seeks input from his subordinates, and Houston had several aides and officers that he consulted. His closest friend and advisor in the field was Colonel George W. Hockley. In a letter to Thomas J. Rusk, dated March 23, 1836, Houston wrote, "I have had no aid or assistance but (for) my friend Hockley, who now fills your former station." In a subsequent letter, dated March 29, Houston told Rusk, "I find Colonel George W. Hockley, of my staff, a sage counsellor [sic] and true friend."[2]

Hockley and Houston became acquainted while Hockley was serving as a clerk in the War Department in Washington, D.C. When Houston moved to Tennessee and became governor in 1828, Hockley followed. When Houston set out for Texas, once again, Hockley followed him.[3] Having a trusted friend in the field as an aide and advisor was advantageous. Still, Houston had to be careful of what he communicated lest prying eyes and ears learn things they should not.

From the time he assumed command of the Texians at Gonzales until reaching Beeson's Crossing, Houston sent correspondence back to the Texas government in Washington via James Collinsworth, Chair of the Military Committee. Like Hockley, Collinsworth had been an ally of Houston in Tennessee. In fact, Collinsworth introduced the resolution that made Houston the commander in chief of all Texian forces.[4] When Collinsworth left Washington on March 17, 1836, along with most of the rest of the convention delegates, Houston's correspondence to the government went to the Republic's new Secretary of War, Rusk.[5]

Though there may have been a friendship between Houston and Collinsworth, the tone of the letters that Houston sent to Rusk was quite different. Correspondence with Collinsworth included the necessary status reports and requests that a commander in chief might make. But Houston was much more candid when writing to Rusk. In his letter to Rusk dated March 23, Houston lamented, "You know I am not easily depressed, but, before my God, since we parted, I have found the darkest hours of my past life! My excitement has been so great, that, for forty-eight hours, I have not eaten an ounce, nor have I slept."[6] This was a far cry from the fact-based status reports sent to Collinsworth. This letter from Houston to Rusk contained a modicum of despair, not something typically associated with the Texian leader. He vented to his friend with clear emotion. This relationship with Rusk would prove to be important going forward.[7]

Despite Houston's rant, things were looking up for the Texian army. The ranks were quickly swelling due to the volunteers joining. With the new arrivals, the number of Texians at Dewees' Ford increased to nearly

General Sam Houston, with aide and confidant Colonel George W. Hockley, conferring over a map of the Colorado River area.

280, while at Beeson's Crossing they numbered over 800. The Mexican forces across from them seemed susceptible to a determined attack. The outlook would not continue to be as rosy going forward, however, and Rusk would prove to be a key figure in the Texians' actions in the weeks ahead. A consistent message from the officers of the Texian army was that the Colorado River would be where they would make a stand and that victory was inevitable. There was no reason to worry, and no reason to retreat. They only asked people to support their efforts by sending reinforcements and supplies.

Despite the optimism being broadcast to the citizens of Texas, Houston remained clearly concerned about desertions. In his letter to Rusk, he stated, "All would have been well, and at peace on this side of the Colorado, if I could only have had a moment to start an express in advance of the deserts; but they went first, and, being panic struck, it was contagious, and all who saw them breathed the poison and fled." He added, "Do devise some plan to send back the rascals who have gone from the army and service of the country with guns."[8]

Houston's appointment as commander in chief conferred authority to return deserters to the ranks, and although there was no law for drafting individuals into the military, there was a policy in place to impress provisions from individuals who were deemed to be fleeing Texas. But while it was common for personal belongings, such as blankets and clothing, to be confiscated, men who wanted to avoid military service would often find ways to avoid pressure to join the army. For example, scouts and river guards might encounter a single family accompanied by several well-armed men under the guise of protectors. These 'skeedadlers' were not pressed into service but were disarmed, dismounted, and left to fend for themselves.[9] Rosa Kleberg, relating her experiences during the Runaway Scrape, wrote, "Deserters were constantly passing us on foot and on horseback. The old men who were with families laughed at them and called to them, 'Run! Run! Run, Santa Anna is behind you.'"[10]

In the March 24, 1836 issue of the *Telegraph and Texas Register*, the editors noted:

> In consequence of false reports respecting the approach of the Mexican army, which at one time was said to be east of the Colorado River, a great panic seized the citizens of this place [Washington] and other neighborhoods, and we are informed, even the convention itself. Much bustle and scramble ensued.[11]

The reference to the convention was to the delegates at Washington who, it seemed, succumbed in large part to this panic. News of the fate of the men at the Alamo, which "spread like fire in high grass," had reached them on March 15. According to one witness, it caused a "complete panic" among those attending the convention.[12]

Two days later, the panic had not lessened. William F. Gray, a land agent visiting Texas from Washington, D.C., observed, "They were thrown into much agitation by a report spread by a person, unknown, who passed through the town to the eastward, without stopping, but stated in his transit that the enemy's cavalry were passing the Colorado at Bastrop, about sixty miles from Washington." Within the span of two days after news of the Alamo had arrived, the convention members elected an ad interim government, adopted the new constitution, and largely departed Washington, heading east. Gray in his diary for March 17, 1836, wrote, "The members are now dispersing in all directions, with haste and in confusion. A general panic seems to have seized them." Concerning the residents of Washington, Gray added that "The families are exposed and defenseless, and hundreds are moving off to the east. A constant stream of women and children, and some men, with wagons, carts and pack mules, are rushing across the Brazos night and day. The families of this place, and storekeepers, are packing up and moving."[13]

Considering that his army was just crossing the Colorado itself on March 17, Houston was none-too-pleased to hear that the Texian government had abruptly fled Washington. It would be hard to instill confidence that victory was imminent among the citizens when the government was in flight. Again, in his March 23 letter to Rusk, Houston complained, "The retreat of the government will have a bad effect on the troops, and I am half-provoked at it myself." In an addendum of the same letter, Houston lamented, "Oh, why did the cabinet leave Washington?...Oh, curse the consternation which has seized the people!"[14]

The Mexican army camp was only a short distance from the Colorado, but not that near to settlements and houses in the area, which tended to be closer to the two crossings guarded by the Texians. Thus, when Mexican soldiers foraged for provisions, they ventured into settlements that were close to the Texian encampments. While the soldiers encamped at Beeson's Crossing made their foray against the Mexican army, the Texians at Dewees' Ford were not idle. The new community of Columbus was directly across from Sydney Sherman's camp. Despite the paucity of settlers in the new town, the Mexican army could not afford to overlook potential sources of supplies, and this led to yet another encounter on the Colorado.

Colonel Sherman watched closely for any activity across the river. His attentiveness paid off on March 23, 1836. Three Mexican soldiers foraging for food were surprised by Texian troops. They offered no resistance and were captured and quickly escorted across the Colorado and to headquarters at the Texian camp downriver at Beeson's. Young Moses Austin Bryan, nephew of Stephen F. Austin, was called to help translate the interrogations of the three recently captured Mexican soldiers.[15] Despite being questioned separately, their accounts meshed well. General Joaquín Ramírez y Sesma had 500 to 600 infantry, plus 150 cavalry and two pieces of artillery. The prisoners further indicated that "his troops are badly clad, and the state of the weather such as to render them almost ineffectual from cold." They also said that the Mexicans intended to build a boat and cross nearby.[16]

The intelligence gathered from the three prisoners was not only useful but uplifting. If correct, the Texian army had numerical superiority over the adjacent Mexican forces, although they did possess artillery, which the Texians did not. In Houston's letter to Rusk on March 23, he reported, "the force of the enemy in this quarter [is] less than I had heard it. Let the Mexican force be what it may, if the country will turn out, we can beat them." In an addendum to the same letter dated the next day, Houston added that "[the prisoners] represent the enemy [to be] much weaker than all former reports."[17]

If Houston was going to engage a Mexican army on the Colorado, he needed additional supplies. The Texians received some much-needed munitions on March 23. One wagon arrived filled with arms and ammunition. Among the weapons were forty-eight muskets. According to Colonel Hockley, the Texian army still lacked good horses, sabers, and pistols, all of which the Mexican forces presumably had.[18] It also still had no artillery of any variety.

Houston searched all corners of Texas for supplies. On March 23, he wrote to Captain B. J. White, ordering him to "repair to Cox's Point or Dimit's Landing and remove or secure supplies at those places." He added, "You are ordered to use and command all the means of the country in securing supplies, and removing the families, and placing them on the east side of the Colorado. You have much discretion left with you, and I hope you will employ it to the best advantage for the preservation of the country."[19] Little did Houston know that Mexican General José de Urrea had been extremely efficient in his sweep along the Gulf Coast. The previous day, the remnants of William Ward's command, after finding Victoria occupied by enemy troops, tried to escape by ship from Dimitt's Landing on Lavaca Bay only to be overtaken and captured by Mexican cavalry units.

With a growing army, one of Houston's challenges was to feed his soldiers. Settlers in the vicinity of the Texian army were pressed into providing whatever provisions they could muster. The primary responsibility for procuring rations fell to the quartermasters. For the troops at Beeson's Crossing commanded by Colonel Edward Burleson, the regimental quartermaster was Edward Winfield. Winfield assigned assistants to procure and eventually slaughter whatever animals could be obtained for meat. One of these assistants was Martin D. Ramsey, a resident in the area near the Colorado where the Texian army camped. A key provider of meat to the army was William Alley, the younger brother of Abram Alley who was a neighbor to Ramsey and a closer neighbor of Benjamin Beeson, who lived just north. Alley provided between 225 and 300 hogs while the Texians camped on the Colorado. Additionally, he contributed thirty to forty head of cattle. Ramsey stated that he slaughtered them on the edge of the prairie east of the river.[20]

The bulk of the Texian army was camped near Beeson's Crossing. With the transfer of Captain Henry Teal's regulars the previous day, Houston may have felt that Sherman's position at Dewees' Ford needed reinforcements. He sent one hundred volunteers to strengthen his post. Among those that went were most of Captain Robert McNutt's company.[21] As the volunteers were marching to Dewees' homestead, they passed a guard detail escorting the three recently captured Mexican prisoners to Houston.[22]

Since his arrival in Gonzales, Houston had on multiple occasions sent orders to Colonel James W. Fannin at Goliad to fall back. His orders had been met with silence. After more than a week, it had to be disconcerting for Houston to hear nothing from Fannin. Though the Texian army at the Colorado was growing, Fannin's command represented a sizable and essential component in Houston's strategy. While writing a letter to Rusk, Houston received a courier with news that the troops under Fannin had been attacked near La Bahía. Though there was no further report on the outcome of the battle, Houston must have been both concerned and irritated. He doubtlessly had expected that Fannin would be far removed from La Bahía. The letter indicated that Fannin began his retreat on Saturday, March 19 and was attacked shortly thereafter. An hour and a half before sundown, he was surrounded.[23] Houston did not hide his irritation with Fannin: "If what I have heard from Fannin be true, I deplore it, and can only attribute the ill luck to his attempting to retreat in daylight in the face of a superior force. He is an ill-fated man."[24] The courier also reported that Ward's command had not returned.[25]

10

BEESON'S & DEWEES' DAY 9, MARCH 24

"All the troops that can be raised I wish placed at my disposal, as on the Colorado I make my stand."[1]

SAM HOUSTON

THERE WAS PLENTY OF EVIDENCE that the Texian army would engage the Mexicans on the Colorado River. In a letter to Richardson R. Royal, Texian revolutionary leader at Matagorda, Sam Houston boldly proclaimed "All the troops that can be raised I wish placed at my disposal, as on the Colorado I make my stand, and it is deemed necessary to concentrate all the effective force at this point for the present."[2] This was an impressive statement by Houston considering that only one day earlier he had received discouraging news regarding the status of James W. Fannin's command. Perhaps it was the most recent intelligence gathered that gave Houston the optimism. Interviews with prisoners led him to believe that the Mexican army across the river from him was not as strong as he previously thought.

Newly promoted Lieutenant John Sharp was ordered by Houston to ride to Velasco with dispatches intended for Major William T. Austin. A week or so earlier, Houston had sent Austin, his former aide-de-camp, to report to Colonel John A. Wharton at Velasco near the mouth of the Brazos River and investigate the availability of supplies. Austin had taken temporary command there while Wharton traveled down the coast to Matagorda. Houston expected Sharp to relay his intentions. "Whilst receiving my papers, General Houston told me to tell the people down in that part of the country not to run any further. They were safe; there would be no more retreating; and that the next news they would hear from the army would be of a battle, the results of which no one could doubt."[3] This seemed a clear indication that Houston had every intention of battling the Mexican forces soon.

Houston's impending decision to engage General Joaquín Ramírez y Sesma on the Colorado would likely have been met with enthusiasm by his troops. Captain Robert J. Calder, in whose company Sharp served, remembered, "There was a strong desire on the part of a large portion of the army to attack this division of the enemy, numbering about seven hundred men, and a considerable murmuring was heard at the commander in chief's refusal to gratify this desire. That we might have routed them, I have no doubt."[4]

At Dewees' Ford, Lieutenant Colonel Sidney Sherman and his men were prepared to fight. Jonathan H. Kuykendall recalled the attitude at Sherman's camp: "Very anxious were our men to be led against the enemy, who, it was confidently believed, was completely within our power. Daily, hourly, were orders expected for an attack. None doubted that we would be permitted to strike a blow."[5] Young William P. Zuber later wrote: "We believed that we could easily defeat any force of the enemy, if they did not outnumber us more than two to one."[6]

On March 16, 1836, Mexican General Eugenio Tolsa was ordered to march in support of General Sesma, who was proceeding eastward from Gonzales toward San Felipe de Austin. Tolsa was in command of approximately 550 men from the Guerrero and Mexico City battalions. Additionally, he was authorized to select a hundred cavalry, but owing to the lack of grain for the horses, only half that number actually accompanied him. Colonel Juan N. Almonte, aide-de-camp and close advisor to General Antonio López de Santa Anna, was ordered to accompany Tolsa. Almonte kept a thorough journal of most of his time in Texas, which became a key source of Mexican movements throughout the campaign. His departure was delayed a day and a half because the mules that had been requested by Sesma were not ready. However, despite his delay, he quickly caught up with Tolsa late in the day on March 20 as they were preparing to cross the Guadalupe River near Gonzales. With Gonzales reduced to ashes, no provisions could be had there, and the Mexican army quickly marched through and beyond the remnants of the small village by noon the next day.[7]

On March 22 as the Mexican troops slowly journeyed eastward, Almonte noted, "At La Baca, coming from Gonzales...the road from Goliad passes to Washington [on the Brazos] and Nacogdoches." This description clearly corresponds to the La Bahía Road. Perhaps more of interest was his observation on March 23, when he recorded, "At the farms of the Navidad, the road to Washington branches off as seen by the wagon tracks; it crosses the Colorado about 7 leagues higher up than where the division was." Neither of the two maps that Almonte favored from his trip through Texas in 1834 show a road at the location he described.[8] However, having traveled extensively through Texas, he may have been aware of roads that were not on the maps. Because of the land grants awarded to settlers along the Navidad, it would not be surprising that there was at least a very rudimentary road in this area. The location of this road, however, does not correspond with Austin's map of 1837, which shows the road to Burnam's Ferry crossing the Gonzales Road nearer Rocky Creek several miles behind them.[9] Because of the prevalent rain in the region at that time, the ruts he observed may well have been the route taken by Houston's troops, with accompanying civilians, as they moved off the Gonzales Road toward Burnam's Ferry. Whether this was

Portrait of Juan N. Almonte, a close advisor to Santa Anna who meticulously documented many events of the revolution.

an unmarked road or just a cross-country route that Houston had decided to use is subject to debate.

General Tolsa arrived on the Colorado during the late afternoon of March 24, 1836. Almonte noted in his journal that day: "About a league before coming to the river, the road from Atascosito and La Bahia del Espiritu Santo separates." A review of maps of the time does not show a split where he indicated, but there might well have been a trace connecting the Atascosito Road and the road to Beeson's Crossing on the west side of the Colorado. Almonte noted that General Adrián Woll reconnoitered six leagues, presumably along the same road, that night. This would prove to be an important maneuver, considering later plans.[10]

Three days earlier, Houston had sent a considerable force of cavalry and infantry to test the Mexicans. On March 24, the Texians may have noticed an increase in activity in the Mexican camp as Tolsa's forces began to arrive. Whether it was to monitor this unexpected activity or because Houston was still planning an attack, another expedition crossed the Colorado for a reconnaissance. Captain Henry W. Karnes again led the cavalry in this operation but, this time, no supporting infantry was included.

What little is known of this expedition is that it was composed of between thirty or forty mounted men. The Texian cavalry crossed using the ferry at Beeson's Crossing. Using what cover they could, they worked their way close to the Mexican lines, eventually overcoming a picket and capturing his horse. However, the Mexicans soon spotted the Texians and "opened fire on them with one or two small field pieces." Mexican cavalry tried to pursue but the Texian riders, with their captured horse, outran them. It was about dark when Karnes reached the ferry and began to recross with his men. After some difficulty in recovering their horses, they finally returned to camp.[11]

Sherman, meanwhile, also planned to engage the Mexicans. There is no indication that the actions from his encampment at Dewees' Ford were coordinated in any way with those of the Texians under Houston at Beeson's Crossing. While Houston had a strategic reason for sending Karnes' company across the river, Sherman's decision may have been more because his men wanted to fight, and he was determined to accommodate them. Jonathan H. Kuykendall recalled that "a prairie extended from the opposite bank of the river to the position of the enemy in the edge of the postoak woods... A ravine nearly opposite our camp extended from the river for some distance in the direction of the enemy." This 'ravine' was likely Ratliff Creek.[12] Like many rivers and creeks in the region, the waterway was lined with foliage that provided some cover. Kuykendall continued, "At the head of this ravine, Sherman posted a strong party of men and caused two or three horsemen to approach near the Mexicans, whose cavalry, it was hoped, would pursue our men and be drawn into the ambush. But the ruse failed. The enemy could not be tempted to leave his camp."[13] The reticence of the Mexicans to engage the Texians may have been due to their experiences in recent operations. Just as likely, however, was that Sesma was simply obeying orders from Santa Anna to not engage the Texians.

Unlike the Mexican army, which received major reinforcements with the arrival of Tolsa's troops, the reinforcements coming to the aid of the Texians arrived intermittently and in small groups. Many of the volunteers for the Texian army came from units that organized in various regions of Texas and traveled independently to the camps on the Colorado. These companies were usually under the leadership of an elected captain and associated lieutenants. One small company, composed of twenty men and raised in what is present-day Fort Bend County, arrived around this time under the command of Captain Daniel Perry.[14] They joined many notable men who had arrived with other captains, such as Anson Jones, who served as a private with Captain Calder's company, found Almonte's journal after the Battle of San Jacinto, and had a political career in the Republic of Texas that led to his election as its last president.

There were, however, instances where Texians volunteered without having joined a particular group. Such was the case for the men who arrived from the Washington area on March 24, 1836. Among this high-profile group was Colonel Wharton, whom Houston had sent to New Orleans to secure supplies in December 1835. He later commanded at Velasco in March 1836 and became Houston's adjutant general, replacing Major Benjamin F. Smith.[15] Another notable, if not infamous, individual who arrived with a letter of introduction from President David G. Burnet was twenty-five-year-old James H. Perry (no relation to Daniel Perry). Houston would later state, "He came to the camp on the Colorado with letters of introduction from the President and other members of the cabinet to the Commander-in-Chief, recommending him as a graduate of West Point, or having been a student there. Being a good looking gentleman, plausible in his manner, unembarrassed by diffidence, not very cultivated, still would do well for a soldier or officer, the general appointed him a member of his staff."[16] Houston's indifference towards Perry would change markedly for the worse. Perry would become not only a detractor of the General but also an accused enemy spy. Despite Houston's distrust of Perry, he allowed him to fight at the Battle of San Jacinto.

11

BEESON'S & DEWEES' DAY 10, MARCH 25

"On the 25th, Peter Kerr brought the disastrous...news of the defeat and surrender of Fannin...This intelligence was most unfortunate and produced a chilling effect upon the army."[1]

DANIEL SHIPMAN

COLONEL JUAN N. ALMONTE, recently arrived with General Eugenio Tolsa, noted in his journal on March 25, 1836, that "In the afternoon about 50 cavalry of the enemy started off in small parties, and carried with them about 50 cattle that were grazing in the plain, within sight."[2] It would seem that efforts to deprive the Mexican army of provisions, in this case beef, were still underway whenever the opportunity arose. Almonte's entry also suggests that Texian excursions across the river were not all that unusual.

On the morning of March 25, the Texians heard three reports from their enemy's artillery. Colonel Almonte noted in his journal that "the division cleaned their arms" that morning.[3] This exercise may well have been the reason for the cannon fire. Nevertheless, the Texians were on alert, thinking that the shots were a prelude to an impending attack, perhaps as retribution for the engagement with Captain Henry W. Karnes' cavalry the previous day. Despite this, nothing of consequence happened during the remainder of the morning hours.

During the early afternoon hours, Texian pickets gave the alarm that the Mexicans were advancing on their position near the Dewees encampment. Though the Texians had crossed the river numerous times, the Mexicans had yet to attempt it. News of the enemy approach toward the river was startling, and Lieutenant Colonel Sydney Sherman's men quickly took cover in their entrenchments. Soon afterward, Mexican cavalrymen, reportedly about eighty strong, were spotted on a bluff overlooking the river. It did not take too long for the two parties to start firing at one another.[4]

The modern Colorado River near this site is at least one hundred yards wide. Considering the rain and resulting high water that the Texians were experiencing during this timeframe, there is reason to believe that the distance across the river was probably a fair bit more. Though they had approached the river, the Mexican troopers never dismounted their horses, evidently content to harass the Texians with rifle fire. Whether they could reasonably be expected to hit a target from horseback from that distance was problematic. The Texians claimed that they consistently overshot their targets and did no damage to the defenders in their trenches. Texians meanwhile eagerly returned fire, but they were shooting uphill as the Mexican cavalry were on horseback atop a bluff overlooking the river. Like the Mexicans, there seemed to be no damage until one Texian sharpshooter reported that he thought he had found his target at least once since one of the enemy commanders flinched as if he had been hit. Shortly thereafter, the Mexican cavalry withdrew.[5]

There is no record of this encounter in Mexican communications or official Texian reports. The motive for the Mexican movement toward the river is unclear as well. Perhaps, like the Texians, they were restless and wanted to spur some activity from their enemy. Alternatively, this small engagement may have given some of the Texians an indication that

Entrenched Texian soldiers, under command of Lieutenant Colonel Sidney Sherman, fire across the Colorado River at Mexican cavalrymen at Dewees' Ford.

a larger fight was imminent. They would soon find out that was not going to be the case.

In his March 23, 1836 letter to Thomas J. Rusk, Sam Houston had seemed upbeat after the interrogation of recently captured Mexican soldiers. He reported, "I have examined the spies, and they represent the enemy much weaker than all former reports."[6] Colonel George W. Hockley's letter to Rusk on the same day, was perhaps even more optimistic. He stated, "General Sesma is on the opposite side of the river, about three miles from our encampment...His troops are badly clad, and the state of the weather such as to render them almost ineffectual from cold."[7]

Of course, this positive news was offset by the arrival of a courier who reported that the Texian forces near La Bahía were under attack. This news in part gave answer to the ongoing silence from Colonel James W. Fannin over the past week. Perhaps Houston held out a glimmer of hope that Fannin could extract himself from the dire situation. The results of the battle were not yet known. Reality would soon arrive, however, by way of a man named Peter Kerr.

In February, Fernando de León was appointed aide-de-camp to provisional Texas Governor James Robinson and took charge of the local militia. After Mexican General José de Urrea had captured Fannin and his men at Coleto Creek, De León was arrested and Kerr, a close friend of the family, was confined to De León's ranch. Knowing the importance of the news about Fannin, and perhaps cognizant of his own perilous circumstances, Kerr managed to escape. He traveled nearly seventy-five miles while evading Mexican forces, crossed the Colorado unseen, and reached the Texian encampment at Beeson's Crossing on March 25, 1836. After an exhausting and dangerous journey, Kerr might have expected sympathy for such a difficult journey and congratulations for his bravery in delivering important news. His reception, however, proved to be anything but warm.

While Kerr was understandably eager to share what he knew with whoever would listen, the surrender of Fannin at Coleto Creek was not the type of information that Houston wanted to be disseminated without his permission.[8] After hearing of his arrival, Houston immediately had Kerr brought to him and listened to his story. Kerr's version of events was probably little more than confirmation of what was already suspected. Nevertheless, the news was sobering, erasing any notion that Fannin would escape his situation. To try and quell the unrest Kerr had helped to precipitate, Houston did with Kerr exactly what he had done with Andres Barcena and Anselmo Bergara in Gonzales when they had learned of the fall of the Alamo only two weeks earlier. Houston ordered Kerr arrested for spreading false information.[9]

Kerr's arrest by Houston was just another turn in his busy life since arriving in Texas many years earlier. Peter Kerr and his partner William Kerr were among Stephen F. Austin's Old Three Hundred, receiving a grant of land in present day Washington County. Unlike many of the other settlers, however, Peter's interests in Texas were far-ranging and his exploits were not confined to his grant of land, nor Austin's Colony. Whereas William settled on the property in Washington County near present-day Burton, Peter set up shop as a merchant in Victoria. After three years or so of moderate success, Peter was robbed on a trading expedition among Indians northwest of Victoria, which ruined him.[10] After a visit to his family in Pennsylvania, Peter eventually made his way back to Texas in 1835 and became well acquainted with the De León family. The head of the family, Martin de León, who had died two years prior, was the founder of Victoria and empresario of the only predominantly Mexican colony in Texas. Kerr became fast friends with his son, Fernando de León.

Many Tejanos were opposed to Antonio López de Santa Anna when he assumed control of the Mexican government and revoked the Constitution of 1824. As the Texas Revolution began to take shape, Fernando de León, his brother-in-law, José María Jesús de Carbajal, and Peter Kerr

Peter Kerr reacts with outrage when Sam Houston has him arrested for spreading false rumors about Colonel James W. Fannin's defeat near Goliad.

drove livestock to New Orleans to trade for munitions in support of the Texian army. After the men succeeded in their endeavor, they boarded the ship *Hannah Elizabeth* bound for Texas. Unfortunately for them, the Mexican warship *Bravo* pursued and ran them aground. The crew of the *Bravo* then boarded the *Hannah Elizabeth* and took prisoners. Kerr was eventually set free, but Carbajal and De León were taken to Matamoros. De León later bribed his way to freedom, but Carbajal was subsequently imprisoned in Monterrey.[11] Kerr was fortunate not to have been taken to Mexico as a prisoner, but goods that he was transporting were in jeopardy. Luck seemed to be on his side, however, when the Texas privateer *William Robbins* recaptured the *Hannah Elizabeth* from the Mexicans. The ship's captain, however, decided to confiscate the cargo. After heated negotiations, Kerr was able to recoup some of the supplies by paying half its value to the captain.[12]

When the Texian army withdrew from the Colorado, Peter Kerr left as a prisoner. His status as a prisoner, though, did not deter him from continuing to tell whoever would listen about what he heard had happened to Fannin at Coleto Creek. Hockley, in a letter to Rusk on April 1, 1836, noted that "from information received the evening after leaving San Felipe, the Cmr-in-Chief [Houston] ordered Peter Carr [sic]...to be taken—a guard was sent to San Felipe and he was brought into camp next morning."[13] On April 3, Houston reported to Rusk, "I send you, in charge of Mr. Este, two prisoners, Peter Kerr, and Beregardo, a Mexican. I have nothing pointed against them; but suspicion has fallen upon them, and they are to be secured."[14] Despite this seeming setback for Kerr, his fortunes would improve considerably going forward.

12
MOVING EASTWARD
DAY 11, MARCH 26

"One battle must be decisive of the fate of Texas."[1]

SAM HOUSTON

SAM HOUSTON HAD ALL but announced his intent to do battle with General Joaquín Ramírez y Sesma across the Colorado River. The Texian soldiers cleaned their rifles and prepared for what they thought was an imminent engagement. On the morning of March 26, 1836, Houston forwent his usual inspections and instead paced alone, seemingly deep in thought. As was often the case, he sought no council as to what actions should be taken. The General finally arrived at a decision–though it was one that was unexpected and would be wildly unpopular. He directed his troops to break camp and be ready to march by sunset.[2] The order read as follows:

> Camp near Beason
> 26 March 1836
> Army Order
>
> Colo Wallace will notify all persons that the Army is moving out of the post oaks, and probably may fall back towards the Brazos.

Troops coming from lower country after today ought to fall back on Columbia, and the mouth of the river as well as supplies. I wish no persons to fall into Enemys [sic] hand on surprise. The Army will march slowly. Great caution should be used.

Sam Houston
Com. In Chief[3]

By early evening, Houston must have gotten enough feedback to determine that it was in his best interest to speak to his men. He called them together to explain the reasons for his decision.

Accounts differ concerning what he exactly said. One account stated that his principal reason was to relocate to a place where fresh grass was available for the animals.[4] That seems to be consistent with the dispatch he had purportedly sent to Lieutenant Colonel Sydney Sherman at Dewees' Ford.[5] Another account states that he provided great details about how the defeat of Colonel James W. Fannin's army meant that they were the last significant Texas forces and the fate of the country depended solely on their first battle with the enemy.[6] More than likely, if a speech was indeed given, it probably did not get into the detail suggested by the latter account. However, he almost certainly would have had to provide an explanation beyond moving out for the sole purpose of grass for the animals. Regardless, it is likely that the men, at least the ones at Beeson's Crossing, that were in Houston's immediate command at the time, realized that their movements were not temporary, but were a full-fledged retreat to the Brazos River.

It took several hours for the soldiers to be ready to march. Upon learning of the retreat, many of those who had families in the vicinity would have had concerns for their wellbeing. It would have been only natural to help remove them to a place of safety. Part of the delay of Houston's march may have been to accommodate furlough requests. It is hard to say whether these requests might have been approved, but the fact is that the Texian army was considerably smaller at the Brazos than it was when Houston left the Colorado. Some accommodation was likely made for many anxious Texian soldiers. Of course, some may have successfully departed without formal leave.

At the time the orders were given, there were perhaps more than 1,000 men at Beeson's Crossing. Equipment and provisions that had been accessible for a week had to be packed for the long march ahead. Houston would have to send dispatches to the encampments at Dewees' Ford, whoever was guarding the Atascosito Crossing, and any outlying areas. Additionally, he needed to forward his plans to the government. All of this would add to the amount of time the Texians needed to commence their march.

Some have claimed that at Beeson's Crossing, just as at Gonzales, the Texian retreat happened so rapidly that the pickets did not receive word of the order to move out. Captain William J. E. Heard later wrote, "When the army commenced retreating from this place, a man called Moses Lapham, and two others, were left on picket guard, and remained in this condition several days without provisions, and frequently in sight of the enemy." There was a happy ending to this tale: "For days, the friends of poor Lapham believed him to have fallen a victim, but he afterwards came up to the camp [and] fought at San Jacinto."[7] This statement would lead one to believe that Lapham and others were a victim of Houston's negligence. Lapham never took the time nor seemed to have the inclination to clarify the situation. In a letter to his parents, Lapham, no admirer of Houston, would often refer to him as "our crazy General."[8]

A letter sent by Thomas Borden to Amos Lapham, the father of Moses, does not suggest a sloppy retreat without calling in the sentries. In that letter, Borden made a point of proclaiming that Moses had been an "active spy" and noted that he and three others had stayed four days at the Colorado after Houston's departure.[9] Perhaps young Lapham's experience as a surveyor with Borden and his knowledge of the Texas landscape helped him in his work as a spy, or scout, for the Texian army, which Borden reported proudly to his anxious father.[10]

Houston had another key item to consider, however, while he led his retreat. What would be the response of the Mexican army? He knew that his troops could be just as vulnerable to an attack during their retreat from the Colorado as they were when they left Gonzales only a couple of weeks earlier. To conceal his retreat, or at least try to delay the crossing of Mexican forces, Houston designed a ruse to give the impression that the Texians were alert and perhaps preparing for an attack. To accomplish this, he reinforced his outposts and sent scouting parties along the river.[11] The houses in the area that remained standing were burned, further adding to the great commotion on the eastern side of the river.[12] At dark, he ordered bright campfires lit to indicate more movement among his men with the hope that this action would put the Mexican army in a defensive position. The maneuver seemed to work as both Henry W. Karnes and Erastus "Deaf" Smith reported that General Sesma had withdrawn further into the woods.[13] The first of Sesma's men did not cross for another three days and did so further south at the Atascosito Crossing.

Meanwhile, Houston ordered his wagons loaded and made ready for retreat. In the evening of March 26, the Texian army quietly broke camp and moved eastward.[14] Owing to their late departure, darkness, and the heavily wooded area, the Texians traveled barely five miles before camping for the night.[15] It was reported that up to seventy-five families were encamped in the area awaiting the outcome of the inevitable battle.[16] The sudden order to retreat meant that those families had to quickly pack and leave as well. Though the urgency of the situation was perhaps not as dire as it was at Gonzales, civilians still needed to be protected, and this may have also contributed to the slow pace of the Texians.

At Dewees' Ford, Sherman had his adjutant, Henry Stouffer, read aloud his dispatch from Houston. In it were instructions for Sherman to march to the edge of the river bottom to a point where there was plenty of grass for his animals. It further informed him that at the fork of the road he would meet a guide, who would lead him to the main body of the army.[17] Perhaps coincidentally, Sherman had earlier ordered an extra supply of beef to be slaughtered but not cooked. This helped facilitate the preparation for departure. In short order, Sherman's command, numbering about 250, were ready to march.[18] This was advantageous since Dewees' Ford was located almost four miles further west than Beeson's Crossing, whence Houston departed with his troops.

William P. Zuber recalled, "We fell into line and marched down the river, in the bottom, not knowing why we were marching, or whither we were going, but judging that, of course, we were going to join the main army, at the lower encampment." He and his comrades continued down the Colorado bottom until they eventually slowed to a single-file crossing of a small and shallow creek about twenty or thirty feet broad. This creek was undoubtedly what is today referred to as Sandy Branch. The Texians continued for about six or seven miles before finally leaving the Colorado bottomlands. Eventually, Sherman's command paused around midnight in a thicket of dead saplings which were used as fuel to cook the beef they had slaughtered that morning. After a short respite, they continued their march eastward.[19]

Houston's sudden order to retreat did not immediately stop the inflow of volunteers coming to join his army. On the day of the retreat, a sizable force under the command of Major John Forbes arrived, albeit split into two separate bodies. Forbes was an aide-de-camp of Houston, who on March 5, 1836, shortly before departing Washington for Gonzales, had dispatched the Major to Velasco to aid Adjutant General John A. Wharton in forwarding troops and ammunition to the Texian army. When Forbes arrived in Velasco, he found that Wharton was in Matagorda and Captain George W. Poe was in temporary command. Forbes assumed command and Poe went to join Houston on the Colorado.[20]

Forbes found that two companies of men, mostly from New Orleans,

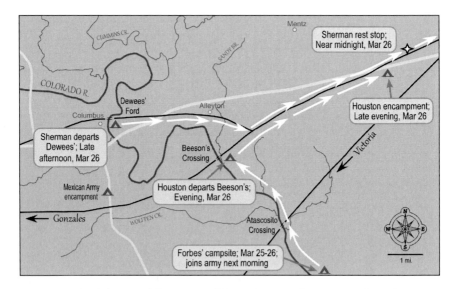

Projected route of the retreat of the Texian army from Dewees's Ford and Beeson's Crossing on March 26, 1836. Map also shows the arrival of Major John Forbes and company the morning of the retreat.

had arrived in late January at Velasco. Amasa Turner, commissioned as a lieutenant, had been sent to recruit men from around his home in Mobile, Alabama. Having no luck there, he moved on to New Orleans, where he was considerably more successful in his recruiting efforts. Ultimately, the men arrived at Velasco by ship from New Orleans. Turner and Richard Roman were elected captains of two companies. Major Forbes also found enough men around Velasco that he helped organize a third company who were eventually nicknamed the "Velasco Blues." The customs collector for the Port of Brazos, William S. Fisher, was elected captain of this company.[21]

Forbes was well satisfied with these recruits. He declared the "Three companies of Infantry well armed and desciplined [sic] & under the command of Excellent Officers." In accordance with his orders, he seized a cargo schooner in Velasco with the intent of sailing down the coast to Dimitt's Landing and marching inland to join the Texian army. Those plans were soon scuttled, however, when he learned "through a reliable source of the unhappy Defeat" of Fannin near Goliad. Forbes' informant also indicated that the Mexican army was advancing in "strong force."[22] Forbes immediately elected instead to lead the three companies overland to join Houston's army and to transport as much of the munitions as possible.

Under Forbes' command, the three companies marched quickly up the Brazos to Columbia. There he procured enough wagons with ox teams to help transport munitions and personnel.[23] From Columbia, Forbes's men traveled along "the old contraband trace leading from there to the Colorado." This road angled to the northwest across open prairie to the San Bernard River, on to Eagle Lake, and hit a point near the Colorado just south of the Atascosito Crossing. Not long after they commenced their trek, Forbes decided that it would be most beneficial to move ahead of the slow pace of the ox-pulled wagons. He selected Captain Turner's company to accompany him on a forced march toward the Colorado while Captains Roman and Fisher remained with the munitions. On the night of March 24, 1836, Forbes with Turner's company camped "at the fartherest [sic] point of timbers skirting the prairie west of the Brazos." Having covered about sixty miles in a couple of days of marching from Columbia, the exhausted Texians reached the Colorado about three miles south of the Atascosito Crossing where they camped on the night of March 25. By 11:00 the next morning, they reached Houston at Beeson's Crossing. One can only imagine their frustration when they discovered that instead of getting ready to do battle, Houston was preparing to retreat toward the Brazos that very evening.

Captains Roman and Fisher slowly made their way west with their men and heavily laden wagons filled with munitions. Major Forbes later stated that the two companies camped on the night of March 26 at the same site as Captain Turner the previous night.[24] This so-called 'campsite' would have provided scant comfort since the Texians would likely have found a messenger waiting to inform them of the army's imminent retreat. Rather than proceeding north along the Colorado to Beeson's Crossing, the group would more likely have traveled along an old cut-off from the Atascosito Crossing northeast toward the road to San Felipe. Reports indicate they did indeed join the retreating army during the night of March 26–27, 1836.[25]

General Houston was not the only one to receive volunteers on the day of his retreat. On the morning of March 26, another company of volunteers, numbering about thirty-five men, arrived at Sherman's camp at Dewees' Ford.[26] This company had organized in Nacogdoches on March 6. While on route, Leander Smith, brother-in-law to Secretary of War Thomas J. Rusk, was elected captain.[27] The company received news of the defeat at the Alamo, which expedited their trek towards the Colorado.[28] After marching down the La Bahía Road from Nacogdoches, the troops stopped at Asa Hoxey's plantation at Cole's Settlement (modern-day Independence), where they procured provisions. The receipt was signed by

DAY 11: MOVING EASTWARD | 157

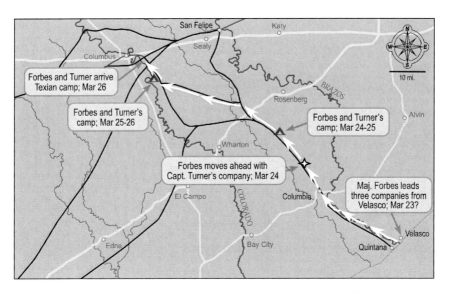

Projected route of Major John Forbes and three companies from Velasco toward Beeson's Crossing.

Lieutenant Hayden Arnold, who soon afterward assumed command of the company.[29] From there, the Texians proceeded south on the Coushatta Trace/La Bahía Road to the Colorado. Upon arriving, the Nacogdoches Volunteers would have first encountered Sherman's encampment at Dewees Ford. Shortly after that, an express rider arrived with a message for Colonel Sherman. Just as Major Forbes had learned upon his arrival in the camp at Beeson's Crossing, the members of the Nacogdoches Volunteers discovered that they would be falling back instead of fighting.[30]

Some of the Texians on the Colorado were relatively new to military service. Others had been with the army since Gonzales. It was safe to say, however, that all were outraged at the massacre at the Alamo. While there may have been nervousness or even panic among some of the men, the recent news of Fannin's defeat at Coleto Creek likely motivated the majority of the men to exact retribution from the Mexican army, who had been sitting across the river from them for the past few days. To say that the men upon being ordered to retreat were unhappy would be an understatement. Outraged would probably be more appropriate.

Evidence that some Texians were not happy with their commander can easily be found. Lapham, one of the Texian spies, wrote, "On hearing of the defeat of F. [Fannin,] we retreated to the Colorado river, and then... our crazy Gen. Houston, ordered all his army of 1200 men to retreat to the Brassos [sic]."[31] In a letter dated November 1855 to Sherman, James Tarlton, a member of Moseley Baker's company, wrote, "Gen. Houston's 'little army' was at least 1800 men the morning he ordered the shameful retreat from the Colorado."[32] Thomas J. Rabb was captain of the volunteers recruited from families who lived along the Colorado. He reportedly told Houston that he had better not let the Mexicans cross the river or he would lose half his army. His sister-in-law, Mary Crownover Rabb, in giving her account of his actions, wrote, "old Sam was affraid [sic] and would not fight."[33] Baker also provided a scathing review of Houston's actions on the Colorado:

> You were now...encamped on the eastern bank of the Colorado. You now have an army of from fifteen hundred to seventeen hundred men, and notwithstanding the terrible panic that has seized the country, you have every reason to believe that a short time will make it two thousand. On the opposite side Gen. Siesma [sic], the Mexican general, is encamped with seven hundred men....You hesitated so long that the most mutinous feeling began to show itself, and to allay the storm, you unequivocally assured the army that you would fight on the next morning at daybreak....You had promised in the morning to fight at daybreak of the next; but on the evening of that same day you called the army together and made it a speech. You represented the imperative necessity of the encampment being removed to a place where water and grass could be had, and although this seemed unaccountably strange, when you were engaged to fight the next morning, yet your order was obeyed, and you retreated seven miles that evening. No one had the most distant conception that you were retreating from the enemy.[34]

Baker was prolific with his criticism of Houston. He later wrote, "Sherman, who commanded the crossing at Dewees', earnestly entreated that he might be permitted to cross over with 300 men, promising to rout the enemy or not return alive. Had you crossed the river and captured Siesma [sic] and his army, as you could easily have done, you would have had such hostages as would have saved Fannin and his men from the cruel fate to which they were destined."[35]

The ludicrous idea that a victory over General Sesma's army might somehow have saved Fannin resurfaced in the *Texas Almanac of 1860*: "If Gen. Houston had fought, or permitted contradiction to all experience, to suppose he would have failed to capture from 200 to 400 of the enemy's infantry... The company of cavalry would probably have fled to Urrea's camp, and conveyed prompt intelligence of the disaster." The writer added, "Is not the corollary obvious, that the massacre of Goliad would not have occurred: that Gen. Urrea, knowing his enemy were in possession of prisoners as numerous as his own unfortunate ones, would not have dared to imbrue his hands in their blood?"[36]

According to Baker, the victory at San Jacinto was unnecessary. The path taken should have been thus, "By routing Sesma, you could immediately have fallen upon Santa Anna on his way from Gonzales and have given him battle with nearly two to one in your favor. A victory over him would have given you the choice of attacking Gaona or Urrea, as you might have deemed proper."[37] This perspective was presented rather poetically by Henry S. Foote in a scenario of what might have transpired:

> At the head of fourteen hundred victors flushed with success, whose ranks would have swelled by scores and hundreds as they dashed onwards, the Command-in-Chief of the valiant Texans, like Frederic of Prussia, or Napoleon, or Jackson, might have pushed rapidly in pursuit of the remaining divisions, into which...Santa Anna had broken his grand army of barbarian soldiers. Encountering the nearest of these, he might have demolished it with such men as fought at San Jacinto, at a single blow; and victory still perched aloft upon the Banner of Freedom, would herself have led the rushing, triumphant charge against the surviving squadrons of the Tyrant. This was the critical moment; now might the yet unburied martyrs of the cause of Independence have been sublimely avenged; and the scenes of devastation, on both sides, have been brought to a close.[38]

It should be considered no coincidence that the criticisms directed at Houston came from men who, at one time, were under Baker's command. Captain Baker was not shy about voicing his displeasure with the commander in chief, and that attitude may well have been passed along to many who served under him.

Criticism of Houston within the ranks of his army certainly was not confined to Baker's company. Robert J. Coleman, one of the signers of the Texas Declaration of Independence and a soon-to-be aide-de-camp for Houston, wrote,

> [Houston] ordered the farm houses in the vicinity of the camp to be burned, and a retreat to San Felipe to be commenced. Thirteen hundred Americans retreating before a division of 800 Mexicans! Can Houston's strong partizans [sic] presume to excuse such dastardly cowardice under the pretence [sic] of laudable prudence?[39]

In September 1857, Captain Jesse Billingsley's narrative of the retreat appeared in the *Galveston News*. He claimed that "the Army earnestly besought Gen. Houston to come to an engagement. This Houston declined…to the disgust of many a galland [sic] soldier, as the apparent salvation of the country depended on the successful issue of an immediate engagement."[40] Some recalled that the decision to retreat prompted the first widespread talk among the ranks about replacing Houston as commander in chief. These talks increased the further east that the Texians marched. Nicholas D. Labadie wrote, "We at once perceived that Houston had commenced his retreat…Many of us declared it was necessary to have a better leader, and that, if we could do no better, we would elect some one better fitted to command." Jonathan H. Kuykendall remembered: "Soon after leaving the Bernard, Ben Fort Smith. . . rode along for a few minutes near that part of our rank in which I marched, and conversed with some of us freely in regard to this policy of this second retreat. He found that we were much opposed to it, and strongly censured General Houston for his non-combative policy." Later regarding the same conversation with Smith, Kuykendall wrote, "[Smith] did not say a word in defense of the general, and, when something was said about depriving Houston of the command and electing some one in his place, Smith neither said aye nor nay to the suggestion."[41]

Even the passage of a century did not deter some from their bitterness toward Houston's decision. In *An Early History of Fayette County*, written to celebrate the centennial of Texas independence, authors Leone Weyand and Houston Wade proclaimed in one of their footnotes, "We of Fayette County have ever contended and still contend that the Battle of San Jacinto should have been fought on the Colorado at Dewees' Ford. A comparative inspection of the ground and the San Jacinto battlefield will convince any fair minded person that our locality is by far the most advantageous from a military point of view."[42]

Of course, the natural consequence of this retreat was that men would leave the army–with or without approval. Considering that a significant portion of the population of Texas resided between the Colorado and Brazos Rivers, it is only natural to expect that some men in the army would want to assist in removing their family from harm's way. The author of an article in the *Texas Almanac of 1860* was more than poetic in citing the displeasure at Houston's decision to withdraw from the Colorado and the impact it had on the army. He wrote, "From the moment the retreat was plainly begun, the indignant army dissolved away like the untimely snow of the hill-top before a vertical sun. The citizens of Western Texas, whose families had been left at home, in the hope that the enemy would be met and defeated, were compelled by the first and holiest promptings of nature, to abandon their dishonored flag draggling in the dust, and provide for the imminently exposed ones of their own household."[43]

Heard, as the first lieutenant in Captain Rabb's locally raised company of volunteers, was selected by those who lived further south along the Colorado to ascertain Houston's full intention and, if he found it to be true that the General intended to retreat, demand furloughs for them all so they could remove their families from harm. Houston granted the furloughs, and many of the men temporarily left the army.[44] Though not specifically stated, it is likely that Heard took that opportunity to make his way south toward Egypt, about twenty-five miles south of Beeson's Crossing, to also help move his family.

A week later, Captain Rabb, probably upon the return to the company of Lieutenant Heard, was assigned a new task. Contrary to reports that Rabb quit the army because of his disgust with Houston, a detail led by Rabb was assigned by Houston to guard Mercer's Crossing at Egypt and to act as a rear-guard for families retreating eastward.[45] While on that assignment, Rabb worked to ensure his family was out of harm's way. Nevertheless, the Rabb family became victims of the hardships of the Runaway Scrape. Rabb's infant nephew died within a few months of leaving their home on the Colorado. His wife died the day after their arrival back.[46] Rabb fell sick while on the Brazos River. Although he remained in the army, his company would be commanded by Heard during the Battle of San Jacinto.

William B. Dewees recalled that it was on the day of Houston's retreat that he also requested a furlough and left the army to assist his family.[47] Dewees was married to Benjamin and Betsy Beeson's daughter Lydia, so he probably assisted the Beesons in their evacuation. Dewees noted that there were about seventy-five families encamped in the vicinity who hoped a Texian victory would remove any necessity to evacuate. Families along the Colorado further south were suddenly left vulnerable with the Texian army's abrupt retreat and had to evacuate, leaving everything behind. With Houston's sudden order to retire, any Texas soldier connected with families or others in the prospective pathway of the Mexican army would have been eager to leave to help facilitate their departure. Even Colonel Edward Burleson asked for a furlough during the Texas retreat to tend to his family.[48]

Of course, not only were there departures from the existing Texian army, but the steady stream of volunteers that had been rapidly inflating its numbers quickly dwindled. Volunteers understandably seemed less enthusiastic about joining an army in retreat, especially not knowing how far the troops would eventually withdraw. To many, the only way to ensure the safety of one's family would be to remove them east of the Sabine River, into United States territory.[49] Given the rapid change in the enlistments while on the Colorado, it was virtually impossible to precisely know the number of soldiers present at the time of the retreat. It is probably safe to assume that the number was between 1,360 and 1,600.[50] Thanks to the retreat, this was the high-water mark for enrollment in Houston's army. Ultimately, Rabb's pronouncement that Houston would lose half his troops if he did not attack the Mexicans on the Colorado proved prophetic. The Texian army dropped to about 750 men while camped at Jared Groce's plantation on the Brazos River just a few days later.

The circumstances on the Colorado changed dramatically and in a very short period. To illustrate this, one needs only to read a letter penned by Lieutenant John Sharp, who had been sent by General Houston to Velasco on March 24 to check on supplies:

Brazoria, March 27, 1836

Having just returned on express forty hours from camp, and finding great alarm prevailing among the people, many of them flying with their families to the United States, and being called upon by the Committee of Safety and Vigilance in this place, to give a statement of facts, in relation to our army, and what its movements are, &c.: I take this method of informing them, that there is no cause for the excitement now prevailing in this part of the country. Our army, now encamped at and near Beason's on the Colorado, consists of from 1,000 to 1,200 men, and reinforcements hourly coming in, they are all well armed, with plenty of provisions, ammunition, &c, are in good spirits, and have perfect confidence in themselves and their officers. From all the information we can gain, either through our own spies, or prisoners, taken from the enemy, they cannot have more than six to eight, hundred men in the army, now encamped about five miles above us on the opposite side of the river. The prisoners say that there were but from twenty five hundred to three thousand men at Bejar after the Alamo was taken; of this number one thousand were sent to attack us at Gonzales, and the remainder were sent to retake Goliad. Of the army opposed to us at Beason's, from two to three hundred are cavalry, and the remainder infantry, with two small pieces of cannon; this body are under the command of Gen. Siezma [sic]. An attack has been made on them, I think, ere this, and if it has, who can doubt of the result? Circumstances rendered it necessary that we should retreat from Gonzales, but our army now will never leave the Colorado, but to go westward, & every day will bring news of a fresh victory, until not a Mexican Soldier, opposed to us, can be found this side of the Rio Grande! Let but the men of Texas turn out, with arms in their hands, resolved to be Free or Die! and families will be as safe here as on the other side of the Sabine.

John Sharp

P.S. On my way down I met several small companies pushing on for our camp, and those that came from the Eastward report from 300 to 500 men on their way from that quarter.[51]

Part of Sharp's mission was to convey Houston's intentions to the settlers. He had no way of knowing that, as he was penning this letter, the Texian army, rather than having engaged in a victorious battle against the Mexican army, was instead in full retreat. The reassurances he put forth soon rang hollow, and the very people he sought to comfort would quickly find that they were in danger from an advancing enemy.

Until the day of retreat, plenty of evidence suggested that the Texian army would engage the Mexicans on the Colorado. In fact, there are indications that Houston planned to attack Sesma from the east and south specifically on March 27.[52] Instead, he decided to retreat to the Brazos, a decidedly unpopular decision among the ranks and the government. Why? The most common explanation assigned to the decision was learning of Fannin's defeat at Coleto Creek. Houston's actions immediately after receiving the news from Peter Kerr seemed to precipitate the retreat. The commander in chief was counting on Fannin's troops in his overall strategy. He expected that Fannin would fall back and eventually join the main army.[53] However, with Fannin's defeat almost a full week prior, General José de Urrea and his troops could conceivably be crossing the Colorado at any time and marching north to flank the remaining Texian army. Still, Kerr's report only seemed to confirm what Houston already suspected. On March 23, he had received reports that Fannin was in dire straits, yet he still proclaimed, "on the Colorado I make my stand."[54] The confirmation of Fannin's defeat most certainly would have impacted Houston's decision, but it seems that this was not his sole reason.

One of the important advantages that the Mexican army led by General Sesma had over the opposing Texians was their artillery. Having disposed of his cannons at Gonzales because of the hasty retreat, Houston had sent Major William T. Austin to requisition additional munitions from Colonel Wharton at Velasco and return to the camp on the Colorado. Though some supplies and ammunition did arrive, there was no sign of any new artillery. When Colonel Wharton arrived in camp on March 24, he may have provided a status report to Houston suggesting that artillery was not coming in the near term, and certainly the arrival of Major Forbes from Velasco would have further confirmed this. The Mexican army would maintain their advantage in this aspect, and years later Houston would cite this as a key reason for the Texian withdrawal.[55]

When General Sesma's army arrived on the Colorado, the opposing armies were probably of similar manpower. A constant inflow of volunteers during the next several days ballooned the Texian numbers considerably, giving them a decided manpower edge over the Mexicans. The Texian soldiers were clamoring for a fight, and at that time their numbers suggested that they may have had an edge. However, that advantage evaporated on March 24, when Sesma was reinforced by General Eugenio Tolsa's troops. With these reinforcements, the Mexican army numbers were certainly comparable to the Texian army. Was this reinforcement a reason for retreat? Indeed, Houston did not mention enemy reinforcements in any subsequent dispatches and Tolsa's arrival is hardly ever mentioned among the reasons for Houston's reluctance to attack. He may have been unaware of the reinforcements, but he very logically expected it to happen.[56] It also it seems difficult to believe that he was oblivious to the arrival of an additional 500 Mexican soldiers, especially since there was a report that the recent arrivals had encountered Texian cavalry.[57] In fact, it may well be that Houston's reconnaissance led by Captain Karnes was precipitated by activity occurring in the opposing camp. With their manpower advantage gone, the prospects for a Texian victory would seemingly be diminished.

Even if a Texian engagement had resulted in victory, logistical issues still might impair the army. Houston, in a conversation with Captain Robert J. Calder during their retreat toward San Felipe, stated, "To be sure, we could have whipped the Mexicans back at the Colorado, but we can't fight battles without having men killed and wounded. But we actually have not the means of conveying as much ammunition and baggage as we need, much less the means of conveying wounded men after an action."[58] These were realistic issues that would have led Houston to reconsider his decision to attack.

There of course were strategic problems even if the Texian army engaged the Mexicans and won. What then? Santa Anna was still headquartered at San Antonio de Béxar. Fighting would continue even after a Texian victory. Several other Mexican commands in Texas posed a substantial threat. And despite the opinions of some optimistic participants, it would have been unlikely that the Texians could have marched from one Mexican army to the next, claiming one victory after another. It is fair, however, to wonder what the Mexican response might have been if the Texian army defeated General Sesma. Santa Anna's attitude after the fall of the Alamo, and the defeat and subsequent execution of Fannin's men at Goliad, was that the Texas rebellion was virtually over. He was preparing to leave Texas and return to his responsibilities in Mexico City. Only the unexpected Texian presence at the Colorado and his staff's pleas to stay changed his mind. A victory by the Texian 'rebels' might have further revitalized Santa Anna's attitude. Rather than multiple commands around Texas, a defeat might have prompted him to consolidate. Houston said as much to Calder: "defeat to the enemy at the Colorado would inevitably have concentrated the other divisions of the Mexican army against us."[59] It is likely that Santa Anna would have been more cautious and not have been found in a vanguard facing the Texians, as he eventually was at San Jacinto. A battle might have been won by the Texians on the Colorado, but winning the revolution might have ultimately become much more problematic.

The original order from Santa Anna was for General Sesma to proceed from San Antonio through Gonzales, cross the Colorado, and encamp at San Felipe de Austin, where Santa Anna would make his headquarters.[60] Those plans changed once Sesma came upon the Texian army covering two of the primary crossings on the Colorado at Dewees' and Beeson's. Santa Anna advised Sesma that reinforcements were on the way.[61] Sesma seemed content to await these reinforcements without taking any action against the Texians, despite repeated attempts to draw the Mexican army into an engagement. The first reinforcements arrived late in the afternoon of March 24, 1836, led by General Tolsa.

Once reinforcements arrived, General Sesma needed to devise a strategy as to how to proceed. He summoned a council of the appropriate officers to determine a suitable course of action. The consensus seemed to be that, despite their perceived slight numerical advantage, a contested crossing, with the Texians entrenched on the high banks, would be too costly.[62] Additionally, they were likely unsure whether the Texians had acquired any artillery, which would have compounded the potential problems in crossing. In a report to Santa Anna dated March 25, Sesma recommended that additional soldiers be sent to cross the Colorado upriver, thereby flanking the Texian army while Houston was otherwise engaged with the forces across the river from him.[63] Of course, this action was exactly what Houston feared most, and it was certainly a factor in Houston's plans going forward.

Whether Sesma thought that Santa Anna would accept his request for more troops to flank Houston's army, he decided to avoid the Texian positions and locate a different crossing. As mentioned previously, the Atascosito Crossing, located a short distance south, was prominent on the maps carried by the Mexican leaders. These maps were critical to the Mexican generals since there seemed to be few adequate local guides. In a March 16 letter to General Vicente Filisola, Sesma complained of the lack of competent guides who knew the crossings.[64] The fact that the Atascosito Road had become virtually obsolete was unknown to the Mexican generals.[65] Ironically, this was the very crossing that Houston had neglected to guard upon his arrival at Beeson's.

Colonel Juan N. Almonte, who accompanied General Tolsa to the Colorado, noted that on the morning of March 26 the Mexicans commenced their march toward the Atascosito Crossing. Presumably, Tolsa's command was trailing Sesma's men. Almonte recorded that they traveled three leagues (approximately 7.8 miles), stopping at least three times. Eventually, they camped on the banks of the San Antoñito, a short distance upriver of their destination. This creek may have been present-day Wolfpen Creek, since it is the only waterway between the Mexican campsite and the Atascosito Crossing. Assuming that Tolsa's command would have camped to the rear, or west, of Sesma's, the distance of march would likely have been closer to two leagues (5.2 miles). Almonte also recorded that the enemy reconnoitered them that day.

The next day, the short journey to the Atascosito Crossing was completed. While scouts were dispatched to determine the Texians' position, rafts were constructed to facilitate the river crossing.[66] Ironically, the move to the Atascosito Crossing was ultimately unnecessary, since the Texians had earlier abandoned both of the crossings they guarded near Columbus.

13

TOWARD THE BRAZOS

"Ascertaining Houston was determined on continuing the retreat, Col. Burleson left the army for the purpose of removing his family to a place of safety. Col. Sherman was therefore ordered to put the army in marching order. The retreat was continued through the day."[1]

NICHOLAS D. LABADIE

AFTER MIDNIGHT ON MARCH 27, 1836, the two parts of the Texian army had not yet merged. Lieutenant Colonel Sydney Sherman's smaller battalion, though further west, had marched out promptly and was ahead of the remainder of the Texians. An amusing incident shows, in part, why the troops under Sam Houston moved more slowly. As Houston was preparing to march on the day after leaving his Colorado River camp, he saw a wagon that was unhitched, with its oxen grazing nearby. The commander angrily demanded an explanation, bellowing "[W]here is the d----d scoundrel that drives that team?" The men pointed to Jim Wilson, who was lazily stretched out before a campfire. Houston exploded: "You d----d infernal s-n of a b---h, why don't you hitch up?" Wilson pointed to his feet with nothing more than rags as shoes and, matching Houston's fury, responded, "Do you think I am going to drive a wagon for a d----d little one-horse army and my feet in that fix? No sir, I will see you and your d----d army further in h-ll than a pigeon could fly in a month first." Houston knew Wilson and wasting no time, bent down to take off his boots and offer them to him to facilitate a departure. Wilson interrupted: "No sir, I could not get my big-toe in one of them; and if I could, do you think I'm going to take your boots? A h-ll of a purty general you'd make, 'stride of a Spanish pony and no boots on. I always liked you, general, but I like you better now, but d----d if I touch your boots." Houston resorted to quiet cajoling until finally the big man bellowed, "Well general, I'll do it for you, but d----d if there is another man on top of this green earth that Jim Wilson would drive that wagon for, without shoes."[2]

Soon after leaving the woods skirting the Colorado, the remainder of Major John Forbes' command from Velasco joined the main Texian army.[3] Two of his companies, led by captains Richard Roman and William S. Fisher, had several ox-pulled wagons carrying munitions and provisions and were thus moving slower than Forbes and Captain Amasa Turner's company, who rendezvoused with Houston on the Colorado. Houston undoubtedly sent word to them, perhaps via one or more of the men guarding the Atascosito Crossing, that Roman and Fisher should join the main army on the road to San Felipe. Maps of the time show a cutoff from the Atascosito Crossing northeast toward the San Felipe Road.

Houston's command finally joined Sherman near the San Bernard River, where he had arrived an hour or so before noon on March 27. There Sherman's Texians stopped, slaughtered a cow, and ate a beef lunch while waiting for Houston to join them.[4] After a while, the main body of the Texian army came marching up the road. The sight made an impression on young William P. Zuber, who had never seen such a large group of people. More notably however, Zuber was more interested in Houston. Having never seen the General, Zuber inquired as to which one he was. When a comrade pointed him out, Zuber was surprised. "What, that plain-looking man on the gray horse?" Zuber was further struck by his

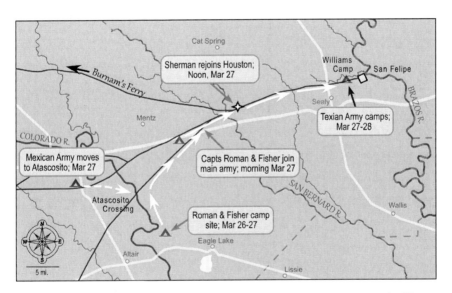

Projected route of companies commanded by Captains Richard Roman and William S. Fisher to the Texian army and their continued retreat to the Brazos River. Map also shows the movement of the Mexican army from their previous campsite to the Atascosito Crossing. Historic roads are in black and modern roads are in gray.

demeanor. He made note that upon reaching Sherman, Houston politely wished him a 'good morning' and asked if he would move his battalion to form the left flank of the army.[5] Jonathan H. Kuykendall, however, was less impressed with Houston's directive: "General Houston's main forces formed a marching battalion on the road, while Sherman's battalion, instead of joining the main column, marched thirty or forty paces to the right through the tall prairie grass."[6]

The reunified army marched another twelve miles until the late evening, stopping at about 9:00 at the home of Samuel May Williams on Arroyo Dulce, only a couple of miles west of San Felipe.[7] Williams was a prominent figure in San Felipe and Austin's Colony. Having spent time traveling extensively in Latin America, he was fluent in Spanish. In September 1824, Stephen F. Austin appointed him as secretary of the local government of the colony, which was confirmed by the governor. Williams assumed responsibilities that included writing deeds, keeping records, collecting revenue, and dispensing paper stamped by the State of Coahuila and Texas. During Austin's absence from 1833 to 1834, it was Williams who managed the colony.[8] But the tired Texians probably took no notice of who owned the property on which they camped. As they had done before on their retreat, the army supplied themselves with fuel for their fires by using fence posts, since readily available timber was too distant. Once again, beef was their main ration. After a quick meal, the men collapsed, exhausted by their rapid trek from the Colorado.

Any lingering doubts Houston may have had regarding the news brought by Peter Kerr on the evening of March 25, 1836, were put to rest as supporting evidence made its way to the Texians. During their retreat to the Brazos, several survivors of the Goliad Campaign joined his army. On March 27, three men from Captain Albert C. Horton's company arrived. Horton was in command of a cavalry unit during James W. Fannin's retreat from Goliad. As Fannin ordered the army's fateful rest stop, Horton and his mounted men scouted ahead for the crossing at Coleto

Creek. As they explored the area, they suddenly heard the echo of gunfire. They hurried back and were dismayed to see that they had been cut off from Fannin, who was surrounded by forces from Mexican General José de Urrea. Many of Horton's men abandoned their comrades at that point. Though Horton evidently showed a willingness to engage the enemy to support the Texian forces, the size of his remaining company was too small, and he reluctantly withdrew.[9]

The three men riding with Horton who eventually made their way to the Texian army were Thomas J. Adams, Garret E. Boom, and John W. Baylor. Adams enlisted in Captain Thomas J. Rabb's company, while Boom joined Captain Jesse Billingsley. Both men fought at the Battle of San Jacinto.[10] Baylor, nephew of the Baylor University namesake Robert Baylor, seemed to have fortune on his side during his tenure in the Texian army. He was initially stationed at the Alamo but was one of the couriers that William B. Travis sent to Goliad to solicit help and was thus spared the fate of the other defenders. Upon joining Fannin's command, he became part of Captain Jack Shackleford's Red Rovers. Only a few days prior to Fannin's decision to abandon La Bahía, he joined Horton's company and thus was spared the fate of most of Fannin's men. Upon his arrival with Houston's command, he joined Captain William Patton's company. He fought at the Battle of San Jacinto, where he received a thigh wound. Baylor considered the wound so minor that he did not report it, which might have been his ultimate undoing. In July, while visiting family in Alabama, the wound became inflamed, and his health began to fail. After developing a fever, Baylor died in early September 1836, an uncounted casualty of the Battle of San Jacinto.[11]

The three recent arrivals from Horton's company were undoubtedly happy to have finally found friendly faces when they joined Houston's command. Little did they know or probably could have imagined at the time that, while they were joining forces with Houston, their former comrades at Goliad were being executed by their Mexican captors. Over the coming days, other survivors from the Goliad Campaign made their way to the Texian army. Of the twenty-eight men who escaped the Palm Sunday execution at Goliad, six joined Houston's command while on the Brazos. Each of these men—Charles Shain, Thomas Kemp, David J. Jones, William Brenan, Nathanial C. Hazen, and Daniel Murphy—fought in the Battle of San Jacinto.[12] Not everybody was so lucky, however, after their initial escape. Colonel Juan N. Almonte of the Mexican army noted in an April 1, 1836, entry that "six Americans were discovered up the river on the other side, who took to the woods; three were caught on foot, and three on horseback." It is not known who these individuals were or what happened to them, but Almonte further noted that, during the night, someone named Adams, who was "supposedly one of those who were routed at Goliad," had been captured near the Colorado.[13]

Some men from William Ward's command also managed to escape capture and find their way to the Texian army. There were many incredible stories concerning their perilous journeys from disaster, but the story of one brave young man is particularly compelling. In August 1835, Fannin, a native of Georgia, sent an urgent appeal for money and volunteers to his friends back home. In November, prominent citizens of Macon, Georgia, gathered to discuss the Texas situation. One of the leaders was Ward, who was among the first to volunteer and ultimately became the leader of the group headed to Texas. For Samuel G. Hardaway, a sixteen-year-old boy with an elderly father, the lure of adventure in a faraway land must have been too much to resist.[14] He eagerly enlisted and became one of the first members of the "Georgia Battalion" to leave for Texas. As he started his journey west, he could not have imagined the adventure that lay ahead would be laced with tragedies and hardships.

The Battalion traveled from Georgia to New Orleans, picking up volunteers along the way. In New Orleans, they embarked on the schooner *Pennsylvania* and landed, after eleven days at sea, at the port of Velasco just before Christmas in 1835. At that time, they officially mustered into the Texian army.¹⁵ Three companies organized, and Hardaway became a private in the company commanded by Uriah Bullock.¹⁶ After a month of camp duties, the Battalion sailed further down the coast to Copano and marched fifteen miles north and west to Nuestra Señora del Refugio Mission. They remained there for three weeks before traveling further north to La Bahía in Goliad. Seven months after Fannin's letter arrived in Georgia, young Hardaway finally reached his destination. Coincidentally, he celebrated his sixteenth birthday about this time.

Decisions made by Fannin led to tragedy for Hardaway and many of his comrades. Fannin dispatched Amon B. King and his small company to evacuate settlers near Refugio, who were under attack by Hispanic militia loyal to the Mexican government. King gathered the settlers, but rather than return to Goliad, he decided to exact revenge.¹⁷ This was one of many mistakes that would haunt the Texians during the Goliad Campaign. The militia forced King back to the local mission, where he was surrounded by forces that included some of Urrea's cavalry. He sent a courier to Goliad to plead for reinforcements. Fannin sent Ward and the Georgia Battalion to Refugio to support King and then withdraw to Goliad. The contingent of about one hundred left La Bahía at 3 o'clock in the morning and arrived in the early afternoon on March 13, when they found King and his company in the mission with the Mexicans camped nearby, across the river. Ward's group made their way to the church and remained there until night when, after fording the river, they successfully drove off the Mexicans.¹⁸

It is difficult to know for sure what happened next, but evidently a disagreement ensued between the two leaders as to who commanded.¹⁹ Newly promoted Lieutenant Colonel Ward clearly had the higher rank, but Captain King had trouble accepting his authority. Neither seemed to appreciate the Mexican reinforcements that were arriving. Because of Ward's long forced march on March 13, it was determined that the group would fall back on the following morning. King, however, had other ideas. Whether through an agreement with Ward or not, in the early morning hours of March 14 King took some Texians scouting. Sometime after his departure, the mission was attacked by Mexican forces, which had been increased by the arrival of Urrea and the rest of his cavalry. Hardaway recalled:

> By this time, the enemy began to reinforce so fast in our sight that we had to return forthwith to the church, and at which we were very soon attacked by their whole force; but having blockaded all the entrances with the images, benches, pews, &c, we had greatly the advantage in position: they came up bravely for a while, received our rifle balls, fell and were carried off, and others took their place, but after a while we could see that it was with great difficulty the officers could whip up their soldiers with their swords to make a charge.

The Texian defenders managed to repulse four assaults, during which only three of them were wounded. Hardaway claimed they killed no less than two hundred Mexican soldiers, but the Mexicans reported losing only eleven killed and thirty-seven wounded.[20]

Despite the Texians' success, it was not hard for Ward to see that the position in the mission was untenable. He did not know that King's contingent had been captured. Ward's group waited until nightfall when they crept from their position and temporarily escaped the impending threat.[21] The Texians pushed through swamps and woods to inhibit any pursuit by the Mexican cavalry. Ward's destination was Copano, but he could not find the right road. The detachment wandered through the night and then found that they had circled back the way they had come. Eventually, Ward decided to march for Victoria and found the route toward that destination. For several days, the weary group trudged slowly toward Victoria, wary of Mexican patrols. Joseph Andrews described the ordeal: "The first day they marched on slowly, without interruption;

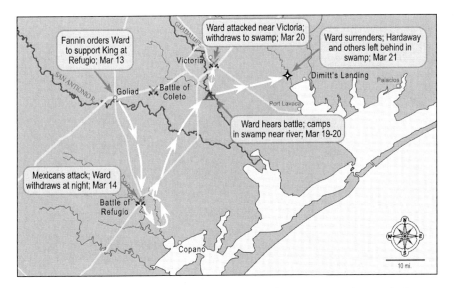

Projected route of Lieutenant Colonel William Ward's command from Goliad to the Battle of Refugio and their subsequent withdrawal to the Guadalupe River and the site of their eventual surrender to the Mexican army. Modern roads in gray."

on the second day the same; but on the third day in the evening, they suffered greatly for the want of water."²² One evening, the weary group heard a battle raging, but by evening the sounds dissipated, and they quit trying to reach the site. Of course, what they heard was the Battle of Coleto Creek, where Urrea captured Fannin. Ward's group settled in a swamp on the Guadalupe River on the night of March 19.²³

The next morning, the Texians made their way toward the prairie and Victoria. Expecting reinforcements, they were surprised when they were promptly attacked by Mexican cavalry. The group fired their remaining ammunition and retreated to the cover of the swamp. Hardaway continued his account, "every man was told to take care of himself. We there got scattered, and I never saw Colonel Ward or the company again, but understood that at night while I was asleep in the cane, that he rallied all the men he could, and made his way towards Dimmit's Landing."

Hardaway awoke on the morning of March 22 and realized his company had departed without him: "I found myself alone in a swamp, in a country full of Mexicans, near 200 miles from the main army of the Texans, and thirteen or fourteen hundred miles from my home, then without a mouthful of provision for five or six days."²⁴ But what seemed a misfortune proved to be anything but that. Shortly after departing, Ward and the men with him were surrounded and surrendered to General Urrea's forces.

Hardaway hid in the swamp during the day and through the night. The next morning, he walked down a path for a couple of miles and came upon a house that had several Mexicans in and about. Hunger will force a person to do things he might not otherwise do. With every bit of resolve he could muster, Hardaway marched up to the house to inquire about something to eat. The men, all Mexican soldiers, were astonished to see a scraggly young American appear out of nowhere. Hardaway asked a woman there for something to eat and she was quick to oblige. The soldiers went outside, no doubt watching for any accompanying Texians.

Hardaway recounted what happened next, "As soon as they all left the house, the woman told me in broken English, that they were all Mexican soldiers, and I had better leave as soon as possible. In a few minutes we saw them returning towards the house, and the woman urged me to start; I did so, and ran towards a swamp which I saw 200 or 300 yards distant; as I ran they fired 12 or 15 guns at me, but without effect: they pursued me to the swamp, but I escaped them."25

His belly temporarily satisfied, Hardaway stayed in the swamp all day. That night, he could hear drums beating at Victoria. The next morning, he crept close enough to see Mexican cavalry there. Discretion being the better part of valor, he decided to retreat again to the relative safety of the swamp where he stayed the rest of the day. That night, he made his way up the Guadalupe until he found a place to cross. To his great luck and relief, it was here that he met three others who had evaded the enemy by hiding in the swamp at the same time as he did. The other three escapees were Joseph Andrews, M. K. Moses, and James P. Trezevant. Like Hardaway, Andrews and Trezevant served in Captain Bullock's company. Moses served in Captain William A. O. Wadsworth's company. It must have felt like a godsend to young Hardaway to see some familiar faces who were in similar straits.

At the crossing, the refugees were fortunate to find an abandoned house that still had some food. They stayed at the house the night of March 24 and the next day began the trek toward the Colorado. By this time, they were beyond the reach of Urrea's troopers but were now traveling directly toward General Joaquín Ramírez y Sesma's command. Hardaway recalled:

> [We] made our way through the woods towards the Colorado river, and that night got to a place where the Mexican army had camped a night or two before: here we remained all night, and next morning we reached the river and crossed it on a bale of

Samuel G. Hardaway and James P. Trezevant trudge through a swamp as they try to evade capture and make their way to General Sam Houston's command.

cotton which we found on the bank, and about two miles above where the enemy were crossing at the same time."²⁶

This description suggests that Hardaway's group traversed the river near Beeson's Crossing. It is certainly consistent with his account that they found a bale of cotton near the Beeson homestead, as the family was very industrious. The Mexican army had moved south and were crossing the river at the Atascosito Crossing, which is a little more than two miles below Beeson's Crossing. The timing of the Texian group's arrival thus may have been fortuitous. Hardaway's statement that "the Mexican army had camped a night or two before" was accurate. General Sesma had only just moved his army toward Atascosito the previous day. Had the Texians arrived a day or so earlier, they would have encountered substantial enemy forces.

After crossing the Colorado, Hardaway and his comrades sequestered themselves again in a nearby swamp for a day. That night they heard a drum and supposed it was the Mexicans. The next morning Hardaway and Moses determined to go and see the campsite that was the source of the previous night's drumming. They moved south along the river and saw the Mexican army in the process of crossing the river. This would have been General Sesma's enhanced force of about 1,500 men. As the pair retreated, they saw six riders charging toward them. Fear quickly faded to relief when they realized the horsemen were Texian scouts. Hardaway later identified four of the six as Cawmack and Johnson from Tennessee and Shipman and Lapham of Texas. He did not recall the names of the other two. The spy party had been sent to determine the locations and movements of the Mexican army. "They were astonished to see us at that place, and when I say we were glad to see them, I but feebly express the feelings of my heart," Hardaway declared. "I was then without hat or shoes, and only a few rags for clothing."²⁷

As glad as Hardaway and the others were to see the Texian scouts,

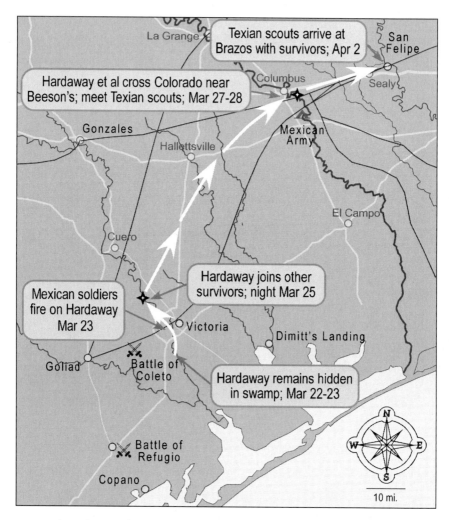

Projected route of Samuel G. Hardaway from the Guadalupe River, where he was stranded, to the Colorado River, where he met Texian scouts, and then to the Brazos River, where he joined Captain Mosely Baker's company. Historic roads in black and modern roads in gray.

they were even more relieved when they finally reached the safety of the Texian encampment. Hardaway described the moment: "[T]he spies carried us to General Houston's army, where we arrived, I think, on the 2d day of April, our appearance being such as to excite the sympathy of every soldier–and on meeting some gentlemen who had known us in this country, the noble tear of compassion was seen to trickle freely on their cheeks."[28] Moseley Baker, in a report to Houston that day, noted the arrival of someone from Ward's command: "Mr. Shipman has just arrived in camp from the Atiscosita [sic] crossing having left there about 12 Oclock yesterday…He was for some time in the Neighborhood of the Enemys Camp…One of Wards party has arrived here. He says Wards party consisted of 102 men & at the mission were attacked by about 1000 Mexicans."[29] This report from one of Ward's party most likely came from Hardaway. He remained with the army, attached to Baker's company.

On the morning of March 28, 1836, following breakfast, the Texian army had moved into San Felipe, and Houston had ordered Baker to post a guard at the ferry. The town was essentially abandoned by this time, with only a few store clerks remaining. While Houston took the time to acquire some much-needed supplies in San Felipe, his quartermaster decided to acquire some more provisions from the Colorado.

William Alley had contributed more than 225 head of hogs and thirty head of beef to the Texian army while it camped at Beeson's. Surprisingly, his contribution did not stop there. In his claim to recover costs several years later, Alley stated that "after the Texian Army marched from the Colorado to San Felipe on the Brazos River, a Commission was sent from the Commander there…to the Colorado River for a supply of Beef and other suitable Cattle." It is astonishing that Alley remained at his home on the Colorado after the Texians evacuated, especially since the Mexican army would have literally moved past his place on the opposite side of the Colorado, when they shifted their operations toward the Atascosito Crossing. Nevertheless, Alley accepted the request and began to drive more than three hundred head of cattle toward San Felipe. His neighbor, Leander Beeson, at this point part of Captain Rabb's company, and his cousin, also named William Alley and who had only days earlier joined Captain Wyly Martin's company, helped him drive the cattle east.[30] Officers also requested that Abel Beeson, Leander's older brother, help take the cattle to San Felipe. However, Abel, who was not in the army, probably refused the request because he was busy trying to help evacuate the rest of his family from the area.[31] Assistant Quartermaster Martin Ramsey noted that "he continued slaughtering and delivering to the army during their march to the Brazos and during their encampment on the east bank of the Brazos, often killing 7 to 8 a day." He estimated that on average the amount of beef consumed daily was more than 4,000 lbs.[32] Many years later, William Alley would submit a personal affidavit testifying that he contributed a total of 350 head of cattle and 200 head of hogs.[33] There is no record that Alley's claim was paid. Later, with his home in Mexican hands, leaving him "deprived of his whole dependency as a Farmer," William Alley joined Captain Martin's company at Fort Bend.[34]

When the forced march of Houston's Texians ended at San Felipe, the ill will that he had garnered for his unexpected retreat from the Colorado began to manifest into a tangible problem. Houston decided to evacuate San Felipe, but rather than cross the Brazos River and defend the crossing as he had along the Colorado, he elected to move north to Groce's Landing. Jared Groce was the wealthiest of all of Austin's colonists and, besides his substantial land holdings, also had an abundance of supplies. Houston's decision to move north was too much for the volatile Baker. Upon receiving his orders from Sherman, he refused to move from San Felipe. Captain Martin did likewise. Houston was in an awkward position, facing an open mutiny. His solution helped avoid further conflict. Rather than confront Baker and Martin and force Texians to choose a side, he simply ordered their companies to do what they wanted to do. He told Baker to defend the Brazos crossing at San Felipe and assist any civilians needing to cross. Martin's company was ordered to do the same downriver at Old Fort.[35] Meanwhile, Houston would slog through wet conditions, over muddy terrain and overrun creeks, marching at a snail's pace to finally reach Groce's Landing.

The Texian army's time on the Colorado had passed. To the disappointment and ultimate criticism of many, no battle was fought there. The ultimate fight for Texian independence would have to wait for another three weeks or so. Meanwhile, the Mexican army was still active along the Colorado. On March 27, the Mexican troops began constructing rafts, laboring until midnight without success. The rain was heavy, and the river continued to rise. The next day, they tried to build a bridge, but the currents proved to be too strong for that endeavor. The bulk of the army remained on the right bank, west of the river, while attempts continued to build suitable rafts. Slowly, soldiers crossed in canoes and other small craft. While this time-consuming exercise continued, the first troops to cross focused on reconnaissance and confirmed that the Texians had withdrawn from the area. By March 29, 1836, a couple of Mexican battalions and one piece of artillery had managed to successfully traverse the Colorado. However, the river continued to rise. Colonel Almonte noted that by 9 a.m., it had risen four and a half feet, and during the next day he estimated that it rose another ten feet. The crossings continued at an exceedingly slow pace. Almonte reported that when the river was at its highest, the rope used for the ferrying process broke four times and two men drowned while crossing in a canoe.[36]

While the crossings continued, Mexican scouts continued forays along both banks of the river. One unit reported a small, abandoned camp where they estimated fifty Texians camped. They erroneously reported that a small cannon had been there as well. On April 1, six Texians were observed upriver and purportedly captured. That night, a man named Smith was also taken prisoner. Though Colonel Almonte made no report in his journal of the interrogation of the six men captured earlier in the day, he did write that Smith was likely an escapee of the executions at Goliad. The Mexicans used this prisoner to scout the area to the north across from Dewees' Ford. From his report, they ascertained that "the Americans had abandoned the country; and [abandoned] the trenches which they had made on the bank of the river; and had taken the road to San Felipe de Austin, with cattle, etc.—that they had not burnt the houses, and that he did not see a single inhabitant on the road, not a single track."[37] This report was further evidence that, while it was strategically important for Sherman to burn William B. Dewees' house to prevent it from being used as cover by Mexican troops, he did not think it necessary to do the same with Robert Moseley's place, which was on the east bank where the Texians camped.

By April 2, Sesma's command had finally completed their crossing. Having been ordered by Santa Anna to await his arrival, Sesma sent a large contingent north along the left (east) bank of the river toward Dewees' Ford. As might be expected, the roads were in poor condition and the Mexicans struggled through the slop. Colonel Almonte reported that they found iron tools and cables in Moseley's house.[38]

With reports of resistance coming from Sesma, General Antonio López de Santa Anna sent orders to Urrea and General Antonio Gaona to assist him. Gaona had been dispatched along a northerly route through Mina while Urrea led a sweep along the coastal areas.[39] Santa Anna left San Antonio de Béxar on March 30, 1836, leaving a relatively small force to guard the town. He quickly outpaced some of the support divisions he had ordered to the Colorado and arrived at the Atascosito Crossing late on April 4. Sesma arrived the next morning, after a reconnaissance of the east bank.[40] Since his arrival in Texas, Santa Anna had experienced nothing but victories from his armies. The defeat of Fannin at Coleto magnified his confidence. He all but considered the war won but was convinced by the presence of Texian forces on the Colorado and the advice of his staff that it would be best if he remained and directed the final defeat of the rebels. With confidence in his position, Santa Anna quickly moved ahead with the forces of Sesma and Tolsa to San Felipe, where he arrived on April 7, 1836. He left General Adrián Woll at the Atascosito Crossing to supervise the construction of additional barges that would facilitate the crossing of artillery, transport wagons, and other equipment.[41]

General Vicente Filisola, in charge of the remaining Mexican forces bringing up the rear, finally got them across the Colorado on April 13, 1836. He arrived at San Felipe on April 15, when he found that Santa Anna had already moved south toward Old Fort. He likewise marched south to reunite with his commander in chief.[42] As the last of the Mexican army departed the Atascosito Crossing, little could they have imagined what events lay in store for them. In just a few weeks, the bulk of the Mexican soldiers would visit the Atascosito Crossing again, this time from a different direction after having suffered a humiliating defeat at San Jacinto. After miles of slogging through endless mud in the Gulf Coast prairies to the south, the morale of the Mexican army was in tatters. Despite initial plans for it to re-group once the troops crossed back to the west of the Colorado, the dejected forced instead moved southwestward, never again to see the Colorado as a victorious army.[43]

14

AFTERMATH

"We arrived on the east bank of the Colorado...Here all was gloom and desolation! Our once happy homes were now in ashes. The cattle had all been driven off and there was naught to welcome us back again to the homes which we had left but a few weeks before."[1]

WILLIAM B. DEWEES

THE HOPES OF THE CIVILIANS encamped nearby and those living in the immediate vicinity were dashed and the reality that they were indeed leaving their homes loomed when the Texian army withdrew. The exit of Texian troops from the Colorado River, however, was not as chaotic as it had been from Gonzales. This time, civilians had ample warning of the impending retreat and likely started their journey eastward ahead of the military withdrawal. Unlike the bulk of the Texian army, however, the civilians would cross the Brazos River at San Felipe and continued eastward.

The Beeson family likely stayed on the east bank of the Colorado near Sam Houston's encampment and watched anxiously as the events unfolded around the ruins of their former homestead. Benjamin Beeson's son-in-law, William B. Dewees, along with his considerably smaller family, may have been waiting with Beeson or perhaps closer to Sydney

Sherman's encampment across from his smoldering house on the west side of the river.

Elizabeth "Betsy" Beeson wrote to Texas President David G. Burnet on April 10, 1836, from Robert's Plantation on Spring Creek. This place was located about twenty-five miles east of the Brazos, where Dewees noted that many settlers went after San Felipe de Austin had been burned. Beeson was remarkably optimistic in her letter considering the circumstances:

> Our family having been compelled to remove from the Colorado and our family being on the Point of suffering for the necessaries of life, I have thought that it might be possible we might make a living in Harrisburgh [sic] and in this Emergency I hope you will Excuse me for Taking the Liberty of Enquiring [sic] of you (not being acquainted with any other person in Harrisburgh) what would be the prospect of getting a House in your place, one suitable for a Public House if you think a living could be made at that business we have some servants & if we could make a living only we would try it please give me your views on this subject by return of Mr. Kokernot.[2]

Her intention of running a "Public House" was in keeping with what her family had done on the Colorado. Though the timing of her letter was dreadful, it showed that despite recent setbacks, Beeson was an enterprising woman. Obviously, her request did not yield any opportunity since the Mexican army soon crossed the Brazos and burned Harrisburg.[3]

The reference to "Mr. Kokernot" was Captain David Kokernot, who had been sent by Houston to Harrisburg to warn Burnet of the approach of the Mexican army. In this light, it is puzzling that Beeson would send such a letter; however, Kokernot probably did not tell her what his purpose was in traveling to Harrisburg, and likewise she did not reveal the contents of her letter to him.

The evacuees on Spring Creek became part of an even larger exodus eastward that ended only with Houston's victory at San Jacinto. Dewees recorded that a company of men escorted their large group to the Trinity River. It was while they camped between the Trinity and the San Jacinto River, along with 150 to 200 other families, that the Beeson and Dewees refugees learned of the joyous and probably unexpected victory at San Jacinto.[4]

The Texas Revolution seemed to be won in the Battle of San Jacinto and the related capture of General Antonio López de Santa Anna, but thousands of Mexican soldiers remained in Texas. While Santa Anna had ordered his second in command, General Vicente Filisola, to leave the rebellious province, much uncertainty lingered about the latter's intentions. Despite this, many Texians wanted to return to their homesteads. One of the earliest to do so, Dewees, described what he saw upon his return to the Colorado on May 10, 1836: "Here was all gloom and desolation! Our once happy homes were now in ashes! The cattle had all been driven off and there was naught to welcome us back again to the homes which we had left but a few weeks before. All was stillness round and the angel of gloom seemed to be hanging over the once lovely place." Dewees, and those accompanying him, were reluctant to recross the river, not knowing where the Mexican army was located.[5] From near the charred remnants of his house, Dewees rode downriver to determine the exact location of the Mexicans.

Just as the Mexican army had crossed the Colorado at the Atascosito Crossing, they also retreated across the river at the same point. Dewees arrived at the Atascosito Crossing in time to witness their crossing. Despite his group's proximity to a large contingent of Mexican soldiers, Dewees felt confident that they were in no danger. He rode back upriver and began to help them construct rafts so they could recross the river.[6] Perhaps Dewees' optimism that they were in no danger was based on his observation that the Mexicans seemed to be in disarray. Upon receiving Santa Anna's letter with orders to withdraw from Texas, Filisola decided that his troops would withdraw across the Colorado, and then he would reassess the situation. Only after the army's morale-killing trudge through the quagmire that became known as the "Sea of Mud" was the decision made to leave Texas.[7]

As others made their way back to their homes, many found, like Dewees, that their houses and livelihoods were in tatters. Beeson, Abram Alley, and Jesse Burnam, all prominent citizens who were essential to the growth and prosperity of Austin's Colony, found themselves virtually destitute. John H. Moore was fortunate that his homestead was clear of the advancing Mexican army and therefore was spared the destruction others experienced. Regardless of the condition of their property, they all decided to return and rebuild. Certainly, it was a testament to the fortitude of these individuals and families.

CONCLUSION

During his tenure as commander in chief of the Texian forces during their fight against Mexico, Sam Houston participated in exactly one battle, which he won. However, a multitude of significant decisions led to that fateful day. Houston was not known to take council from many, and his decisions were often made in the face of incredible opposition. The discipline it took for him not to give in to this opposition, whether from soldiers, officers, or government officials, meant that he had an overarching strategy that he felt was paramount to employ. Alternatively, as some of his critics were apt to point out, Houston was nothing more than lucky in the ultimate outcome and he did nothing more than stumble and bumble along the way until his fortuitous outcome at San Jacinto in April 1836.

One criticism from his contemporaries was his decision to retreat from Gonzales upon learning of the defeat at the Alamo. He was castigated for not immediately engaging the Mexican army at that time. Yet most objective assessments of the situation would agree that Houston was correct in his decision to withdraw from Gonzales. It is, however, interesting to consider what Houston was thinking as he rode toward Gonzales from Washington. Was he considering the best way to help those stranded at the Alamo, or was he considering the bigger picture and formulating a larger strategic plan? How would Houston have proceeded had he arrived a few days earlier in Gonzales and General Antonio López de Santa Anna had delayed his attack on the Alamo? For days, men had been traveling to Gonzales with the intention of organizing and riding to the relief of those trapped at the Alamo. Given a few days to prepare, would General

Houston have indeed started to march toward San Antonio?

Considering his subsequent actions and his prior recommendation to Governor Henry Smith that the Alamo be abandoned and destroyed, it is hard to imagine that Houston would have had much impetus to march on the superior Mexican forces at San Antonio de Béxar. This would likely have been true even if he could have efficiently coordinated his actions with Colonel James W. Fannin at Goliad. There was incredible concern and sympathy throughout Texas for those trapped in the Alamo, so it is doubtful that Houston would have outright refused to march on San Antonio. Instead, Houston might have delayed under the guise of preparing and training. Perhaps he would have delayed while waiting for Fannin's approach. Regardless, considering his force was considerably smaller in number and firepower, it is hard to imagine a scenario where Houston would have decided to move toward San Antonio and engage a fight in relatively open country. If this was indeed his attitude, it would have meant that in his mind, those at the Alamo were beyond help.

Houston's immediate reaction upon learning of the demise of those at the Alamo was to withdraw. Unless circumstances proved otherwise, the last thing Houston would have wanted was to engage with the Mexicans. In addition to dealing with a rag-tag untrained army, he had the wellbeing of a civilian population to consider. Strategically, the defeat of the Texians at the Alamo gave him the excuse to move further east, toward the heart of the Austin Colony and other population centers. The impending engagement with the Mexican army could best be fought closer in proximity to reinforcements and in more favorable terrain.

Upon leaving Gonzales, he employed a tactic that he would continue to use throughout the campaign. He did what he could to deprive the advancing Mexicans of any easily obtainable resources. A large army needed to be fed and supplied, and he intended to make it difficult for them to live off the land to the extent that he could. This meant burning places that were well-stocked and driving livestock eastward. This strategy may not have occurred to the average Texian at the time until they viewed the distant flames at Gonzales while resting miles away at Peach Creek. Little would they realize that they would soon witness the destruction of many other places along their march.

This desire to deprive the Mexican army of supplies and resources likely accounted, at least in part, for Houston's unusual route eastward. On his journey to assume command of the army at Gonzales, Houston stopped at Jesse Burnam's homestead. He must have noticed the abundant supplies available there. Much to Burnam's dismay, Houston later decided to destroy his house, depot, and ferry. Since the Mexican troops in this area ultimately never crossed Burnam's land, he was understandably upset at Houston's decision. Of course, Houston could not know what course the Mexicans would pursue, and he deemed it necessary to make sure the enemy could not take advantage.

Once established on the east bank of the Colorado River, Houston began sending scouting parties to help establish the location and strength of the oncoming Mexican forces. The first of the encounters, led by Henry W. Karnes, skirmished with Mexicans near the Navidad River. The capture of one of the enemy provided the Texians with invaluable information. This encounter also deterred Mexican General Joaquín Ramírez y Sesma's approach, allowing time for Houston to retreat down the Colorado and establish positions at Beeson's and Dewees', the two primary crossings along the Gonzales–San Felipe Road.

As reinforcements continued to arrive, the Texians soon had a numerical advantage over their adversaries. During their time on the Colorado, Houston's command increased to nearly 1,500 men, which represented the apex of enrollment for the forces under his direct command. Houston continued to learn as much as he could through scouting expeditions sent across the river to harass the Mexicans. With each day, it seemed that the momentum grew to launch an attack against the Mexican force encamped across the river.

Houston delayed in part because he was expecting an imminent arrival of artillery. On March 14, 1836, he dispatched Major William T. Austin to Velasco with orders to forward artillery and munitions to their encampment on the Colorado. That mission, however, was unsuccessful. When Colonel John A. Wharton, who had previously commanded at Velasco, arrived at Beeson's Crossing on March 24, he likely informed Houston that no artillery was destined to arrive anytime soon. That news likely played a part in Houston's decisions.

Evidence would support the idea that Houston did plan a battle with the Mexican army. He wrote as much in several correspondences. As late as March 24, he wrote: "On the Colorado I make my stand."[1] On that very date, he ordered Lieutenant John Sharp to relay his intentions to the settlers along the coast that he intended to do battle and that they were safe with no reason to run.[2] But within a few days, Houston completely reversed his decision. In that time frame, two significant events occurred. The first was the arrival of Peter Kerr with the unfortunate news that Fannin had surrendered. Despite efforts by Houston to quash this information, concern spread among his men. Although Houston had already learned that Fannin was in a perilous situation, Kerr confirmed the worst possible scenario, one that would become even worse in the coming weeks when reports arrived of the massacre of Fannin's men and other Texians on Palm Sunday. Kerr's grim report meant that Houston had the only army still fighting for Texas independence. However, with Santa Anna's orders for the execution of prisoners at Goliad and the devastating attack at the Alamo, Houston's troops had plenty of motive when the time came to engage the Mexicans.

The second event that may have prompted Houston to delay in seeking a battle with the Mexican army was the arrival of reinforcements led by General Eugenio Tolsa. These brought the number of Mexican troops confronting Houston to a level comparable to the Texians. It seems unlikely that Texian scouts did not notice an uptick in activity in the Mexican camp. It must have occurred to Houston that this may have been related to the arrival of anticipated Mexican reinforcements.

Much to the dissatisfaction of his men, Houston abruptly decided to withdraw from the Colorado. Whether he lost a significant opportunity by retreating is an interesting question to debate. For eleven days the Texian army was stationed on the Colorado River. For much of that time, they were within striking distance of the Mexican army. A great battle seemed inevitable. Would it have been decisive? If the Mexicans had prevailed, it may have been decisive. The Texians' lone remaining army would have been defeated, and only some scattered, unorganized companies would have remained. Santa Anna could have successfully concluded his conquest of Texas in a matter of weeks. Had the Texians prevailed, they would have had vital momentum on their side, but large Mexican forces still operated to the west, south and north. Houston would have to deal with the wounded and been encumbered with prisoners while other Mexican forces approached. A Texian victory would likely have forced Santa Anna to be more conservative and consolidate his forces, making it doubtful that he would be caught in an undermanned forward position as he was at San Jacinto. The Texians, however, would likely have reaped the benefit of additional volunteers and perhaps aid from the United States.

While this potential battle may or may not have been decisive, it most assuredly would have been pivotal. Victory for either side would likely have been the beginning of what would ultimately be a victorious campaign. However, this battle was never fought. Despite enormous pressure from soldiers, officers, and government officials, Houston decided to withdraw from the Colorado. This decision was logical. With Fannin's defeat, Houston was vulnerable to being flanked by General Urrea from the south and potentially General Gaona from the north. Half of his force was recently enlisted and untrained. A retreat to the Brazos allowed time for training, provide additional time for artillery to arrive, and further drew the Mexican army deeper into the heart of the Anglo settlements.

The reward of a possible victory on the Colorado was not worth the risk of defeat, or even a stalemate.

The disparaging words directed at Houston because of his decision to abandon Gonzales were subdued compared to what Houston's detractors directed toward him upon their removal from the Colorado. From their perspective, a Mexican force, inferior in number, was vulnerable to defeat. Considering the desire for retribution, to many an attack seemed justified and timely.

Seemingly pervasive dissatisfaction within the ranks soon led to conversations about a change in command. The mutinous feelings would only grow as they decided to move on from San Felipe. Both Moseley Baker and Wyly Martin categorically refused to follow Houston.[3] Rather than condemning them and inflaming the situation, Houston simply ordered them to guard major crossings on the Brazos. Texas President David G. Burnet was so distraught when Houston did not engage the enemy that he dispatched Secretary of War Thomas J. Rusk to assume command and attack the Mexicans.[4]

Regardless of the vehement opinions put forth by those who served with Houston, or the many who have discussed the issues since then, one indisputable fact remains. Houston, as the commander in chief of Texian forces, successfully accomplished his mission and defeated the Mexican army. That objective was achieved not only from the success on the battlefield at San Jacinto but was also the result of a series of decisions that drew the Mexican army deeper into Texas and onto ground of Houston's choosing. The decisions by Houston while camped on the Colorado River resulted in a battle unfought, but ultimately led to the freedom of Texas.

Except for the tragedy of the Goliad Massacre and the terrible hardships experienced by those involved in the Runaway Scrape, the timeframe between the fall of the Alamo and the Texian victory at San Jacinto is often overlooked. The Texian withdrawal from Gonzales is often depicted on maps by broad arrows without reference to specific campsites and routes. This book has provided support that the Texians under the command of General Houston, camped on the William W. W. Thompson league near the Navidad River on the night of March 15, 1836, and then, the day after, proceeded along an unmapped route from there to Burnam's Ferry, where they encamped on the night of March 16. After spending two nights at John Crier's, just downriver from Burnam's place, the army proceeded to march downriver toward present-day Columbus. The Texians' exact campsite on March 19 is uncertain. Based on accounts of the time, they did not reach Columbus that night, but instead stopped just short of the destination, probably near Cummins Creek. Early on March 20, the Texian army split and proceeded to their respective campsites at Beeson's Crossing and Dewees' Ford.

There is likewise uncertainty as to the position of the trailing Mexican army's encampment on the Colorado. A historical marker on the rise just west of the Columbus golf course designates the site of General Sesma's camp. Unfortunately, these markers, while valuable in giving visitors an account of historical events, provide some erroneous information. The designated site puts the Mexican army directly across from Sydney Sherman's camp at Dewees' Ford, miles away from the bulk of the Texian army at Beeson's Crossing. Instead, the Mexicans likely encamped west of the Colorado, with a line of sight between the two Texian encampments. One physical piece of evidence of this is a Mexican cannonball found near the suggested Mexican campsite that was likely fired during one of the raids led by Captain Henry W. Karnes' Texian scouts. Another historical marker at Beason's Park, just east and across the Colorado from downtown Columbus, indicates the site of Houston's encampment. Ironically, Beason's Park is instead closer to the site of Sherman's camp. Houston's campsite at Beeson's Crossing was located about six to seven miles downriver, which again indicates a different location for the Mexican army's camp.

This book provides a day-by-day account of events that transpired while the Texian army encamped on the Colorado River. This includes skirmishes with the Mexican army, the constant flux of new arrivals, the work done to acquire provisions, communiques sent and received, and attempts to instill training and discipline. Countless people lost their homes, their livestock, and their way of life. Those with fortitude returned and rebuilt and achieved some level of prosperity. Others suffered immeasurable tragedy and never regained the same status as they had before the Texas Revolution. Some never bothered to return. Whether they were prominent in historical accounts or merely a footnote, many of the pioneers and volunteers that first settled and then fought for Texan independence deserve to be recognized and acknowledged.

Karnes, perhaps one of the most underappreciated Texas heroes, was a reliable scout upon which Houston learned to rely. John H. Moore commanded the Texian forces at the Battle of Gonzales. Jesse Burnam was recognized as a leader, often called upon to respond to Indian raids and active in governmental affairs. The Beeson, Dewees, and Alley families settled on the major river crossings in what became Colorado County and became vital members of Austin's Colony. Kerr had done well in colonial Texas but had to suffer the humiliation of being arrested after he brought the news of Fannin's defeat to Houston. Samuel G. Hardaway, a young Georgia boy, came to Texas for adventure and got more than he possibly imagined. The story of what these underappreciated heroes did during an overlooked period of Texas history has been told in this text. Their biographies are continued within the following appendix.

BIOGRAPHICAL APPENDIX

"He whose merit deserves a temple has scarcely found
a grave in the annals of Texas history."

INSCRIPTION ON TOMBSTONE OF JESSE BURNAM

HENRY WAX KARNES

PERHAPS ONE OF THE MOST underappreciated heroes of Texas, Henry Wax Karnes, was an active figure during the time spent by the Texian army on the Colorado River. The trajectory of his life might have propelled him into a higher echelon of Texan heroes, had it not been cut short unexpectedly.

After the Texian retreat from the Colorado, Karnes and his good friend and noted scout, Erastus "Deaf" Smith, continued to be an essential asset to General Sam Houston.[1] Often, when the pair went on a mission, they returned with valuable information. They did not disappoint when Houston sent them on a reconnaissance mission on April 18, 1836. The pair captured a courier with a dispatch from General Vicente Filisola to General Antonio López de Santa Anna. This information gave Houston the first indication of the whereabouts of the Mexican leader and dictated the Texian movements that led to the decisive battle at San Jacinto.[2]

During the Battle of San Jacinto, Karnes led one of the companies under the Texian cavalry commander, Mirabeau B. Lamar. In Houston's official report to President David G. Burnet, he wrote about Karnes:

"Our cavalry had charged and routed that of the enemy upon the right, and given pursuit to the fugitives, which did not cease until they arrived at [Vince's Bridge] which I mentioned before, Captain Karnes, always among the foremost in danger, commanding the pursuers."[3]

Not long after San Jacinto, Karnes and Henry Teal were selected to travel to Matamoros to negotiate a prisoner exchange and recover escaped slaves. Whatever the protocol of wars may be, this would have to be considered a risky venture. Though the pair arrived without incident, they were consistently stonewalled for a meeting by General José de Urrea, who had taken over from Filisola.[4] After some time, the frustrated pair requested passports to return to Texas but were refused. Since they had come under a flag of truce, Urrea was probably reluctant to jail them, but he clearly did not want them to leave.

The treaty that Santa Anna negotiated was officially repudiated by the Mexican government, and there was increasing talk of invading Texas. As the chatter grew, the pair of Texians thought it important to get this information back to the leaders in Texas. Thus came what became known as the "whip-handle dispatch." Teal wrote a letter to Thomas J. Rusk telling him of the need to prepare for an imminent invasion. The letter was hidden inside the handle of a whip and taken by a Mexican courier to Texas. The courier was intercepted by Texian scouts on the Nueces River, who believed he was a spy. Having searched, unsuccessfully, for dispatches, they threatened to hang him unless he revealed what they knew he must be concealing. Fearing for his life, he gave them the whip handle with the enclosed dispatch. The letter was probably not what the scouts were expecting, but they were happy and immediately forwarded the dispatch, not to Rusk, but straight to a newspaper publisher. This of course led to two outcomes. First, it put panic into the frontier settlers. Second, when it reached General Urrea's desk just two weeks later, it resulted in Teal and Karnes being put in prison.[5]

Over time, the security for Karnes and Teal lessened and, after a few months, with the help of friends, they managed to escape. On September 26, 1836, Karnes was issued a promissory note for over $1,400 for expenses incurred in his expedition to Matamoros. This included salary, money for a lost saddle and gun, and payment for the guide who had led his party to Matamoros.[6]

Karnes resigned as a captain in the Texian cavalry upon his return from Mexico, but he was induced to return to the military in January 1837 with a promotion to colonel. He led the cavalry on the Texas frontier through mid-March of 1838. At this time, he was only twenty-six years old, so such an assignment was a testament to the respect and confidence in his leadership that he had earned. During this period, Karnes either negotiated or battled with various Indian groups. In November 1837, he secured a treaty with the Tonkawas, whose leaders agreed to punish anyone in their group who committed depredations on a citizen of Texas. In return, the government agreed to live in peace with the Tonkawas and punish all aggressions committed by Texians, provided enough evidence was found.[7]

In part owing to his successful negotiations with the Tonkawas, in early 1838 Karnes was appointed as one of the commissioners to negotiate with the Comanches. His success in this venture proved considerably more problematic. His first attempt seemed to go well. In May, 150 Comanches came to San Antonio for peace talks and Karnes sold some goods to them.[8] But in August, Karnes and twenty-one men were attacked by 200 Comanches near Arroyo Seco. Waves of arrows killed most of the Texians' mounts. While they prudently took cover, Karnes, as leader, was not afraid to expose himself when necessary. Ultimately, no Texians were killed, but Karnes was shot through with an arrow while standing atop a riverbank directing his men.[9] This injury plagued him for the rest of his life. The Comanches lost at least twenty killed, and more were wounded. Among the Comanche dead was one of the participants in the San Antonio meeting.

In June 1839, Karnes began to organize another excursion against the Comanches after several Indian raids and killings. The expedition consisted of two separate companies of about fifty-four men each, commanded by captains Juan N. Seguín and Louis B. Franks. Karnes led the group west and northwest of San Antonio toward the headwaters of the Medina and Hondo Seco rivers and Canyon de Uvalde. Eventually, scouts under John C. "Jack" Hays spotted signs of Indian movements. At one site, they came upon a recently abandoned Indian camp. There they found the remains of a body that had been tortured by fire hanging from a tree. It became evident that the Comanches did not wish to engage their pursuers. Karnes thought it best to abandon the chase, but many of his men were reluctant to do so. He sent some back to San Antonio and divided the remainder into three units. Hays' men destroyed a deserted Indian village, killed a few isolated Indians, and recovered some stolen horses. The expedition returned to San Antonio two weeks after leaving, and the Texians led by Franks and Seguín were honorably discharged.[10]

Newly elected President Lamar instituted a different policy toward the Indians than his predecessor, Houston. He intended to expel the Indians from Texas or exterminate them. He signed a bill in December 1838 for a "Frontier Regiment" consisting of fifteen companies. At the same time, the Texas Congress passed additional legislation that authorized Lamar to enroll eight companies of mounted volunteers into active service. This regiment was commanded by Colonel Karnes, who had orders from Lamar to operate as necessary against Comanches or other hostile Indians.[11] After several months, Karnes realized that he was a commander without a command. He became increasingly frustrated as manpower was diverted to other operations, especially the ongoing Cherokee War in East Texas. By July 28, 1839, he finally had enough and resigned as colonel of the Mounted Gunman Battalion.[12]

Karnes remained determined to lead an offensive against the Comanches. In August he met with President Lamar in Houston and secured the services of a newly organized company of mounted gunmen from Galveston. Additionally, he approached some idle Mexican federalists who were in San Antonio and convinced them to help raise a company of Mexicans and Texians.

The men from Galveston were commanded by Captain William Wilson, the sheriff of Galveston County. By September 22, Wilson's company was moving through Columbus. As they moved west of the Colorado, they passed dwellings which had been deserted after Indian raids. It was while they camped near the Navidad that Karnes joined them. This site was probably very close to the point where Karnes had led a group of riders three and a half years earlier to scout the location of the approaching Mexican army while General Houston moved his army south toward Beeson's Crossing. Karnes' scouts had killed one Mexican and captured another, who provided valuable information to his captors at the time.

The 1839 expedition stopped at this location because Karnes became ill. For two days, he struggled with a fever while the company waited. His illness might well have been attributed to ongoing problems with the wound he had received at Arroyo Seco a year earlier. After two days, Karnes was well enough to continue. His command passed through Gonzales on September 30. Like other areas, Gonzales was feeling the effects of Indian depredations, and local settlers were willing to support Karnes' efforts. The group finally arrived in San Antonio on October 3.

Karnes' men temporarily quartered in Mission Concepción. While there, they quickly got a sense of the problems the area had been experiencing. One of Wilson's company remembered, "Those Comanches keep them [the San Antonio residents] in such awe they dare not venture without the outskirts of town without going armed and two or three in company, and very seldom lose sight of the spire and cross of their cathedral." The new arrivals moved their quarters once, settling closer to the San Antonio River. During the first night, Indians managed to sneak into camp and steal three horses. Several Texians pursued, killed one of the thieves, and recovered one of the horses. Clandestine raids continued for the next three nights, however, until the Texians decided to relocate their camp once more.

Karnes' expedition left San Antonio on the morning of October 20, 1839. It was not until November 1, when the battalion was near present-day Fredericksburg, that they were notified by a terrified scout that Indians were approaching. Karnes ordered a retrograde movement for about eight miles, where they camped. He directed Hays to lead scouts to find out the Indians' location and strength. Hays reported that he counted thirty well-mounted Comanches.[13] He then guided Karnes' command to the Comanche encampment, arriving just before daybreak. A startled horse alerted the camp and a firefight erupted, but the Texians had the upper hand, and the rout was on. Ten to twelve Comanches were killed, and one was taken prisoner. The Texians also nabbed forty horses and mules, along with other loot.

By November 5, the Texians moved into the Llano River valley. As he had when he joined Wilson, Karnes again fell sick, and the expedition stalled. This time, however, his illness lasted longer and, worse yet, the weather became progressively colder. Inactivity and frigid weather do not go well together, and the men increasingly expressed a desire to return home. By November 19, Captain Wilson himself resigned. The expedition did finally make its way back to San Antonio on November 21, when the remainder were released from service.[14]

Still in San Antonio, Karnes wrote to Secretary of War Albert Sydney Johnston on January 10, 1840, that on the day prior three Comanche leaders had arrived in San Antonio announcing a desire for peace. They said that eighteen days earlier they had a council and chose a prominent chief to represent them in negotiations. Karnes told them that no peace treaty would be possible unless they brought in all prisoners and stolen property that they held. To this they agreed and promised to return in twenty to thirty days with a large party ready to negotiate a settlement.

Karnes, having been ambushed about a year and a half earlier and still coping with continual depredations, was skeptical of the promise. Nevertheless, an agreement was reached, and the meeting was scheduled.

Unable to stay in San Antonio due to business in New Orleans, Karnes recommended to Johnston that one or two commissioners meet the Comanches in San Antonio upon their return. President Lamar agreed with Karnes' suggestion and dispatched Hugh McLeod, Texas adjutant general, and William Cooke, the First Regiment's quartermaster general. Johnston issued orders to Lieutenant Colonel William S. Fisher, who replaced the recently resigned Edward Burleson as commander of the First Regiment, to take charge of the peace negotiations. Three companies of the regiment accompanied him.[15] One other significant point that Karnes made was that, should the Comanches fail to bring in the promised captives, their leaders should be held hostage until the prisoners were returned. This was a significant departure in typical Indian negotiations, but Johnston evidently approved it, since he forwarded those suggestions as orders to Fisher.[16]

As he had anticipated, Karnes was not present when the Comanches returned to San Antonio. Their delegation included sixty-five men, women, and children. They brought with them only one captive, Matilda Lockhart, who had been captured about fifteen months earlier. She was in terrible condition, showing clear signs of torture. She also indicated that "she had seen several of the other prisoners, at the principal camp a few days before she left; and that they brought her in, to see if they could get a high price for her." Hearing this, the Texians believed the Comanches had acted in bad faith. Once troops were in position, the translator informed the Comanches that their leaders were now prisoners. While the women and children would remain free, the young warriors would be sent to bring back the captives being held. Moments later, the melee began. When it was done, thirty-five were dead, including the Comanche leaders and most of their warriors along with three women and two children. Twenty-nine were prisoners, mostly women and children. Seven Texians were killed and eight wounded.[17] This incident, called the Council House Fight, would bring future Comanche attacks.

On June 24, 1840, Karnes advertised in the Houston paper, hoping to raise six companies to march to Laredo with the objective of protecting the border. By late July, he was preparing to depart when he suddenly became sick with fever (either yellow or typhoid). While awaiting recovery, he allowed the men to cut corn on his property for food. Recovery was slow and by the time he started to feel better, he felt it necessary to travel to Houston to confer with President Lamar. Only a single day into the trip, Karnes suffered a severe relapse and returned to San Antonio. This time, there was no recovery, and Karnes died on August 16, 1840, about three weeks before his twenty-eighth birthday.

Karnes was well respected and, unlike many of his time, seemingly free of controversy. Lamar was planning his infamous Santa Fe Expedition for the purpose of solidifying Texian jurisdiction over the area and to establish much-needed trade. The President planned to have Karnes lead the operation before his unexpected death.[18] A memorial in the *Brazos Courier* for Karnes was glowing. It read, in part, "One by one the brave hearts who were the strength of our country during the darkness of the revolution, are sinking into the grave: and among these, none deserve more honorable mention than Karnes. He was an active and efficient officer during that struggle, and since that period he has rendered us the most important services on our Western frontier." The writer added, "In private life he was beloved by all who knew him—as a friend, he was constant—as a citizen, he was worthy—and as a man, he was above all reproach. His heart was open and generous as the day, and his conduct guided by the noblest principles of honor." He concluded, "Our country never mourned a braver soldier or a better man."[19] Robert M. Potter, in his article about Karnes' escape from Matamoros, described him as follows: "Though of humble origin and almost illiterate, he was a man of large brain, by nature a gentleman as well as a soldier, and of the kind of material which in Napoleon's day so often supplied the great leader with field marshals from the ranks."[20] Both Karnes City and Karnes County are named after the heroic Texan scout and military leader.

JESSE BURNAM

WHEN THE FRENZY of the Runaway Scrape had finally subsided and Texas independence had seemingly been won, Jesse Burnam faced the stark reality that he had a large family but no home. William Owen and John Hickerson, his oldest sons, were young adults who had served in the Texian army. Jesse's oldest daughter, Mary, had wed William S. Townsend a few years earlier. The next oldest daughter, Minerva, died of pneumonia at the age of fifteen in November 1836 and was the first to be buried at the family cemetery.[21] But Jesse had many other offspring, and he would excel as a supportive father, engaged citizen, and restless pioneer.

The younger remaining Burnam children were quick to point out that what they needed was a mother.[22] They were specifically interested in Nancy Ross, wife of the late James J. Ross and daughter of James Cummins, first *alcalde* of San Felipe de Austin. Burnam clearly thought that their idea had merit. Practicality often trumped love when it came to frontier marriages. The fact was that Burnam needed a mother for his children and Nancy Ross, recently widowed, was alone with four children.[23] So it was that they wed in August 1837.[24] However practical this might have been, the pair stayed together for over twenty-five years and had seven children of their own!

Jesse's oldest child, William, was ready to settle down soon after his stint in the Texian army. He married Caroline Zumwalt, daughter of Adam and Nancy Zumwalt, a prominent family that settled in Green DeWitt's colony about 1829. Colorado County records list the wedding date as August 1, 1837.[25] It is interesting and probably no coincidence that the date coincided with the marriage of Jesse to Nancy Ross. Perhaps even more curious is that the same date is recorded in Colorado County for the marriage of Mary to William Townsend. Family records indicate that they married in 1834, which seems logical since they had two children by August 1837. It is likely that since that marriage, and many others, occurred in Mexican Texas, citizens wanted to ensure the legality of their marriage by having a Republic of Texas record. Regardless of whether the ceremony was the result of addressing a technicality or not, it was likely a good excuse for a grand party. William and his family settled for a time near Gonzales. Mary and William Townsend lived near present-day Round Top.[26]

After the Texas Revolution, organizing and sustaining the new government was key, and Jesse became part of that. John G. Robinson, the local representative to the Congress which met at Columbia in October 1836, was killed by Indians during a congressional recess. Jesse replaced him and remained in that seat during the next session, which met at Harrisburg in May 1837.[27] However, due to the needs of his family and the priority of rebuilding his homestead, Jesse then quit his position in the Texas Congress and other political roles. One significant exception was his later work in opposition to the annexation of Texas into the United States.[28]

Jesse did remain actively involved in civic duties. He was twice a grand jury member in the earliest Fayette District courts, held in 1838 and 1839 at La Grange.[29] A more dangerous duty was membership in the militia, usually mustered in response to Indian depredations. One of his most prominent forays was joining the October 1840 expedition led by his wife's brother-in-law, Colonel John H. Moore. The large expedition was formed to pursue the Comanches, who had plundered settlements along the coast months earlier, into the upper Colorado River region.[30] In 1852, Burnam received a warrant for his 1840 service.[31]

Brothers George Tandy Holman and John Thompson Holman relocated to Texas from Virginia in May 1836, shortly after the Texian victory over the Mexicans at San Jacinto. George settled on Jesse's 1831 land grant north of what would soon become Prairie Point (now Oakland) on the Navidad River. He may have leased the property for some time. His dealings with Jesse allowed him to meet Jesse's daughter, Nancy. The two became enamored and married just three days prior to Christmas in 1840.[32] They lived on the Navidad property and raised a couple of children. In 1846, George officially bought 800 acres from Jesse.[33]

In December 1841, another of Jesse's daughters wed. Amanda married Jerome Alexander, a young man who became the first district clerk for the third judicial district of the Republic of Texas, which included Fayette County.[34] Unfortunately, the young couple's marriage lasted less than a year. Jerome was part of the Fayette County contingent of men led by Captain Nicholas M. Dawson in September 1842 to the Battle of Salado Creek. Although the Texians won the fight with Mexican invaders, Dawson's men were almost wiped out in what became known as the Dawson Massacre.[35] Jesse's family suffered additional tragedy during military operations in 1842. John, Jesse's second oldest boy who served during the Texas Revolution, died of exposure in 1842 while in military service.[36]

Two years after she became a widow, Amanda Burnam Alexander married John Holman, the brother of her sister Nancy's husband, George. John had become a clerk in a general store in La Grange, a few miles north of Jesse's homestead. In 1841, he wed a widow, Mary Shields, but she died not long after having their first child. Given that John and Amanda were widowed with young children and had a relationship through their respective siblings' marriage, it is perhaps not surprising that they formed a relationship. Jesse must have approved of the union. Just a few days before they wed in December 1844, he sold some of his property to John for $1,200.[37] Amanda thus moved back to the property where she had been a child.

The acreage Jesse sold to John included the site of Burnam's original homestead and ferry, which had been destroyed by the Texian army in 1836. In short order, John built a two-story southern-style manor. The impressive structure included four chimneys, upper and lower galleries, gables, and four rooms on each story. John and Amanda Holman developed the property, reproducing much of what Jesse had originally built. Outbuildings included a carriage house, barn, smokehouse, blacksmith shop, and a detached kitchen.[38] The plantation became known as Holman Valley. Years later, the small community of Holman, located on FM 155 between La Grange and Weimar, would be established.

As the new couple worked to improve their new property, Jesse decided to move a few miles downriver on the same league of land. Soon, he had a large two-story brick residence to accommodate his seemingly endless family. His new homestead was dubbed Burnam Station.[39] According to the 1840 census, Jesse owned 9,088 acres in Fayette County and eight town lots in La Grange. Additionally, he owned 6,666 acres of land in Colorado County and was executor for 4,444 acres for the heirs of James J. Ross, his wife Nancy's first husband. Jesse also served as guardian of the four Ross children.[40]

Tragedy struck Jesse's clan in 1848. While giving birth to twins, Nancy, married only seven years to George, died. Adding to the tragedy was the fact that neither twin survived. Nancy and the infant twins were buried on their property near Oakland. Since George had to tend to his property on the Navidad, the two surviving children were sent to live with their aunt Amanda and uncle John at Holman Valley. Years later, George joined his brother and acquired property from Jesse in Holman Valley.[41]

As Jesse was completing his new home, his household was about to grow larger still, though under unfortunate circumstances. The Townsends were a prosperous family, part of which settled near present-day Round Top. Mary, Jesse's oldest daughter, wed William Townsend, and they settled three miles east of Round Top, where they quickly began a family. Records are unclear, but evidently Mary died sometime around 1846. Less than two years later, in January 1848, William also passed away, leaving five minor children.[42] In December 1849, Jesse became the legal guardian for William and Mary's five children.[43] Jesse also took in two nieces, Delzey and Narcissis, and one nephew, Joe, who were orphans of one of Jesse's brothers. Delzey eventually married Jesse B. Holman, a cousin of the Holman brothers, further cementing close relations between the two families. Jesse Holman bought property in 1853 on the Navidad from Robert J. Burnam, one of Jesse's sons.[44]

Jesse took whatever steps were necessary to ensure his children had a proper education. This meant extended periods away from home for the children. In a letter dated February 1851, Jesse Bennett Burnam wrote to his older brother William that he was in school at La Grange and his sister Emily and their cousin John Townsend were going also. In September of 1852, Emily, who was at boarding school in Independence, wrote to her brother Robert, saying that she was pleased with school but terribly homesick and hoping that her mother would send for her.[45]

By the 1850s, Fayette County was developing, with the nearby county seat of La Grange well established. Before coming to Texas, Jesse had allegedly said, "When neighbors got close enough to hear them call hogs, I got cramped and had to move."[46] Jesse was feeling crowded again in 1853.[47] He had moved from Tennessee to the warmer climate of Texas as a young man because of health considerations. This time, family considerations determined his destination. In July 1853, the heirs of his late son John received 320 acres of land in Burnet County due to his military service. To supplement this grant, brothers William and Robert bought thousands of additional acres along and near the Colorado River in Burnet County.[48] Jesse then purchased 984 acres in south Burnet County and, more importantly, 1,023 acres on nearby Double Horn Creek from his son William.[49] It was on the latter property, near a spring among a grove of oaks, that Jesse decided to build a new homestead.[50]

Jesse constructed a temporary two-room log cabin where his family could live while he worked on the larger permanent house. However, considering the size of his extended family, he was forced to add two wings and a second story to accommodate everyone.[51] He started raising sheep, one of the first men to try.[52] He used slave labor to harvest wheat and corn. Since Austin was the nearest market in the early days, Jesse traveled there with his oxen to buy provisions.[53] By the early 1860s, he and his oldest son William were farming while two other sons, Robert and Jesse, raised livestock. Jesse had substantial pens to corral the stock. At one point, all the nearby ranches made a sale of 1,500 steers, which were gathered and penned at his place.[54]

Jesse's family again suffered great losses during the Civil War. There are no details on how, but Jesse's son Jesse Bennet died from exposure in Arkansas in 1862 while serving in Company B of the Twenty-First Texas Cavalry. In March 1863, Jesse's second wife Nancy died. Then, in November, his daughter Amanda, wife of John Holman, passed away. Amanda's young son Edward died about eight months later.[55] Jerome, Amanda's son by her first husband, also joined Company B of the Twenty-First Texas Cavalry, was captured, and died in a St. Louis hospital while he was still a prisoner.[56] In 1866, Amanda's husband, John Holman, married Amanda's half-sister, Emily, who was widowed when her husband Henry H. Hunter was killed at home while on leave from Confederate service.[57]

One of the consequences of the war was that, with manpower scarce and state resources devoted to the Confederate cause, the frequency of Indian attacks increased significantly. It was not uncommon for Indians to sneak in, cut fences and hobbles, and then drive the horses away. A tenant of Burnam's during the war wrote to her husband in 1863 that "Mr. Burnam has been sick a few days. He is better now. He talks of going to the army as soon as he is able. I think that what few men there is here in the country ought to stay. I think they can do as much good here as anywhere, and if they all leave, the Indians and 'Tories' will take possession. Last week they killed two in the Snow house."[58] Perhaps the combination of illness and Indian raids made Jesse more aware of mortality. In 1864, he divided his property among the four children still living at home. He conveyed his home, acreage, improvements, livestock, utensils, a steam engine, furniture, etc. Additionally, he conveyed to these four children plus Emily, his oldest child from his second marriage, property across the river and his slaves.[59]

Once the turmoil of the Civil War had abated and life returned to some semblance of normalcy, Jesse began once again to hear the sounds of the hog callers. He became restless and wanted to move—this time to California. However, with his family well settled, he received no enthusiasm from his kinfolk for a move. Because his sight was failing him, the old man could not make the move by himself. The patriarch of the Burnam family would forever remain in Texas.

For years after it happened, Jesse resented Sam Houston for destroying his homestead. Objectively, Houston may have had a good military reason to do it, but it is difficult to forgive the destruction of years of hard work. Jesse periodically applied to the Texas government for compensation. His losses included not only his place on the Colorado but also property destroyed on his land grant on the Navidad. In his last petition, Jesse said that

> On the retreat of the Army of Texas from the Colorado in 1836, His house and ferry were burned by order of the Commander of Texas forces that he sustained great loss in other property by said order. That he has borne all his losses this long with patience and resignation hoping that the Country would finally do him justice, and pay for what he conceived, an act of unnecessary destruction such remuneration as in your judgement may be entitled to sustain him in his worn out old age.

Jesse included testimony from William Patton and William H. Smith, who claimed to have been ordered by George W. Hockley and Houston to burn his premises.[60] Evidently, Texas legislators agreed that Jesse deserved compensation, but there is no evidence that he ever received anything for the loss of his property.

After the Texas legislature in 1870 passed a law providing compensation for veterans of the Texas Revolution, Jesse applied for a pension. Having participated in some of the battles in 1835, he applied multiple times. In each application, he cited his indigent circumstances and signed the document with an 'X' due to his blindness. Affidavits from John H. Moore and Joel Robinson were provided to support his claim. Unlike his application for loss of property, Jesse succeeded in collecting several hundred dollars for his military service.[61]

On his ninetieth birthday, Jesse's relatives hosted a party for him, which was evidently well attended. He was described in a newspaper article thusly: "His hoary locks and emaciated frame bears evidence of the weight of years. His feebleness grows more apparent day by day, and in a little while the gallant soldier, the noble patriot the loving and indulging father, must answer the bugle call of the Great Commander, and silently take his place in line among the noble chieftains whose brave deeds are the best and only inheritance of a God-fearing and loving people."[62] A few months later, Jesse did "answer the bugle call of the Great Commander." He was survived by only five of his children, having outlived both wives and eleven offspring.

Jesse's grandson, Jesse Austin Holman, described him as "an uneducated man, but endowed with a fair share of good common sense and made a success of all his undertakings; except to make and save money. Out of about ten thousand acres of land, he got very little out of it. He virtually gave many men homes."[63] This assessment seems fair. He lost everything in the Texas Revolution, but he built again, not once, but twice. And he gave "homes" to "many men." Family, friends, and even strangers often lived with Jesse or on his properties.

Jesse was buried in a stone vault on his property at Double Horn. An inscription on his tomb reads, "He whose merit deserves a temple has scarcely found a grave in the annals of Texas history." Jesse was not a hero in the conventional sense, but his mark on Texas was indelible.

There is a historical marker on FM 155 at Holman in Fayette County that recounts his time on the Colorado. A founder's plaque for him is also present on the town square in La Grange, and there is another marker commemorating him located south of Marble Falls in Burnet County.[64] Finally, a small road between Highway 71 and the Colorado, just inside Colorado County, is called Burnham Ferry Road.

JOHN HENRY MOORE

JOHN H. MOORE WAS SPARED the loss of property suffered by many settlers in the path of the retreating Texian or advancing Mexican armies. His property instead was only visited by a few small Texian companies that were not burning homesteads or stores.[65] After returning with his family upon hearing of the success at the Battle of San Jacinto, he found his property largely intact, although what remained of his livestock was likely scattered in all directions. This good fortune allowed him to continue a career that made him one of the notable leaders in early Texas.

Although Moore chose to resume his duties with farming and raising livestock, the location of his home was every bit as valuable as before the Revolution and perhaps even more so. With the growing population of the area, there was a push to carve out a new county, which would need a county seat. Moore's property, located where the La Bahía Road intersected the Colorado River and centrally located within the new county, made an ideal location for a seat. Moore partnered with J. S. Lester and William M. Eastland to create a town. Local residents successfully petitioned the Texas government and on December 14, 1837, the Texas Congress established Fayette County with La Grange as the seat. Both names were chosen in honor of the Marquis de Lafayette who provided French assistance against the British during the American Revolution.[66]

Before Congress could approve the application, Moore and his partners were extolling the virtues of their new town in Texas newspapers.[67] By the summer of 1838, La Grange was growing. There was an effort to establish a town called Colorado City across the river in an attempt in part to blunt Moore's efforts to promote La Grange.[68] This site did show some early promise in that it was recommended by state commissioners as a site for the permanent capital. Evidently, Moore was not jealous of the proposal, as he donated land for the effort.[69] Although the Colorado City capital site was approved by Congress, President Sam Houston vetoed the proposal. With the growth of La Grange, and perhaps because floodwaters from the Colorado (with accompanying mosquitos) would sometimes push near his front door, Moore decided to purchase a quarter league of land (1,107 acres) for himself approximately six miles northeast of La Grange.[70] He built a home and started raising cotton to support his growing family, which expanded at this time from three children to six, with the last born in 1844.

As much as Moore may have wanted to settle down as a farmer or rancher, he would often be absent from home, busy dealing with matters of the Republic. Most particularly, the frontier continued to be harassed by Indian raids. Notably, the Comanches were increasingly becoming a problem. Rather than waiting to counter the raids, however, Moore decided to attack them. He began raising a force from his district in late 1838. Ultimately, fifty-five men answered his call. Additionally, Moore solicited the valuable assistance of forty-two Lipans and twelve Tonkawas, who were enemies of the Comanches as well. As Moore's force moved westward, his scouts reported a Comanche camp on the San Saba River. Moore attacked at dawn on February 12, 1839. Castro, with some of his Lipan warriors, stampeded hundreds of horses that had been grazing nearby toward the middle of the camp. The remainder of Moore's men rushed upon the enemy, firing as necessary. At first, it appeared the surprise attack succeeded as many Comanche warriors were cut down. However, as daylight came, Moore realized that he had made a grave error. The scouts had underestimated the size of the camp, and his men were only attacking one end of a much larger encampment.[71]

The Comanche forces quickly became overwhelming, and Moore realized that retreat was his only option. Moore's men managed to fight their way back to the horses only to find that the Comanches had stolen them and were quickly surrounding them. Moore's group was forced to hunker down and fight defensively. This they did for several hours without loss. Eventually, the Comanches pulled back and the weary Texians and their Indian allies extricated themselves from the onslaught. With no horses, Moore's group was forced to walk over a hundred miles across rough terrain with the possibility of a surprise attack at any time. Nevertheless, they returned home without incident. Amazingly, Castro had already arrived, having somehow recovered the stolen horses, which he promptly appropriated for his own followers.[72]

During Houston's first term as president of the Republic of Texas, the policy toward the Indians was trying to maintain peace through negotiation. His successor, Mirabeau B. Lamar, had a decidedly different policy. He was determined to rid Texas of the Indian problem through use of force and chose Moore to help implement his plan. On August 31, 1839, Lamar wrote to Moore: "Sir—You are...hereby authorized and requested to raise Two hundred mounted rangers for a time of Three months and to employ them in scouring the country... chastising the Comanches whenever overtaken."[73] Moore obediently formed a ranger company and patrolled the area specified without much incident. The Council House Fight in March 1840 precipitated a big change in Comanche attitudes toward the settlers. Feeling as if they had been betrayed, their leaders intended to exact revenge for the deaths of dozens of Comanches who were slaughtered in San Antonio.[74] The activity of the Comanches thus increased dramatically.

Lester, one of Moore's partners in the founding of La Grange, wrote a letter to Lamar on July 16, 1840, that read, in part:

> In consequence of...the disturbances by the hostile Indians visiting nearly every settlement on the east side of the river from the City of Austin to some distance below La Grange, stealing a great many horses besides, committing some other depredations, there appears to be considerable discontentment & confusion among the Citizens....I candidly believe they [an expeditionary force] would be able to effect more, for the safeguard & protection of our frontier settlers, than has been done since the existence of our Govt. Yes, I believe they would do it too, in 3, or 4 months, by marching to & destroying their villages...

Lester was not hesitant to recommend a leader for this expedition. "I believe Conscientiously that Colo. Jno H. Moore would be the most suitable person to Command it of any other."[75]

The culmination of the Comanche raids occurred in August 1840 as a vast Comanche army, led by Buffalo Hump, swept through the Guadalupe River valley, killing and looting along the way. Pleas went out to the citizens of Texas to help stifle the massive Indian raid. One such plea was sent in a letter dated August 9, 1840, to John H. Moore in La Grange. J. H. Kerr wrote: "A large party of Indians...have surrounded Victoria they made their appearances on Thursday afternoon, many of the Citizens have been Killed and all the horses taken, the town of Linnville has been burnt to the ground, on Saturday afternoon...We ask for assistance and that too speedily, for without an immediate reinforcement, the whole country will be laid desolate."[76]

Many Texians gathered and pursued. The culminating battle occurred near present-day Lockhart in Caldwell County. In the Battle of Plum Creek, Texian forces numbering about two hundred, led by General Felix Huston and Captain Mathew Caldwell among other notables, intercepted a band of 600 to 1,000 Comanches. Though the battle was technically a victory for the Texians because the Comanches took the brunt of the losses, the raiders still retreated largely intact and escaped with much of the plunder from their coastal raid. Moore, with 150 additional volunteers, arrived at the scene only after the battle was winding down.[77]

The Battle of Plum Creek did not accomplish Lamar's objective. To diminish the Comanche threat, Lamar felt the Texians needed to carry the fight into the heart of their homeland. It was Moore that Lamar relied upon to carry this out. Following the battle of Plum Creek, Moore sent out circulars calling for volunteers to join a campaign against the Comanches along the upper Colorado River basin. Within the three-month time frame that Lester had referenced in his letter to Lamar, Moore had his expeditionary force. They left Austin in late October 1840. This ninety-man force came mostly from the frontier counties of Fayette and Bastrop. As with many of Moore's expeditions, Thomas J. Rabb and Nicholas M. Dawson served as company captains. Also as before, Moore had twelve Lipan Apaches under the command of Castro.[78] The Texians moved up the Colorado until they reached the area around present-day Colorado City in Mitchell County. The Lipans, acting as scouts, informed Moore that a Comanche encampment was about fifteen miles ahead on a horseshoe bend of the river. Moore moved to within a mile or so of the camp to survey the situation and develop a plan. Once this was done, the Texians waited, shivering on the frost-covered ground while the Comanches slept comfortably under buffalo robes in their teepees.

At dawn, the Texians mounted their horses and silently moved to within three hundred yards of the Comanche camp. Finally, the sound of the horses alerted an Indian scout who gave a shrill cry of alarm to rouse his comrades. Hearing that, Moore ordered a charge, and the fight began. The surprise was so complete that many Indian warriors had little chance to resist. The Texians used their guns to advantage and afterwards engaged in hand-to-hand combat. Shortly after the hostilities commenced, many of the Comanche forded the river and tried to climb the bluff across the river. Some of Moore's men shot them while climbing. The ones that made it to the top were slain by a Texian contingent that had been posted there for that very reason.

The results showed 130 Indians left dead. Thirty-four women and children were captured. The Texians also recovered several hundred horses and considerable goods taken at Linnville the previous August.[79] The Texians and their Indian allies had ventured about 250 miles beyond Austin. Never had the Comanches been pursued so far. The distance and the cold weather gave them a sense of safety, making the attack even more effective. This defeat would prove to be an effective deterrent against the Comanches significantly harassing Texian settlements again.

Though perceived primarily as an Indian fighter, Moore had experience leading men into more conventional military conflicts. Perhaps most notable was his presence as commander of the Texian forces at Gonzales in October 1835, during the early stages of the Texas Revolution. He was not quite done with his military leadership, though. By the winter of 1841, the last of the various rebellions had been snuffed out in Mexico and Antonio López de Santa Anna, again in charge, turned his eyes toward his lost province of Texas. Word came through friends below the Rio Grande that a raid was planned, with the objective of occupying San Antonio.

John C. "Jack" Hays, as the leader of a ranger company in San Antonio, decided the information was credible and sent scouts to track the Mexican army's progress. He also sent requests for aid from other communities. As usual, Moore was quick to respond and organized a force with his two reliable captains, Dawson and Rabb. Moore reportedly arrived in San Antonio on March 5, 1842, with a force that numbered about thirty-six, bringing the Texian total to 107.[80]

About the same time, Colonel José María Carrasco, a Mexican officer, approached San Antonio with a white flag. Carrasco informed the Texians that the Mexican army, 1,400 strong and commanded by General

Ráfael Vásquez, was nearby. He added that Vásquez had demanded an immediate and peaceful surrender.[81] The Texians convened a council of war to discuss the matter of fighting or retreating. Ultimately, they decided that, since the Mexican forces had such overwhelming numbers, it was most prudent to withdraw. Hays and his men, along with many American civilians in San Antonio, withdrew to the Guadalupe River. Immediately afterward, General Vásquez and his force occupied San Antonio. It was likely no coincidence that the city was occupied on the anniversary of the fall of the Alamo six years earlier. But Vásquez' mission was not conquest, but rather a warning of things to come. Just two days after capturing the city, scouts brought word to Hays that the Mexicans were retreating, evidently carrying away all the plunder their wagons and carts could hold.[82] The Texians pursued them far enough to ensure they had left Texas. Afterwards, the volunteers disbanded.

In August 1842, Moore became very ill. In fact, the illness was so serious that the August 17 issue of the *Telegraph and Texas Register* reported the sad news that Moore had died! A retraction of this news was quickly issued in the next week's paper, reporting that Moore was "rapidly recovering."[83] Moore did indeed survive what was obviously a serious illness, but that illness may have had a profound impact on upcoming events. Six months after the invasion led by General Vásquez and less than a month after Moore's illness, Mexican General Adrián Woll led a force of nearly 1,500 troops to San Antonio, capturing the unprepared city on September 11, 1842. Caldwell was the first to answer the call for help, moving with 125 men to join forces with Hays and his company, who were waiting near Salado Creek a few miles outside the city.

A council of war was held, and it was decided to hold the position and try to lure the Mexicans into an attack. The plan was more than successful. Hays led a group of riders into town and then, after being noticed, fled back toward the Texian lines. Rather than just a dozen or so cavalry following, however, several hundred set off in pursuit. After

Portrait of General Adrián Woll, quartermaster general of Santa Anna's army during the Texas Revolution. He later led a Mexican expedition to capture San Antonio in September 1842.

they located the main Texian force, Woll ordered infantry and artillery brought up. Fortunately for the Texians, Woll's artillery was ineffective through the numerous trees. Mexican infantry advanced several times on the Texian position but were repulsed each time. By late afternoon, the Mexicans retreated. The Texians reported over one hundred of the enemy had been killed or wounded, while the Texians only lost one. Woll's report, as might be expected, was wildly different. He reported a loss of twenty-nine dead, with fifty-eight wounded. He further claimed that the Texans lost not one, but rather 120, with fifteen captured.[84]

The Texians' victory was not without tragedy for them. A group of Fayette County men left La Grange to assist Hays and Caldwell. The small group added volunteers as they moved west.[85] Dawson, a captain in Moore's previous expeditions, was this time elected to lead the company. As his men rested after their hard ride, a courier from Caldwell warned them of the impending battle. With this news, Dawson pushed his command onward. Near Seguin, Dawson dispatched scouts to determine Caldwell's location. As Dawson slowly moved toward Salado, he met the returning scouts, who told him that the battle was underway and that several hundred Mexicans were being held in reserve. Realizing that he was outmanned, Dawson suggested waiting until additional reinforcements arrived. However, he was talked into proceeding. With bleary eyes and jaded horses, the contingent of fifty-four men moved forward. It proved to be a disastrous decision.

In the afternoon, Dawson's men spotted a group moving toward them, which they assumed was Caldwell's. In fact, they had run into the rear of Woll's large force. When Woll realized that there was activity behind him, he sent a couple of hundred men back to make sure that he would not be caught in a trap. With tired horses, Dawson's men were in no condition to retreat. They took cover in a small thicket of mesquite. Quickly, the small group was surrounded and taking heavy fire. When the Mexicans brought in artillery, Dawson realized he was in an untenable position. With losses mounting, he tried to surrender, but both sides continued firing. When the firing ceased, thirty-six Texians had been killed, including Dawson, and fifteen were prisoners. Only three managed to escape.[86]

Dawson, as noted earlier, had been a captain in Moore's previous expeditions against the Comanches. Due to Moore's illness, however, this time leadership was left to Dawson. Had Moore been healthy, would the expedition have met the same fate as it did with Dawson? Would he have pushed ahead with tired men and worn-out horses? Would he have attacked a superior force under these conditions? Of course, the answers to these questions will never be known.

Moore was not absent from all events, however. On September 20, Caldwell learned that Woll had abandoned San Antonio and immediately set out to intercept the Mexican army. As they moved south, Caldwell continued to gather additional volunteers. James Mayfield, with one hundred men from Bastrop, and Moore, with about the same number from Fayette County, arrived. By the time Caldwell approached the Mexican army, he had a force numbering almost five hundred. He divided his contingent into two battalions, with Mayfield in charge of one and Moore in command of the other.[87]

About 3:00 in the afternoon on September 22, Hays' rangers encountered Woll's rear guard and exchanged gunfire. After this, Woll fell back to Arroyo Hondo to make a stand. Hays informed Caldwell of the action and the Texian army moved up quickly. There may be some dispute as to what happened next, but evidently by order, Hays moved to capture the Mexican battery on the opposite side of the creek. This he did rather efficiently. As he was turning the cannons around toward the Mexicans, he noticed them preparing a counterattack. More alarmingly, he realized that he was not getting the support he expected, which led him to abandon the mission and fall back.[88]

If Hays had been indeed ordered to capture the Mexican artillery, where was his support? Caldwell claimed in his later report that he did not order an attack, owing to the boggy ground, tired horses and men, and the lack of ammunition. Contemporaries had other explanations. Mary A. Maverick said that there was a disagreement between Caldwell and Moore about who should be in command.[89] John H. Jenkins recalled that there was not a disagreement on command but rather on the proper course of action. Hays noted that the Texian command lacked "discipline or [a] system of harmony among the officers who could not agree as to the proper line of policy." Jesse Billingsley, who had commanded a company under the direction of Moore at Gonzales in 1835, evidently tired of waiting for action and lined his men up to attack but was subsequently ordered by Caldwell to stand down.[90] Once Hays retreated, it was deemed too dark to proceed, and any action had to wait until the following morning.

The missed battle with Woll was Moore's last chance at combat in the antebellum era. Woll slipped away with his army during the night without the Texians realizing it. By the time they did, the Mexicans were six miles down the road and closer to friendlier territory. After a heated debate, the decision was made to abandon any further pursuit and most of the Texian army went home. Moore was not with those who rebelled, crossed the Rio Grande, and became embroiled in the military disaster remembered as the Mier Expedition.[91] By 1843, Houston had negotiated a peace with the Comanches, so that menace was greatly reduced. The expeditions that Moore so frequently led were not necessary, and he generally retired to his property to farm and ranch.

It was not until the Civil War that Moore tried to resume military service. He attempted to join the Eighth Texas Cavalry (Terry's Texas Rangers), but since he was over sixty years of age, he was deemed too old and instead was recruited to sell war bonds. Reportedly, Moore went to Kentucky during the war to deliver clothing and supplies to Confederate troops there. Three of his sons and a son-in-law also served the Confederacy.[92]

Toward the end of Moore's life, an incident occurred that may have adversely impacted his legacy. In October 1878, Ira G. Killough, the husband of Moore's oldest daughter Tabitha, was gunned down. This news quickly appeared in newspapers throughout the state. What made the reports particularly sensational was that Killough was highly regarded as a war hero, former Texas legislator, and nominee for state treasurer.[93] Tabitha testified that it was her sister's husband John Hunt that was responsible for the murder. Furthermore, she implicated her brother, Robert J. Moore, and nephew, William Byrd Moore, as accomplices. Newspaper writers were generally sympathetic toward her plight and equally harsh against the Moore family members implicated.[94] Robert and Byrd Moore were immediately apprehended and held without bail. A $500 reward was posted for David Hunt, who had fled.

Byrd's trial was a couple of months after Killough's death. Robert's day in court followed one week later. Both men were found not guilty, which spawned renewed outrage in several newspapers. One anonymous letter submitted to the Dallas *Commercial* claimed that Governor Joseph D. Sayers refused a $5,000 fee to defend Robert because "he believed the accused guilty of a cold-blooded murder." Moore replied that he never tried to employ Sayers and that he would never make such a statement. The anonymous letter went on to claim that Moore "boasted that he had for years been collecting together $10,000 to kill his own son-in-law." Moore replied heatedly, "This statement I emphatically denounce as an unmitigated falsehood!"[95]

Family lore says that Moore never intended for his daughter to wed, and that Ira and Tabitha eloped and married against her father's wishes. Moore carried an ongoing resentment against the Killough family for years. Additionally, Ira Killough was a well-liked and respected individual whose influence and clout was growing, while Moore, though well respected, was not known to be a necessarily pleasant fellow. Moore may well have thought that his influence was being usurped by his unwanted son-in-law. Whether true or not, there seemed to be sufficient motive for Moore to be involved in a plot against Killough. The fact that Moore took the effort to print a denial was evidence that there was widespread belief that he was indeed involved.[96]

In April 1879, a full year and a half after Ira was killed, Hunt surrendered to authorities in Galveston and was brought back to La Grange. Three months later, a bail hearing was held and, unlike the two previously accused men, bail was set at an incredible $10,000, which was duly paid![97] The trial convened at Columbus in September 1879. Jury selection was so contentious that only three were seated from the first pool of sixty. The trial was attended by many interested and influential parties, and it ended in a mistrial. The local paper, the *Colorado Citizen*, reported that all the jurors thought Hunt was guilty, but that four were unwilling to sentence him to hang or life in prison.[98] A continuance was granted with the intention of holding another trial, but only twelve weeks later, it was reported that Robert had died. Some said his death at the age of thirty-seven was in part due to his health remaining poor after his confinement in prison for two months while awaiting trial.

Eight months later, John H. Moore died. A belated obituary appeared in the *La Grange Journal* in December 1880. As most obituaries do, the writer extolled Moore's accomplishments during his life. The writer noted that, "By his wife, who died some five years ago, he had six children, of whom two have died and four yet remain, together with a number of grandchildren, to mourn their loss." It further stated, "Moore was a thrifty man and accumulated a handsome fortune, most of which he divided among his children before his death."[99] Such statements were too much for Richard O. Faires of Flatonia, husband to Eliza Killough Faires and son-in-law to Ira and Tabitha Killough. He issued a rebuttal to the Moore obituary that reported that Tabitha Killough had been disinherited and no support was provided to her or her children in Moore's will. Faires further noted the high interest rates Moore charged to his sons-in-law on loans he provided. Lastly, he claimed that Moore did not provide for his orphaned granddaughter because of a grudge against his other late son-in-law, Richard V. Cook.[100]

It was not until September 1881, almost three years after Killough's death, that Hunt was retried for his murder. This time the verdict was not guilty.[101] For some time, there continued to be questions about the veracity of the verdict and whispered murmurs about John H. Moore's role in Ira Killough's murder. Absent more details of the case, there is no way to know if the verdict was just or a travesty. Regardless, Moore's stature toward the end of his life was impacted.

John H. Moore's name will forever be linked with the Battle of Gonzales and the founding of La Grange. Too, he often took the field as a commander in campaigns against Indians during the antebellum years in Texas. Despite the influence a family feud may have had toward the end of his eighty years, his impact on Texas history is undeniable. A historical marker describing Moore's exploits can be found near the site of the Battle of Gonzales and two more stand at his residence northwest of La Grange.[102]

BENJAMIN BEESON

WHILE THE ACTIONS OF MANY of the people in this work were documented through the use of primary sources, the Beesons, despite their prominence on the Colorado River, were not among them. Consequently, it is difficult to know precisely what transpired for the Beeson family after they left their charred home on the Colorado in March 1836. One thing for certain is that they had their share of tragedy. The first in Texas was when the family found themselves between two opposing armies. When the dust settled, their homestead had been burned to the ground, setting the stage for more hardships in independent Texas.

William B. Dewees, who was married to Benjamin and Elizabeth "Betsy" Beeson's oldest child, Lydia, recorded that seventy-five families were encamped near the Texian army in March 1836, waiting to see the outcome of unfolding events.[103] Though Dewees never mentioned the Beesons by name, it can logically be assumed that they were among the settlers who lingered nearby while the Texians and Mexican faced off on the Colorado. The fact that their property was nearby and their son Leander was enrolled in the Texian army supports this assumption.

Like Dewees, when the Texian army suddenly retreated, Beeson and his family probably followed and crossed the Brazos River at San Felipe de Austin. They continued their flight until they reached Robert's Plantation, twenty-five miles east of the Brazos.[104] It was here that Betsy Beeson penned her unusual letter to President David G. Burnet asking about the prospects of opening a boarding house in Harrisburg.[105] The Dewees and Beeson families continued east toward the Trinity River, escorted by a company of men. It was while encamped between the Trinity and San Jacinto rivers that they learned of the unexpected Texian victory at San Jacinto.[106] They soon returned to their devastated homes on the Colorado near Columbus.

The Beeson family must have made some attempt at rebuilding. An ad in the *Telegraph and Texas Register* dated October 25, 1836, asked for a stolen horse, if found, to be returned to the Beeson place.[107] Whatever rebuilding that might have occurred, however, was likely short-lived. The tragedy of losing their home would pale in comparison to the events the family endured over the course of the next year.

On September 21, 1836, Leander and Collins Beeson, two of Benjamin's sons, accompanied by a man named Maxwell Steel, were traveling to San Antonio in pursuit of a runaway slave. As the trio crossed the Guadalupe River a little below Gonzales, they were attacked by about forty Indians. Leander's horse was shot out from under him, and he just managed to dive into the river and swim to the opposite bank. Despite being injured, he made his way to the Beeson home on the Colorado. The party that returned quickly found the body of Leander's unfortunate brother,

Collins. Though there was no sign of Steel, it was reported days later that his head was found at an Indian camp.[108]

While there was documentation of the unfortunate death of Collins Beeson, the details of the subsequent deaths of Beeson family members are less certain. In the March 14, 1837, edition of the *Telegraph and Texas Register*, two notices were printed to settle estates. One, dated February 28, was for the estate of Collins, with William Dewees and Leander recorded as administrators. Immediately adjacent to this one was another notice for Benjamin Beeson's estate, dated March 9. The same two men were listed as administrators with the addition of another Beeson brother, Abel.[109] It is unknown how Benjamin Beeson died. No obituary is known to exist. A map of the division of his property shows part of it being left to John F. and Nepsey Berry's two young sons, James and John. This would suggest that this couple, his daughter and son-in-law, had died prior to his will being written.

No estate announcements could be found for John and Nepsey Berry as there had been for Collins and Benjamin Beeson. Nevertheless, Colorado County records show that on February 27, 1837, Leander and Abel Beeson were appointed as guardians for James and John Berry, "infant minors of the Estate of John F. Berry."[110] The circumstances and date of death of Nepsey Berry are unknown, although she clearly died before her father. Unfortunately, one of the late couple's sons, James, would die in late 1849 or early 1850, before he turned twenty.[111]

The fate of Betsy Beeson is shrouded in even more mystery. The last documentation of her shows her recovering money from the Republic in December 1836.[112] Records show that about the same time that Leander and Abel Beeson were applying to become guardians of their infant nephews, James and John Berry, Leander also applied to become guardian of his younger sister, Mary Ann, who in 1837 would have been about seven or eight years old.[113] Presumably, Betsy died about the same time or perhaps shortly after her husband did. She would have been only forty-three

BIOGRAPHICAL APPENDIX | 235

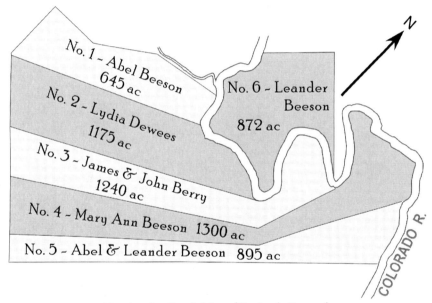

Plat showing the division of Benjamin Beeson's
land grant among his living heirs.

or so, seven years younger than her husband when he died. To date, it has not been ascertained whether these family members died under similar circumstances. Perhaps their deaths were the result of a tragic accident or virulent disease. If so, however, it was not reported in area papers. Both Benjamin and Betsy Beeson were purportedly buried in the Columbus cemetery, though considering the timing of the town organization, it seems more plausible that they were buried on their property several miles south. Regardless, their graves have unfortunately been lost.

Benjamin and Betsy Beeson seemed to have an impressive reputation for hard work and, until the ruin they suffered during the Texas Revolution, they had made an impressive account of themselves. Their son Leander honorably served in the army and fought at San Jacinto. His life beyond that, however, was chaotic to say the least and his name became prominent in district court criminal records.

By 1838, the county had yet to build a courthouse or jail. William Dewees and the first sheriff, Stephen Townsend, who had commanded troops under Sam Houston on the Colorado in 1836, were among a group who pledged funds to build the jail. By August 1838, it had been completed and, ironically, Townsend's brother Spencer and Dewees' brother-in-law, Leander Beeson, were the first occupants.[114] The incident that landed the pair in the new jail occurred on December 12, 1837. Leander was complaining to whomever would listen that Naham Mixon had called his brother Abel "a damn rascal." Spencer learned secondhand that the same man had called him a swindler. Emotions were running high, likely fueled to some degree by alcohol. A mob made its way to the boarding house owned by Mixon's brother to confront him. Mixon wanted nothing to do with them and the mob seemed to dissipate. The respite was brief; less than an hour later, a second mob, this time including William Dewees, returned. In a confused melee, shots rang out and Mixon was shot in the back, allegedly by Leander Beeson. Mixon lasted for a few days before he succumbed to his injuries. Ultimately, Beeson, Townsend and William Dean were charged with the crime. Dean evidently escaped the area before being tried, while Beeson and Townsend were eventually acquitted.[115]

Beeson and Townsend were co-defendants in the situation with Mixon, but that alliance soon faded. The spark that may have precipitated the ill feelings between the families was an accusation, in November 1838, by William S. Townsend, son-in-law of Jesse Burnam, and his brother Stephen that Abel Beeson had branded two of their heifers.[116] The accusation was tried in court and Abel was evidently found guilty, though the consequences of the verdict are unclear.

In 1840, Leander Beeson was again caught up in controversy when he fathered a child out of wedlock. The course of what happened next is unclear, but Leander evidently was well vested in raising the child, which was named Leander Jr. He married Rebecca Giberson in 1842 and they formally adopted the boy in 1845. The child's mother later married someone else.[117]

Leander Beeson's legal problems resurfaced after he married. In 1844, he was arrested for betting on the election for county representative to the Texas Congress.[118] A much more serious charge was levied a few years later. Leander was arrested for assault with intent to murder Moses Townsend in January 1848.[119] The grand jury did not convene on the matter until October of that year, and, evidently, the delay in legal proceedings was unacceptable to the Townsend family. In March 1848, Gideon Townsend, nephew of Moses and newly returned from military service in the Mexican American War, allegedly attacked Leander, presumably in retaliation to his attack on Moses. Charges for assault were subsequently levied against Gideon Townsend.[120] It is hard to ascertain exactly what happened due to the spotty records available. Evidently, the grand jury indictment against Leander was nullified for unknown reasons. Another grand jury, however, indicted him three years later for the same alleged assault on Moses Townsend.[121] Despite the charges against

Leander and Gideon, there is no indication that either one served any meaningful time in jail.

There is evidence in the court records that tension between the families may have eventually eased. One common charge prevalent in Texas was gambling. In January 1854, Leander Beeson, along with his nephew, John Berry, and another individual were accused of playing cards in "a public house...for retailing spirits and liquors." Interestingly, the venue for the gambling was identified as "Townsends grocery."[122] Though the stakes were low, it is interesting that Leander felt secure enough to gamble in a Townsend establishment. Whether there was peace between the families or not, Leander's troubled life did not last much longer. His wife probated his will in January 1857.[123] There are no details of how or exactly when his death occurred, but he would have died at the relatively young age of forty.

Abel Beeson got married and had several children. He named his oldest after his late sister Nepsey and later named twin boys Benjamin and Collins after his late father and brother. As noted earlier, he and Leander served as guardians of their nephews James and John Berry and their youngest sister, Mary Ann. Abel, seemingly with the more stable homelife, was likely the practical guardian.

In March 1846, the youngest child of Benjamin Beeson and the only one born in Texas, Mary Ann, married Basil Sapp when she was just fifteen years of age. Shortly after their first child was born, Sapp abandoned his wife. After waiting three years, her request for divorce was granted by the Texas legislature. Two weeks later, she married George Perry and had three children with him.[124]

Most of Benjamin and Betsy Beeson's children died relatively young. Lydia, their oldest child and William Dewees' wife, died at thirty-eight years of age. Their oldest boy, Collins, died at the hands of Indians at twenty-six. Nepsey died of unknown circumstances at about twenty-five. The Beeson's also had a child, Benjamin, who died as an infant. Leander died at about forty years of age. Abel moved to Caldwell County in the late 1850s. There is no record of him in the 1870 census. He may have been a casualty of the Civil War. If so, he would have been about fifty when he died. Ironically, it may have been Benjamin Beeson, who died at about the age of fifty-one, who had the longest life of anyone in his immediate family.

Beeson's homesite is often mistakenly identified as the early site of Columbus. In actuality, the town was located close to Dewees' Ford. Beeson's Crossing, however, was at the focal point of the standoff between the Texian and Mexican armies during March 1836. With the Texas Revolution behind them, Benjamin Beeson and his family might have expected to rebuild for an even more prosperous future. Unfortunately, that was not to be the case. Perhaps their name might have been more prominent had their family escaped numerous subsequent tragedies. But they are not entirely forgotten. Beason's Park, located on the east side of the Colorado River just across from downtown Columbus, is named after the Beeson family. In that park are historical markers about Benjamin, his crossing, and the military standoff in March 1836.[125]

WILLIAM BLUFORD DEWEES

LIKE BENJAMIN BEESON, William B. Dewees' home stood squarely in the middle of the standoff between Mexican and Texian forces in March 1836. His house was burned, as were most along the western side of the Colorado River. Dewees and his family left with others that had been camped near the Texians, waiting to see the results of what they thought would be an inevitable battle. Ultimately, he was with 150 to 200 families on the Trinity River when word reached them that the Mexican army had been defeated at San Jacinto. That became a turning point in his life, after which he became a local developer and primary founder of Columbus.

Dewees was purportedly one of the first to return to his homestead on the Colorado, where he noted the devastation. Upon arrival, he observed, "All was stillness around and the angel of gloom seemed to be hanging over the once lovely place." Dewees traveled down the river to the Atascosito Crossing, where he witnessed the Mexican troops led by General Vicente Filisola. Feeling confident that he was in no danger, he rode back upriver and began to help construct rafts so his group could recross the river.[126]

A group of citizens, Dewees most prominent among them, had petitioned the government to create a township called Columbus at a site near his home. Obviously, the timing could not have been worse, and any remnants of the budding town were destroyed in the subsequent stand-off between the two armies. Dewees, however, was not deterred and, once resettled into a suitable living arrangement, he started to promote the new town. In an advertisement in the *Telegraph and Texas Register* dated May 1, 1837, Dewees told of "a general sale of Lots in the town of Columbus...Its site is a high and beautiful bluff, supplied by never failing springs, of the purest water the country affords, and surrounded by the richest land and settlements in Texas."[127] Over the course of the next few years, he was involved in a flurry of land transactions in and around Columbus. Notably, he and several other prosperous individuals donated land for the benefit of Rutersville College, the first institute of higher education founded in the Republic of Texas.[128]

Dewees' town developed slowly. In the summer of 1837, it was reported that Columbus comprised only "two public houses, two small stores, and half-dozen shanties."[129] By the early to mid-1840's, however, the town started to grow. Travelers noted thirty homes in the town, along with three stores, two taverns, and a smithy.[130]

As might be expected for a town founder, Dewees was active in the local government. He was elected as a justice of the peace in February 1837 and is recorded as performing marriage ceremonies.[131] Additionally, he was listed in court documents as an associate justice (to William J.

E. Heard as chief justice) in some early county court cases in 1838 and 1839.[132] Dewees was unanimously elected county treasurer in April 1840 and served in that post until Texas became a state. The minutes of his appointment stated that he had to post a bond of $5,000, but he retained a stipend of $250 from the fees he collected. Too, it was "ordered & decreed by the court that the sum of $300 be allowed William B. Dewees for a house to be used by the county for a court house Dist. & County Clks office for the term of one year from the present time April 14th 1840 to be paid by the county out of money arising to the county for taxes & c. Texas promissory rates."[133] A primary function of the treasurer was collecting taxes. Ironically, Dewees was often behind in his tax payments. Ultimately, however, he paid his debts.

Dewees was certainly a prominent citizen and had his hand in numerous ventures, land speculation being an important one. Being as well-known as he was and involved in many issues, it was perhaps inevitable that he would run into some sticky situations. His name appears in two cases involving his brother-in-law, Leander Beeson. In 1837, Beeson was accused of murdering Naham Mixon. Dewees, as part of the mob that was looking for Mixon, was eventually charged as well. In 1848, Dewees was again involved in the case of Beeson and his alleged intent to kill Moses Townsend.[134]

Dewees appeared on the other side of the ledger as well. In September 1838, Colin De Bland was charged with assault on Dewees. A few months earlier, these two men were on the committee assigned to help secure funding for a new jail.[135] De Bland's enthusiasm as a citizen working for the benefit of the new town had since waned. According to one witness, the clash started when De Bland said "something about the people of Columbus being d—m rascals." Dewees took offense and asked if De Bland meant him. De Bland was not shy in replying, "If the cap fit him, he could wear it." The arguing escalated and Dewees told De Bland, "All that he had against him was that he didn't vote for him." This observation may have been the impetus for De Bland's original derogatory comment, as he had evidently lost a local election. Dewees tried to leave, but De Bland attacked him. The two scuffled for a while before the brawl was broken up temporarily. Witnesses provided different accounts, but at some point, De Bland brandished a pistol and Dewees hit De Bland with a chair. The episode ended with De Bland threatening that he would kill him.[136] This episode shows how quickly attitudes could change and how readily frontier residents would resort to violence. Six years later, L. J. Bryan Rhyne, of Fayette County, was also charged with assault against Dewees.[137] The reason for their confrontation is unknown, but witnesses testified that it was Rhyne who started the encounter, and then a wholesale brawl ensued. It ended with Dewees being kicked while on the ground.

In the early days of the Republic and ensuing statehood, two criminal charges were most common. One was assault/attempted murder/murder. The second, seemingly less serious, but more commonplace, was gambling/playing cards. Even the most respected members of the community at some point seemed to succumb to the lure of card playing. Dewees was not exempt from such temptation. He was charged with "betting at a gaming table." Among those charged with him was his in-law, Amos Besch, and the former sheriff and city marshal, Ira A. Harris.[138] One of the vices that often accompanied gambling was excessive drinking. It is not known whether Dewees was truly a teetotaler or not, but it is interesting that in 1853, Dewees was part of a committee assigned to appoint a delegate to the state convention in support of the temperance movement.[139] Considering the all-too-common violence and general carousing, Dewees might have regarded the temperance movement as a positive development in his town.

Whereas Dewees' list of criminal appearances in court, as defendant or as complainant is short when compared to his brother-in-law, Leander Beeson, he was an all-too-common visitor in civil court. Records show over forty cases where Dewees' name appears in a civil proceeding in the

25th District Court. More often than not, he was the plaintiff rather than the defendant. Many of those cases involved payments, or lack thereof, of land deals that he had made.

After about sixteen years of marriage, Dewees' wife, Lydia Beeson Dewees, died in March 1847 at about thirty-nine years of age.[140] On the frontier, life is harsh, and death can come quickly and unexpectedly. Quick remarriages are often for practical reasons as much as romantic ones. But in the case of Dewees, his second marriage may have turned some heads. Within a week after his first wife Lydia died, forty-seven-year-old William B. Dewees married Angelica Besch, the seventeen-year-old daughter of prominent German immigrants.[141]

The circumstances of a quick marriage may not always be as they at first appear. Dewees was left with a child, Emily, who was about five at the time, and he may have felt it a priority for her to have a mother. Whether there was a significant relationship prior to marriage is unknown. Dewees relinquished all claims against Lydia's estate. Records show that her heirs were her siblings and her late sister Nepsey's children. Notably, her daughter Emily was not listed as an heir.[142] Perhaps there was an understanding between the two prior to her death. Deed records show a sale of 300 acres of property from Lydia to her husband William about a month before her death.[143] Perhaps they knew that her death was imminent, and this sale was recorded in lieu of any further claim on her estate by William or their daughter Emily.

After his remarriage, Dewees and the Beeson family did not seem to associate with one another as they had prior to Lydia's death. Perhaps there was gossip among area residents about Dewees' quick union. Whether there were hard feelings between Dewees and his in-laws over this is hard to determine. Dewees seemed to have had clear affection for his late wife, however, since the name of his first child with Angelica was Lydia.[144]

In 1852, Dewees entered a contract with Emanetta Cara Kimball, using the pseudonym Cara Cardelle, to share profits on a book written by Dewees and compiled by Kimball. Entitled *Letters of an Early Settler of Texas*, the work contained letters purportedly authored by Dewees to a friend.[145] Though an advertisement in the *Texas Monument* newspaper for the book assured readers that the letters were genuine, they are almost certainly contrived.[146] Despite this, they likely do contain many accurate depictions of life and events in Texas. In his book, Dewees tended to put himself in the middle of important events. For example, Dewees claimed that Sam Houston consulted with him as to whether conditions were right for the Texian army to attack the Mexicans on the Colorado. Considering that Houston did not consult much with his officers, it seems unlikely that he would solicit Dewees' opinion on such an important decision. Dewees also claimed that Houston sent him to retrieve the Twin Sisters, the cannons that were being delivered to the Texians on the Brazos River. Again, there is no independent documentation to support Dewees' version of events.[147]

The claims by Dewees within his book did not go unnoticed. While giving a lecture in 1871, John Henry Brown, a participant in and prolific documentarian of many early Texas events, gave an account of the great Indian Raid of 1840 and subsequent Battle of Plum Creek. Having taken part in that battle, Brown was incensed with Dewees' claim that he led one of the citizen volunteer companies involved in the famous clash with Comanches.[148] The contract that Dewees executed with Kimball stated that he had completed another manuscript entitled *Life on a Frontier or Adventures of Will Dewees*. However, there is no record of this manuscript being published, and there is evidence that it might have been destroyed in a fire.[149]

As a sign of Dewees' popularity, he was approached to run for the Texas legislature. In a letter in the March 5, 1859, edition of the *Colorado Citizen*, several citizens implored him to run for public office. It read in part, "we know of no man more deserving of the honor of being our representative—more worthy as a gentleman—better qualified to represent our interests, or who would more fully devote all his tireless energies to fulfill the obligations of a legislator for his constituents, and the best interests of our county and State—than our old, long tried and worthy fellow citizen, W. B. Dewees." Shortly afterward, Dewees responded in the same newspaper that while honored, he "would be doing great injustice to the interests of my family, were I to respond affirmatively to the call of my friends."[150]

Dewees' time as county treasurer ended when Texas joined the union. About three years later, the Colorado County court ordered "that the present Treasurer of the County be authorized to employ an attorney by giving a reasonable conditional fee thereof in any suit he may institute against W. B. Dewees on his bond as former Treasurer of the County."[151] This might suggest that there were some irregularities in the treasurer's office during Dewees' tenure. The ultimate result of this order is unknown, but it did not seem to affect Dewees' standing in the community. After all, the purpose of a bond was to atone for any shortcomings. It might have been, however, a precursor of things to come.

In the chaos after the Civil War, Governor Andrew J. Hamilton appointed Dewees to serve as the treasurer of Colorado County until an election could be held to fill the position. After Dewees' term ended, it was alleged by county officials that he failed to transfer $1,440 in county funds to his successor. Dewees' defense was that the funds had been in a law office safe that had been burglarized. Though the alleged crime occurred in March 1866, Dewees was not tried until two years later. The verdict was in favor of the county, and Dewees was ordered to pay $1,728 in restitution. His appeal only affirmed the original decision of the court.[152]

Dewees dropped out of the limelight after his legal problems. His fortunes deteriorated to the point that he was added to the county's pauper list.[153] Two months later, on April 14, 1878, he passed away in Columbus at the age of 79. A simple obituary in the local newspaper noted, in part:

"Judge W. B. Dewees...has held several offices of trust in our county and city, but for the last few years has taken no active part in politics. During the past year his health has been very feeble, and he was greatly reduced in strength. His death was easy and peaceful, as if he dropped off to sleep. A goodly number of our citizens accompanied the old veteran to his last resting place at five o'clock Monday evening. Peace to his remains."[154] Regardless of all other matters, Dewees is widely recognized as the primary founder of Columbus. There is a historical marker in the city that describes his role in its founding, and a street is named in his honor.[155]

ABRAM, WILLIAM, AND CYNTHIA ALLEY

WHILE NEWS OF THE VICTORY by the Texian army at San Jacinto was a welcome relief to the settlers of Texas, the rush to return home for many had to wait as the Mexican army slowly retreated westward. Abram Alley's homestead was directly on that retreat. Just as the Mexican troops had crossed the Colorado River at the Atascosito Crossing, they also retreated across the river at the same point, near the ruins of Alley's home. This marked not only a new era of Texas independence, but also a new start for the Alley siblings.

Of all the Alley brothers who came to Texas, Abram was the only one who married. Like many settlers who evacuated during the Runaway Scrape, Abram and his young wife of barely one year, Nancy, returned to a burned cabin and devastated homestead. The couple began the arduous process of rebuilding. Before the year was out, Alley had constructed, near the same site, a two-room oak log square notch home with stone chimneys on each end. A well was eventually dug, and several outbuildings were erected.[156]

Abram and Nancy had nine children, though only five lived to adulthood.[157] However, the family would expand beyond that. On New Year's Day, 1837, Nancy's mother, Elizabeth Millar Betts, passed away. Two of her children, John and Elizabeth Millar, became wards of Abram and Nancy.[158]

With a growing family and a recent inheritance from Nancy's aunt, Abram decided in 1852 to expand his cabin. He traveled to Bastrop, purchased pine lumber from a sawmill, and then floated it downriver to the Atascosito Crossing. He remodeled his cabin by expanding it into an L-shape, adding a couple of rooms, another fireplace, and a front and back porch.[159]

Abram Alley farmed, primarily cotton. The 1850 census also records that he had seventy hogs, 300 head of beef cattle, and fifty head of milk cattle. The many milk cattle suggest he was dabbling in dairy production.[160] In March 1837, Abram had registered the first cattle brand in Colorado County. He was also a prominent member of the new government. He served as a juror in the first term of the district court that convened in Colorado County in April 1837 with Judge Robert M. Williamson presiding. He was appointed by President Sam Houston as the president of the Board of Land Commissioners of Colorado County in December 1837.[161] He also served a term as a justice of the peace from 1839 to 1841.[162]

As parents, the Alleys advocated education, something not always easy on what was still a frontier. When news started to circulate that a college would be opened, there was considerable interest and excitement. Eventually a site was selected in Fayette County. At first, Rutersville College did well, but when Texas joined the United States and the Mexican American War started, it began to lose students. Concerns of corruption and competition from other institutes worked to further deplete enrollment. Motivated to help the struggling college, Alley sold the trustees 1,000 acres of land for five dollars.[163] Unfortunately, his generosity was for naught, and the college continued its decline.

Alley died in May 1862 at the age of 58. Among the list of claims against his estate after his death were bills from Colorado College in Columbus for tuition for his son John and an unknown student by the name of J. Carter. After her husband's death, Nancy Alley earned a few dollars by tutoring students at her home. She never remarried and, along with her bachelor son William, continued to live in the home that Abram had built until her death in 1893.[164] The Alley house was moved from its site near Atascosito Crossing into Columbus in 1976. It was dilapidated, but some of the descendants of Abram and Nancy renovated it as a museum.[165]

Unlike Abram Alley, who became a dedicated family man, his brother William A. Alley remained a bachelor and devoted his efforts toward more entrepreneurial pursuits. William served for a time as the tax assessor and collector for Colorado County. He was an innkeeper, ran a trading post, and brokered cotton and other crops for area farmers. He also engaged in land development, and this consumed much of his energy.[166] In 1859, William platted the town of Alleyton. Just as William B. Dewees committed significant time and resources to developing Columbus, Alley was just as devoted to Alleyton. Although the emerging town was only three miles east of Columbus, Alley had enough vision to see one of the essential elements necessary for the town to prosper. Using his land and money, Alley convinced the Buffalo Bayou, Brazos, and Colorado (BBB&C) Railroad Company to extend its line from Harrisburg to Alleyton. This was the brainchild of none other than Sydney Sherman, who had camped near the future site of Alleyton in March 1836 while commanding the Texian troops at Dewees' Ford.[167]

After the railroad reached Alleyton, the BBB&C moved its offices there, and for several years the town remained the terminus of the railroad. During the Civil War, Alleyton was not only the terminus of the railway but the beginning of vital trails by which Texas cotton went to Mexico. Cotton, shipped by railroad, would be offloaded in Alleyton and begin the journey to Mexico by wagon, thus avoiding the Union blockades of Texas ports. The lively community became home to several hotels, saloons, and trading posts.[168] It must have been exactly the type of community that William Alley had envisioned. It was not until after the war that the railroad finally crossed the Colorado River and moved past Columbus and towards San Antonio. Though the community prospered for a brief time, Alleyton never usurped Columbus as the primary town

BIOGRAPHICAL APPENDIX | 249

The cabin of Abram and Nancy Alley, originally located near the Atascosito Crossing, was built immediately after the return to property after the Texas Revolution in 1836. The cabin is now located in Columbus.

of Colorado County.

William Alley remained in the town named after him for the rest of his days, and where a historical marker commemorates his family.[169] His half-sister, Eliza McCoy Rolluson, and her husband, Thomas Rolluson, lived with William during his later years until his death in 1869. But a full sister of Abram and William, Cynthia Alley, lived a much different life. Cynthia and her husband, Williamson Daniels, moved from Missouri to the San Augustine area in east Texas in 1831. They supplied provisions to the Texian army during the early days of the Revolution and, when word came that the Alamo had fallen, Williamson joined a company of San Augustine volunteers, led by Captain Leonard H. Mabbitt.[170] His company did not reach San Jacinto until after the decisive battle, however.

Though there was a connection between the young couple with the San Augustine area, Williamson and Cynthia Daniels became prominent in Austin's Colony as well. In October 1832, Daniels received a land grant on the western boundary of Austin's Colony along the Lavaca River.[171] The Daniels' homestead was where the Texian army camped on the first night after their rapid exit from Gonzales in March 1836. It is also where General Joaquín Ramírez y Sesma camped with his Mexican troops a few nights later. Though they must have had a home on their grant on the Lavaca, the couple clearly spent time on land inherited by Cynthia from her brother, Rawson Alley. Williamson Daniels' signature is on the December 1835 petition to make Colorado a separate municipality.[172]

After the Revolution, the couple permanently settled in Colorado County. In May 1838, Williamson Daniels was elected president of the Board of Land Commissioners for the county, succeeding his brother-in-law, Abram Alley. From 1841 to 1842, he sat in the Texas Congress as a representative. In 1842, he volunteered in response to the Mexican raids by Generals Ráfael Vázquez and Adrián Woll. In 1845, Williamson Daniels served as a justice of the peace; three years later, he was chief justice of Colorado County, and in 1850 he was a commissioner for the same county.[173] He had five children with Cynthia before his death in 1872, at the age of seventy-four. She lived until 1899, one of the last of the original pioneering families of Texas.

PETER KERR

ON MARCH 25, 1836, Peter Kerr rode into the Texian army camp bearing important news about the fate of Colonel James W. Fannin's command at Goliad. Much to his surprise and dismay, he was immediately arrested for dispersing lies about the enemy. Though Kerr's report was soon confirmed, he traveled to the Brazos River as a prisoner. When Sam Houston moved upriver from San Felipe de Austin, Kerr remained behind with Moseley Baker's company. Kerr evidently was willing to tell anybody who would listen about what he heard had happened to Fannin at Coleto Creek. Colonel George W. Hockley, in his letter to Thomas J. Rusk on April 1, 1836, reported that "from information received the evening after leaving San Felipe, the Cmr-in-Chief [Houston] ordered Peter Carr [sic]...to be taken—a guard was sent to San Felipe and he was brought into camp next morning."[174] Two days later, Houston wrote to Rusk, "I send you, in charge of Mr. Este, two prisoners, Peter Kerr, and Beregardo, a Mexican. I have nothing pointed against them; but suspicion has fallen upon them, and they are to be secured."[175]

Eventually, the cloud of suspicion against Kerr lifted. After the Battle of San Jacinto, Houston appointed Kerr to be an interpreter to help deal with the numerous prisoners that the Texians had captured.[176] Through a resolution passed in January 1840 by the Congress of the Republic of Texas, Kerr received "full remuneration for three month's service as interpreter for the prisoners captured at San Jacinto."[177] Specifically, he received 320 acres of land in Bastrop County for serving in the Texian army from May 1 to August 1, 1836.[178]

By that time, Kerr's fortunes had already improved. He became associated with cattle buyers who were regularly doing business on the Rio

Grande. Knowing the language and, more importantly, the customs of the people, Kerr was of great benefit to the cattlemen, who made more money than they normally did. For this, he was awarded a share of the purchased stock, which he then drove to the Colorado River below Austin.

In 1849, Kerr leased land for cattle grazing from John Hamilton, who had acquired a league and labor of land in what is now Burnet County. About this same time, the military established Fort Croghan on Hamilton's grant. Kerr managed to obtain a contract with the government to furnish beef to the fort. A couple of years later, he obtained a deed from Hamilton to the entire league minus 600 acres that had been sold to someone else. Shortly after getting this acquisition, Kerr executed a contract with the government for the part of the league lying west of Hamilton Creek, which was the area where Fort Croghan was located. Importantly, the contract included a proviso that if the government surrendered the lease, Kerr would get the title to all improvements on the land. This deal paid handsomely when Fort Croghan was abandoned in December 1853 and Kerr took ownership of all the improvements there. He sold 617 acres west of Hamilton Creek, which included the fort, for a substantial profit.

Meanwhile, on the area to the east of Hamilton Creek, Kerr platted a town to be called Hamilton. He did well by selling town lots and, when Burnet County was organized in 1852, he donated ten lots for a courthouse square. Additionally, he donated one hundred acres of land just to the east for the benefit of the town. In 1857, residents of the burgeoning town petitioned to rename the town Burnet.

Kerr had become successful and won the respect of his many friends and neighbors. He was known for his charity. Noah Smithwick noted that "many a poor family blessed the day when Uncle Peter...brought his herds into the country. Anyone was welcome to take up the cows and milk them." He added rather poetically that "whether the heartless desertion of the senorita chilled his heart, rendering it impervious to the smiles of her sex, I cannot say, but he lived and died a bachelor." Despite Smithwick's romantic speculations, the records of the Fourth Texas Congress show that Kerr applied for a divorce. There is no known documentation of who his spouse may have been, or when the marriage took place.[179]

Despite Kerr's successes, he was starting to feel his age and looking for someone to take over his operations and holdings. In an October 1858 letter to his brother, Andrew Kerr, in Pennsylvania, Peter Kerr wrote,

> I wish you were here I would deed every dollar worth my estate to you as I am annoyed with the care of it. You and your sons could take care of it better than I can. I want you to write me when your time is and that you can come. If you do not in case of death there will be nothing for you. There are at least fifty thousand dollars worth. I am tired of making one more dollars worth. I am getting old and can not be troubled much longer. It is now time to rest if ever I expect to.

Fifty thousand dollars in 1858 was certainly a small fortune. Nevertheless, Andrew Kerr never came to Texas. Peter Kerr did have three nephews, W. S. Carothers, H. K. Peffer, and Gilbert A. Searight, who represented the only other members of his family who arrived in Texas. Carothers came to live with Peter Kerr when he was about fifteen years old after both his parents had died. The other two nephews came after Kerr's letter to his brother.[180]

On November 18, 1861, Kerr recorded his last will and testament. In it, he left his sizable land holdings, over 6,300 acres, to Burnet County, as well as three notes that were due to him for about $23,500. Proceeds of the notes and any sale of the land was intended to be used to build a college on the Hamilton league. To Carothers, Kerr left his livestock, wagons, and implements. Carothers also got the right to use Kerr's land for a period of ten years after his death. Three days after submitting his last will and testament, Kerr died. Carothers served as executor of his estate. That decision would prove to be ill-conceived, as his nephew did nothing but undermine Kerr's last wishes.[181]

Carothers unsuccessfully challenged Kerr's will in the district court, then somehow convinced the Burnet County commissioners to accept a judgment by the Texas Supreme Court annulling Kerr's will. Ultimately, all Burnet County received from the estate was two acres for a public school. Meanwhile, Carothers, Peffer, and Searight were the ones who ultimately enjoyed the estate that was intended to benefit the citizens of Burnet County.[182]

Peter Kerr led an adventurous and ultimately successful life. He certainly played a key role in the development of Burnet County. In recognition of these contributions, the Burnet County Historical Society dedicated a historical marker at the Fort Croghan Museum in 1970.[183] There is also a street in Burnet named after Kerr.

SAMUEL G. HARDAWAY

AFTER RECOVERING FROM his harrowing escape from behind enemy lines, sixteen-year-old Samuel G. Hardaway joined the company commanded by Moseley Baker. Young Hardaway served and fought in the decisive battle at San Jacinto, describing the event and its aftermath thusly:

> When we reached within about fifty yards of them we fired two or three rounds from our deadly rifles, which seemed to produce a tremendous effect, and at this moment a charge from all quarters was ordered...the destruction of human life was speedy and immense... The appearance of the battle-ground can better be imagined than described. Piles and clusters of their dead and dying lay in every direction: indeed the ground was literally covered. But the recollection of the dreadful massacre of our brave companions at the Alamo and Goliad in a great manner relieved our feelings from the horrors of the scene.[184]

There is some dispute as to what happened to Hardaway's fellow refugees—James P. Trezevant, M. K. Moses, and Joseph Andrews—after they rejoined the Texians in March 1836. There is ample documentation that Trezevant remained with the army, working as a commissary and acting quartermaster and becoming a brevet major before resigning in November 1836.[185] There is also an audited claim for reimbursement, signed and dated October 26, 1836, by Moses while in Columbia, suggesting that he too remained in service with the army.[186] The audited claim for payment for Andrews included service from December 23, 1835 up to April 10.[187] It may well be that he left the army at that time. No evidence on any muster rolls could be found that any of the three fought at San Jacinto. Trezevant had evidently been dispatched to help raise an additional battalion of men at that time.[188]

On April 30, Hardaway left the Texian army.[189] It was time to return home to Georgia as a hero. However, Hardaway's trip home would prove to be just about as harrowing as the events he endured in Texas. It took eight days for him to travel by foot to Natchitoches. From there, he traveled by boat down the Red River and on to the Gulf of Mexico via New Orleans. At Mobile, he learned of renewed conflict with Creek Indians. Although warned of the extreme danger of trying to cross the Creek Nation, he was anxious to get home, and he managed to find fifteen others who were willing to risk the trip.

The group left in two mail stages on Sunday, May 15, 1836. After a night of travel, they made their way to Tuskegee, where they got breakfast. It was here that they also learned that the trouble with the Indians was every bit as dire as had been presented earlier. Hardaway relates, "we passed on to the next stand and found that it had been plundered. As we continued on, we found every house and place plundered or burnt, and some burning, until we reached Thorn's Stand, about 20 miles from Columbus; there we saw the houses in flames." The stage drivers put the whip to their horses but did not go far before they came upon the previous day's stage "piled up across the road, with the dead horses and one dead white man, [so] that we could not pass." The drivers had to stop–

exactly what the waiting Indians wanted. The Creek warriors attacked and with no room to maneuver the stages, the drivers and passengers cut loose the horses. It was every man for himself. Not everyone was able to obtain a horse. Those that did tried to flee but were fired upon by Indians attacking from all sides.

Hardaway and four others were the unfortunate ones who were not able to procure a horse. All they could do was run. Two men were shot almost immediately. Hardaway describes the frightening scene as follows:

> The moment after they were shot I run directly through where the Indians were that had fired, and as I passed 2 or 3 others fired at me, but without effect. I made the best of my way towards a swamp, which I saw distant 3 or 400 yards, and discovered I was pursued by two Indians. Just before I reached the swamp I turned and discharged my musket at the foremost, which was in 40 or 50 yards of me; I saw him fall, but before I entered the swamp, I saw him rise again. The other Indian ran up to him and stopped a few minutes; during which time I had got in the swamp and reloaded my gun; he then came down to the swamp and appeared to be searching for me, and while he was in the act of parting the cane, I shot him in the body, not more than 15 or 20 yards distant; he fell dead.[190]

Just as had been the case near Victoria and the Guadalupe River, Hardaway once again found himself hiding in a swamp surrounded by enemy forces; this time, however, he was only a few miles away from his home. He stayed in the swamp, surviving by eating berries. He would sneak out at night to try to find a road. It was not until after three days that he found the road where the stages had been left. He traveled through the night back toward Tuskegee, finally arriving near sunrise on May 20, 1836.

Hardaway stayed in Tuskegee for a few days to recover from his ordeal and regain his strength. Finally, he and two others decided to commence their trip once more, but this time via a safer, more northerly route. On the third day of his travels, he crossed the Chattahoochee River and landed once again on Georgian soil.[191]

Years after the war, the Georgia government filed a claim against Texas for state arms and equipment captured by the Mexicans during the war for Texan independence. The first notice from Georgia came from Governor Herschel V. Johnson in a letter dated November 15, 1855. The letter was accompanied by an affidavit from Hardaway. As one of the very few survivors of the Georgia Battalion, his statement carried weight. Governor Elisha M. Pease of Texas, though ignorant of the details of the Georgians' service, thought their state did deserve some payment and stated as much in a message to the Texas legislature that focused in part on Hardaway:

> The affidavit of S. G. Hardaway, a member of one of these companies who escaped at the massacre, and who is well known to many of our citizens, states that the arms and equipment of these two companies were the property of the State of Georgia, and that they were surrendered to the Mexican Army at the capitulation of Col. James W. Fannin. I know nothing in relation to this matter beyond what is disclosed by these papers, but if the facts are as stated by Mr. Hardaway, and I have reason to believe that this statement is true, this state ought to pay the State of Georgia the value of these arms and equipment.[192]

Ultimately, Texas approved a payment of $3,000. Georgia officials decided to use that money to erect a monument at Goliad to honor the men of the Georgia Battalion who had fought there, but for years nothing was done. In 1976, the city of Albany, Texas, erected a fountain and plaque honoring the sacrifice of the Georgia Battalion for Texas independence.

For serving in the Texian army from December 21, 1835, to April 30, 1836, Hardaway received a certificate for 320 acres of land in Goliad County, which he later sold to Joseph Callahan.[193] Considering the young man had fought in two battles and escaped capture, this award may seem inadequate. In fact, Hardaway should have gotten a donation grant of 640 additional acres for having participated in these battles. The issue may be moot, because he never returned to Texas. Instead, he settled in Montgomery, Alabama. He married twice and had a total of twelve children. During May 1861, he enlisted in the army of the Confederate States of America as a captain in the Sixth Alabama Infantry. After the war, he eventually became an adjutant general in the Alabama militia. Hardaway died in January 1873 at the age of 53. His wife Sallie soon afterward was granted a pension for her husband's service in the Texian army almost four decades earlier.[194]

NOTES

INTRODUCTION

1 W. Roy Smith, "The Quarrel Between Governor Smith and the Council of the Provisional Government of the Republic," *The Quarterly of the Texas State Historical Association* 5 (Apr. 1902): 286. Note that early battles of the Texas Revolution were fought by Texian volunteers. The task of forming a regular army had not commenced, and Sam Houston had virtually no one to command.

2 David M. Vigness, *The Revolutionary Decades: The Saga of Texas, 1810–1836* (Austin: Steck-Vaughn Company, 1965), 178–179.

CHAPTER 1: RUNAWAY SCRAPE BEGINS

1 "Compendium of the History of Texas," in *The Texas Almanac of 1860* (Galveston: Richardson & Company, 1859), 52.

2 Eugene C. Barker, "The San Jacinto Campaign," *The Quarterly of the Texas State Historical Association* 4 (Apr. 1901): 242.

3 Andres Barcena and Anselmo Bergara, Interview, Mar. 11, 1836, in Todd Hansen, ed., *The Alamo Reader: A Study in History* (Mechanicsburg, PA: Stackpole Books, 2003), 508–509; Barcena and Bergara, Letter, Mar. 11, 1836, in Hansen, *Alamo Reader*, 509–510; Bergara, interview, 1860s?, in Hansen, *Alamo Reader*, 511. There were contradictory stories of how Barcena and Bergara came to be in Gonzales and how they acquired the information about the Alamo. In an interview years later, Bergara falsely suggested that he had survived the battle.

4 Henderson Yoakum, *History of Texas: From Its First Settlement in 1685 to Its Annexation to the United States in 1846* (2 vols; 1855; reprint, Austin: Steck-Vaughn, 1961), I: 106. Barcena served in Captain Juan N. Seguín's company at the Battle of San Jacinto. Bergara remained a prisoner for some time before finally being released.

5 Walter Lord, *A Time to Stand* (New York: Harper & Brothers, 1961), 179–180. Santa Anna offered to take Susanna Dickinson and her daughter to Mexico City so Angelina could be raised "properly," which she refused. Joe, despite overtures of friendship and freedom from Santa Anna, escaped and later joined the others on the road to Gonzales. See Jack Jackson, ed., and John Wheat, trans., *Almonte's Texas: Juan N. Almonte's 1834 Inspection, Secret Report, and Role in the 1836 Campaign* (Austin: Texas State Historical Association, 2003), 376. Almonte had hired Ben as a cook while he was visiting the United States in 1835 and brought him back to Mexico.

6 Antonio López de Santa Anna, Proclamation, Mar. 7, 1836, in Hansen, *Alamo Reader*, 342–343.

7 Amelia Williams, "A Critical Study of the Siege of the Alamo and of the Personnel of its Defenders, Chapter 4," *Southwestern Historical Quarterly* 37 (Jan. 1934): 161–163; Lord, *Time to Stand*, 125–127.
8 Barker, "San Jacinto Campaign," 293.
9 Moseley Baker, "Letter from Gonzales to the Standing Committee of San Felipe, March 8, 1836," Texas State Library and Archives Commission, *Texans' Fight for Independence Exhibit*, http://www.tsl.texas.gov/sites/ default/files/ public/tslac/exec/ documents/struggles1_2015001_24.pdf [Accessed May 20, 2020].
10 Robert M. Coleman, *Houston Displayed, or Who Won the Battle of San Jacinto?* (Austin: Brick Row Book Shop, 1964), 11–12.
11 Barker, "San Jacinto Campaign," 293, 317.
12 Ethel Z. Rather, "De Witt's Colony," *The Quarterly of the Texas State Historical Association* 8 (Oct. 1904): 160; James V. Woodrick, *Lost Texas Cannons* (Sugar Land, TX: CreateSpace Independent Publishing Platform, 2016), 8. Rather's article is one of the few early sources that acknowledge there were three cannons at Gonzales in 1836.
13 Yoakum, *History of Texas*, I: 87; Sam Houston to James W. Fannin, Mar. 11, 1836, in John Jenkins, ed., *The Papers of the Texas Revolution* (10 vols.; Austin: Presidial Press, 1973), II: 51–54.
14 Barker, "San Jacinto Campaign," 293–294.
15 "Compendium of the History of Texas," 52.
16 James T. DeShields, *Tall Men with Long Rifles* (San Antonio: Naylor Company, 1971), 131–132.
17 Barker, "San Jacinto Campaign," 296. Measles plagued the Texian army throughout the campaign.
18 Barker, "San Jacinto Campaign," 308, 327.
19 DeShields, *Tall Men with Long Rifles*, 129–130. According to Creed Taylor, he and his brother and several others had been dispatched to reconnoiter prior to Susanna Dickinson's arrival and therefore missed the ensuing turmoil and abrupt army departure.
20 Barker, "San Jacinto Campaign," 294.
21 After the war, Houston consistently denied giving orders to burn Gonzales and other settlements. The actions of the army throughout the conflict makes this hard to believe.
22 Henry S. Foote, *Texas and the Texans or Advance of the Anglo-Americans to the South-West* (2 vols.; Austin: Steck Company, 1935), II: 268.
23 Barker, "San Jacinto Campaign," 294.
24 Barker, "San Jacinto Campaign," 295, 308.
25 Elsie Turk Smothers, "Sarah Ann McClure Braches (1811–1894)," in Evelyn M. Carrington, ed., *Women in Early Texas* (1975; reprint, Austin: Texas State Historical Association, 1994), 40–41; Joe Tom Davis, *Historic Towns of Texas, Volume 2: Columbus, Gonzales, Jefferson* (Austin: Eakin Press, 1996), 31. At this time, only Sarah Ann McClure was present since her husband, Bartlett McClure, had been dispatched to recruit more volunteers in East Texas.
26 Smothers, "Sarah Ann McClure Braches," 41; Davis, *Historic Towns of Texas*, Vol. 2, p. 31.

27 Robert H. Hunter, *Narrative of Robert Hancock Hunter* (Austin: Encino Press, 1966), 10–11.
28 Barker, "San Jacinto Campaign," 295–296.
29 Barker, "San Jacinto Campaign," 296.
30 James K. Baker, "The Lavaca River Trench and Lost Cannon," *Journal of South Texas* 22 (Fall 2005): 145–154.
31 Houston, Army Orders, Mar. 14, 1836, in Jenkins, *Papers of the Texas Revolution*, V: 77–78. It may have been coincidental, but it is no less interesting, that Houston's orders put Austin and Wharton in proximity to one another. John A. Wharton and his brother William were strong and early advocates of Texan independence and became increasingly frustrated with Austin's conciliatory attitude toward Mexico. The hostility grew to the point that John Wharton and William T. Austin (a distant relative of Stephen's) became engaged in a duel. Wharton's hand was permanently injured. By the time of the Texas Revolution, the two families had seemingly reconciled. See Bartee Haile, *Unforgettable Texans* (Charleston, SC: History Press, 2017), 22.
32 Houston, Army Orders, Mar. 14, 1836, in Jenkins, *Papers of the Texas Revolution*, V: 77–78.
33 John A. Wharton to William T. Austin, Mar. 18, 1836, in Jenkins, *Papers of the Texas Revolution*, V: 138–139.
34 Barker, "San Jacinto Campaign," 296. Kuykendall stated that later that night, Houston reprimanded Rhodes and then ordered him released.
35 Stephen L. Moore, *Eighteen Minutes: The Battle of San Jacinto and the Texas Independence Campaign* (Lanham, MD: Republic of Texas Press, 2004), 69–70; Barker, "San Jacinto Campaign," 296.
36 Barker, "San Jacinto Campaign," 296.
37 James E. Brasher, "A Pivotal Battle Never Fought," *The Texas Gun Collector* (Fall 2018): 28.
38 Foote, *Texas and the Texans*, II: 269.

CHAPTER 2: TO THE COLORADO–DAY 1, MARCH 16

1 Barker, "San Jacinto Campaign," 275.
2 Houston, Army Orders, Mar. 14, 1836, in Jenkins, *Papers of the Texas Revolution*, V: 77–78.
3 William P. Zuber, "Notes and Fragments: Capt. Jesse Burnam's Name," *The Quarterly of the Texas State Historical Association* 5 (Oct. 1901): 164. Zuber discussed the inconsistent spelling of Burnam's name. Family member signatures vary through time, but the spelling on Jesse's tombstone is 'Burnam'. It seems that over time, 'Burnham' has usurped the original spelling. In this document, 'Burnam' will be used unless a direct quote uses the alternate spelling.

4 Houston to James T. Collinsworth, Mar. 15, 1836, in Jenkins, *Papers of the Texas Revolution*, V: 82–84; Ernest R. Lindley, comp., *Biographical Directory of the Texas Conventions and Congresses, 1832–1845* (Austin: Book Exchange, 1941), 69–70. Collinsworth, a fellow Tennessean, nominated Houston to be general-in-chief. He later served as Secretary of State for the Republic of Texas, an envoy to the United States to seek recognition as an independent nation, and the first Chief Justice of the Supreme Court of Texas.

5 Barker, "San Jacinto Campaign," 275.

6 Stephen F. Austin, *Original Map of Texas by Citizen, Stephen F. Austin, presented to His Excellency the President by the Author, 1829*, from Texas General Land Office, *Map Store*, https://s3.glo.texas.gov/glo/history/ archives/map-store/index.cfm#item/76201 [Accessed Feb. 2, 2019].

7 Calavera is Spanish for skull. In subsequent maps, this creek would be called Skull Creek, as it is today.

8 Austin, *Original Map of Texas by Citizen, 1829*.

9 Stephen F. Austin and James F. Perry, *Connected Map of Austin's Colony*, from Texas General Land Office, *Map Store*, https://s3.glo.texas.gov/glo/history/archives/map-store/index.cfm#item/1943 [Accessed Feb. 18, 2019].

10 Houston to Collinsworth, Mar. 15, 1836, in Jenkins, *Papers of the Texas Revolution*, V: 82–84.

11 Barker, "San Jacinto Campaign," 275.

12 Moore, *Eighteen Minutes*, 74.

13 Samuel E. Asbury, ed., "The Private Journal of Juan Nepomuceno Almonte," *Southwestern Historical Quarterly* 48 (July 1944): 27.

14 Yoakum, *History of Texas*, I: 75; John H. Brown, *History of Texas from 1685 to 1892* (2 vols.; St. Louis: L. E. Daniell,1893), I: 587; Paul D. Lack, ed., *The Diary of William Fairfax Gray: from Virginia to Texas, 1835–1837* (Dallas: DeGolyer Library & William P. Clements Center for Southwest Studies, 1997), 117; Alexander Horton, "Life of A. Horton and Early Settlement of San Augustine County," *The Quarterly of the Texas State Historical Association* 14 (Apr. 1911): 305–314. Houston purportedly traveled with his friend and confidant Colonel George W. Hockley, Colonel Alexander Horton, Lieutenant Richardson Scurry, Captain William Cook, Captain James Tarleton, and possibly others. Horton claims that Houston arrived in Gonzales with him, Hockley, Scurry, and one other man.

15 William P. Zuber, "Notes and Fragments: Last Messenger from the Alamo," *The Quarterly of the Texas State Historical Association* 5 (Jan. 1902): 263–265.

16 Horatio Chriesman, *Surveys in Austin's Colony by Horatio Chriesman along Mill and Cummins Creeks*, 1830, from Texas General Land Office, *Map Store*, http://s3.glo.texas.gov/glo/history/archives/map-store/index. cfm#item/68 [Accessed Mar. 10, 2019].

17 Galen D. Greaser, Douglas J. Howard, and Michael T. Moore, *Austin's Colony 1821–1836: In Commemoration of the Two Hundredth Birthday of Stephen F. Austin* (Austin: Texas General Land Office, 1993).

18   James L. Haley, *Sam Houston* (Norman: University of Oklahoma Press, 2002), 123; Jesse Burnam, Property Destroyed in 1836 [submitted in 1874], Texas Legislature, Memorials and Petitions, 1834–1929, Miscellaneous, Oversize Box 7 (Texas State Library and Archives Commission, Austin, henceforth cited as TSLA; online, Images 342–355). William W. W. Thompson's testimony was part of Burnam's petition.
19   Amelia W. Williams and Eugene C. Barker, eds., *The Writings of Sam Houston 1813–1835*. (8 vols.; Austin: University of Texas Press, 1938), I: 360–361.
20   Barker, "San Jacinto Campaign," 317.
21   Iris R. Guertin, *Navidad Country* (Sugar Land, TX: CreateSpace Independent Publishing Platform, 2009), 669. In 1837, Thompson would sell his land to Burnam and settle with him at his property on the Colorado River.
22   William H. Smith, July 30, 1830, Texas Comptroller, Republic Claims, Audited Claim Number 7972 (TSLA, online: Reel Number 98, Image Number 374); Moore, *Eighteen Minutes*, 74. Though not much tends to be heard of William H. Smith, Houston promoted him to an important position. Henry W. Karnes and Erastus "Deaf" Smith at this point were still used more for scouting.
23   Burnam, Property Destroyed in 1836. Smith mistakes General Joaquín Ramírez y Sesma's command for that of General Martín Perfecto de Cos.
24   Alsbury, "Private Journal of Almonte," 26–27.
25   Brasher, "Pivotal Battle Never Fought," 28.
26   Some documents say that the Texian army reached Burnam's on March 17, 1836. Houston, in his letter to Collinsworth dated March 17, stated that his men had just arrived at Burnam's. However, he may have arrived on the afternoon of March 16th, but the letter did not go out until the following day and is thus dated March 17. Also, Houston reported that the army was camped at the Navidad on March 15, which would beg the question, what was the army doing on March 16 if they did not arrive at Burnam's until March 17? Note that Somervell's letter to Perry was sent from Burnam's on March 16. Kuykendall, who seems to have documented events well, also puts the arrival at Burnam's on March 16.
27   Houston to Collinsworth, Mar. 17, 1836, in Jenkins, *Papers of the Texas Revolution* V: 122–124.
28   Somervell to Perry, Mar. 16, 1836, in Jenkins, *Papers of the Texas Revolution*, V: 92.
29   Barker, "San Jacinto Campaign," 317–318.
30   Somervell to Perry, Mar. 16, 1836, in Jenkins, *Papers of the Texas Revolution*, V: 92.
31   Moore, *Eighteen Minutes*, 29–31.

CHAPTER 3: CROSSING AT BURNAM'S FERRY–DAY 2, MARCH 17

1   Barker, "San Jacinto Campaign," 297.
2   Walter P. Freytag, ed., *Chronicles of Fayette: The Reminiscences of Julia Lee Sinks* (Schulenburg, TX: Schulenburg Printing & Office Supplies, Inc.), 11. Temperance Burnam's maiden name is sometimes referenced as Baker rather than Nalle. Baker was evidently the name of the family she lived with for some time.

3 "A Texas Nonagenarian," *Burke's Texas Almanac and Immigrant's Handbook for 1883* (Houston: J. Burke, 1883), 39. Nancy Burnam was born in 1822. While Jesse Burnam did not move his family to the Colorado until 1823, Nancy was probably born near Independence, Texas, and was indeed the first Anglo child born in Austin's Colony.
4 Julia Lee Sinks, ed., "Reminiscences of Capt. Jesse Burnam," *The Quarterly of the Texas State Historical Association* 5 (July 1901): 13–18.
5 Militia Election, May 28, 1824, in Eugene C. Barker, ed., *The Austin Papers* (3 vols.; Washington: Government Printing Press, 1924–1928), II, Part 1: 806–807.
6 Sinks, "Reminiscences of Burnam," 14–18.
7 Noah Smithwick, *The Evolution of a State or Recollections of Old Texas Days* (Austin: University of Texas Press, 1983), 23–24.
8 Emma Holman Scott, "Amanda Burnam Holman (1823–1863)," in Carrington, *Women in Early Texas*, 123.
9 Jesse and Temperance Burnam had nine children, but one died in childbirth.
10 Vigness, *Revolutionary Decades*, 192; Ethel M. Willey, *Capt. Jesse Burnam, A Texas Pioneer* (Waco: Davis Brothers Publishing Company, 1997), 15. Willey generated a map depicting the road through Burnam's Ferry as a "Branch of the La Bahía." Even historical markers mistakenly locate the crossing on the La Bahía Road.
11 A. L. Bradford and T. N. Campbell, eds., "Notes and Documents: Journal of Lincecum's Travels in Texas, 1835," *Southwestern Historical Quarterly* 53 (Oct. 1949), 192–193; Lois W. Burkhalter, *Gideon Lincecum 1793–1874* (Austin: University of Texas Press, 1965), 39.
12 Burkhalter, *Gideon Lincecum*, 39, 49–50. In May 1835, Lincecum was on his way home and stopped to see his friend Gail Borden, who was sick in San Felipe. While there, Moseley Baker came by looking for recruits and persuaded Lincecum to join as surgeon for forces west of the Brazos. Though he was eager to participate, some old acquaintances, one of which was William B. Travis, brow-beat him into giving up his position owing to his wife and ten children back home. Despite the displeasure of Baker, Lincecum managed to extract himself from service and made his way back to his home in Mississippi. Twelve years later, he returned to Texas with his family for good.
13 Scott, "Amanda Burnam Holman," 123.
14 Willey, *Jesse Burnam*, 44.
15 Amelia Williams, "A Critical Study of the Siege of the Alamo and of the Personnel of its Defenders, Chapter 1," *Southwestern Historical Quarterly* 36 (Apr. 1933): 271.
16 Louis J. Wortham, *A History of Texas: From Wilderness to Commonwealth* (5 vols.; Fort Worth: Wortham-Molyneaux Company, 1924), II: 336.
17 Lindley, *Biographical Directory of Texas Conventions and Congresses*, 59.
18 Austin to Permanent Council, Oct. 26, 1835, in Barker, *Austin Papers*, III: 212. The Consultation of 1835 was originally scheduled to begin on October 15, but due to confusion over where it was being held and the late arrival of delegates, it was pushed back until November 1.
19 Jesús F. de la Teja, ed., *A Revolution Remembered: The Memoirs and Selected Correspondence of Juan N. Seguín* (Austin: Texas State Historical Association, 2002), 81.

20 Houston to Collinsworth, Mar. 17, 1836, in Jenkins, *Papers of the Texas Revolution*, V: 122–123.
21 M. K. Wisehart, *Sam Houston, American Giant* (New York: Van Rees Press, 1962), 189.
22 Barker, "San Jacinto Campaign," 297.
23 Smothers, "Sarah Ann McClure Braches," 40–41; Davis, *Historic Towns of Texas*, Vol. 2, p. 31. Knowing that Gonzales had been burned, Sarah Ann McClure allegedly penned a letter in both Spanish and English pleading with both armies for her house to avoid suffering the same fate. Although almost everything else was destroyed by the Mexican army, the house remained intact.
24 José Enrique de la Peña, *With Santa Anna in Texas: A Personal Narrative of the Revolution*, trans. By Carmen Perry (College Station: Texas A&M University Press, 1975), 103.
25 Jesse Burnam, Nov. 5, 1836, Republic Claims, Audited Claim Number 1450 (TSLA, online: Reel Number 13, Image Number 490).
26 Burnam, Property Destroyed in 1836. William Patton would also provide an affidavit on behalf of Jesse Burnam, although he stated that it was Hockley that gave the order.
27 Burnam, Property Destroyed in 1836.
28 Burnam, Property Destroyed in 1836.
29 Sam H. Dixon and Louis W. Kemp, *The Heroes of San Jacinto* (Houston: Anson Jones Press, 1932), 208; John H. Burnam, Feb. 17, 1837, Republic Claims, Audited Claim Number 574 (TSLA, online: Reel Number 13, Image Numbers 511–512, 514–516). John H. Burnam was originally omitted from the San Jacinto rolls.
30 William P. Zuber, *My Eighty Years in Texas*, ed. Janis Boyle Mayfield (Austin: University of Texas Press, 1971), 57. James Ross's farm would have been across the river and slightly north of Burnam's Ferry.
31 Andrew Crier, June 18, 1836, Republic Claims, Audited Claim Unnumbered 01 (TSLA, online: Reel Number 21, Image Numbers 527–528). Technically, Andrew Crier joined Houston's army on March 18, 1836.
32 With the news that his expeditions to Refugio had been unsuccessful, Fannin resigned himself to finally withdrawing and slowly began preparations to evacuate Goliad.
33 Houston to Collinsworth, Mar. 17, 1836, in Jenkins, *Papers of the Texas Revolution*, V: 122. Cox's Point, or Cox Point, and Dimitt's Landing are located near the mouth of the Lavaca River. Both increased in importance as Mexican troops occupied other entry points. It was near here that Mexican cavalry captured William Ward and his command. Houston obviously thought that Fannin was in Victoria by this point.
34 Houston to Collinsworth, Mar. 17, 1836, in Jenkins, *Papers of the Texas Revolution*, V: 122–124.
35 Gregg J. Dimmick, *Sea of Mud: The Retreat of the Mexican Army After San Jacinto, An Archeological Investigation* (Austin: Texas State Historical Association, 2004), 37–38.
36 Peña, *With Santa Anna in Texas*, 22.
37 Houston to Collinsworth, Mar. 17, 1836, in Jenkins, *Papers of the Texas Revolution*, V: 122–124.
38 Barker, "San Jacinto Campaign," 297.

39 Hockley to Rusk, Mar. 21, 1836, in Jenkins, *Papers of the Texas Revolution*, V: 152–153.
40 Marquis James, *The Raven: A Biography of Sam Houston* (Indianapolis: Bobbs-Merrill Company, 1929), 235–236.

CHAPTER 4: CRIER'S CREEK–DAY 3, MARCH 18

1 Houston to Collinsworth, Mar. 17, 1836, in Jenkins, *Papers of the Texas Revolution*, V: 124.
2 Houston to Collinsworth, Mar. 17, 1836, in Jenkins, *Papers of the Texas Revolution*, V: 124.
3 Foote, *Texas and the Texans*, II: 269.
4 Stephen Hardin, *Texian Iliad: A Military History of the Texas Revolution* (Austin: University of Texas Press, 1996), 85–86.
5 Hockley to Rusk, Mar. 21, 1836, in Jenkins, *Papers of the Texas Revolution*, V: 152.
6 Foote, *Texas and the Texans*, II: 269–271, 273.
7 Moore, *Eighteen Minutes*, 469; Dixon and Kemp, *Heroes of San Jacinto*, 377.
8 Foote, *Texas and the Texans*, II: 269–271, 273.
9 Baker and Edward Burleson to Franklin J. Starr, Mar. 17, 1836, in Jenkins, *Papers of the Texas Revolution*, V: 98.
10 Jonathan N. Cravens, *James Harper Starr: Financier of the Republic of Texas* (Austin: Daughters of the Republic of Texas, 1950), 15–16. Franklin J. Starr, the brother of James H. Starr, was responsible for making Travis' diary available after his death.
11 Zuber, *My Eighty Years in Texas*, 52–53.
12 Zuber, *My Eighty Years in Texas*, 54–55.
13 Zuber, *My Eighty Years in Texas*, 56–57.
14 Lester G. Bugbee, "The Old Three Hundred," *The Quarterly of the Texas State Historical Association* 1 (Oct. 1897): 113. This Thomas Gray died in 1827 and should not be confused with the Thomas Gray that fought in the Battle of San Jacinto.
15 Fayette County History Book Committee, *Fayette County, Texas Heritage* (2 vols.; Raleigh, NC: Curtis Media, 1996), I: 95.
16 Zuber, *My Eighty Years in Texas*, 51–52.
17 Fayette County History Book Committee. *Fayette County, Texas Heritage*, I: 2.
18 Fayette County History Book Committee. *Fayette County, Texas Heritage*, I: 95.
19 Terry G. Jordan, *Texas Log Buildings, A Folk Architecture* (Austin: University of Texas Press, 1978), 159.
20 James M. Day, comp., *The Texas Almanac, 1857–1873, A Compendium of Texas History* (Waco: Texian Press, 1967), 667–668.
21 Freytag, *Chronicles of Fayette*, 22. James Ross married the eldest daughter of Judge James Cummins, Mariah, before their trip to Texas. Some years later, he divorced Mariah, and married another daughter of the Judge, Nancy, who would later become Jesse Burnam's second wife. John H. Moore married yet another Cummins sister, Eliza.
22 Mirabeau B. Lamar, Information from A. Rabb Colorado [River] Earlieast [sic] Settlers and Indians Toubles [sic], 184?, in Charles A. Gulick Jr. et al., eds., *The Papers of Mirabeau Buonaparte Lamar* (6 vols.; 1921–1927; reprint, Austin: Pemberton Press, 1968), IV, Part 1: 215–216.

23 Wortham, *History of Texas*, II: 335, 353–354.
24 An Old Soldier, "First Breaking Out of the Texas Revolution at Gonzales," in *The Texas Almanac for 1861* (Galveston: Richardson & Company, 1860), 60–61.
25 Old Soldier, "First Breaking Out," 61.
26 Hubert H. Bancroft, *History of the North Mexican States and Texas: 1531–1889* (2 vol.; San Francisco: History Company Publishers, 1889), II: 165.
27 Rather, "De Witt's Colony," 155–156; Wortham, *History of Texas*, II; 336–337.
28 Rather, "De Witt's Colony," 157.
29 Wortham, *History of Texas*, II: 360.
30 Austin to Moore, Oct. 26, 1835, in Jenkins, *Papers of the Texas Revolution*, II:221.
31 Travis to Austin, Nov. 6, 1835, in Barker, *Austin Papers*, III: 242.
32 John H. Moore, Apr. 17, 1838, Republic Claims, Audited Claim Number 7092 (TSLA, online: Reel Number 73, Image Number 634).
33 Zuber, *My Eighty Years in Texas*, 52. Zuber said that the Moore family had left by the time his company reached his property, but they "found six men occupying one of his houses, faring well on his provisions the family had left."
34 Dixon and Kemp, *Heroes of San Jacinto*, 239. Ironically, by the time this company was fully formed, the members of the convention had long since scattered and shortly thereafter, the town was abandoned.

CHAPTER 5: ON THE MOVE–DAY 4, MARCH 19

1 Foote, *Texas and the Texans*, II: 270.
2 John Crier, Aug. 14, 1837, Republic Claims, Audited Claim Number 3124 (TSLA, online: Reel Number 21, Image Numbers 529–535).
3 Zuber, *My Eighty Years in Texas*, 57.
4 Thomas L. Miller, *Bounty and Donation Land Grants of Texas, 1835–1888* (Austin: University of Texas Press, 1967), 199.
5 Moseley's Crossing was named after Robert Moseley who lived in the area, opposite the river from Dewees.
6 Barker, "San Jacinto Campaign," 297.
7 Zuber, *My Eighty Years in Texas*, 58.
8 Barker, "San Jacinto Campaign," 297.
9 Historian Eugene C. Barker, a prolific author and editor of events during this time, seems to agree that March 20, 1836, is the most likely arrival date.
10 The contingent proceeding to Beeson's place had to cross an additional small creek, Sandy Branch.
11 Freytag, *Chronicles of Fayette*, 26–27.

12 Jackson and Wheat, *Almonte's Texas*, 394. There is some controversy as to the date that Karnes and company had their encounter. Sharp put the date on March 16, which is clearly incorrect. His recollections were written many years later and his dates were understandably inaccurate. Hockley, in a letter to Rusk dated March 21, described this incident as having occurred yesterday (i.e., March 20). However, he later described actions that occurred later than March 21, suggesting that he held the letter for some time before dating it and mailing it. The date used here was recorded by Colonel Juan N. Almonte of the Mexican army who, in his very detailed journal, described this incident as occurring on Saturday, March 19, 1836. This date seems to best fit the overall timeline.
13 The Rocky Creek mentioned is the same one where Private Rhoades got in trouble for stopping to drink a few days earlier. That creek extends west as a tributary off the Navidad River into present-day Lavaca County and was commonly referenced in accounts of the time.
14 Foote, *Texas and the Texans*, II: 270.
15 Hockley to Rusk, Mar. 21, 1836, in Jenkins, *Papers of the Texas Revolution*, V: 152–153. Hockley recounted that Karnes encountered twelve of the enemy.
16 Foote, *Texas and the Texans*, II: 270.
17 Foote, *Texas and the Texans*, II: 270.
18 Hockley to Rusk, Mar. 21, 1836, in Jenkins, *Papers of the Texas Revolution*, V: 152–153. Certainly, General Sesma's command was heavily involved in the Battle of the Alamo, and it would not be surprising to see some of the spoils of that battle carried by a Mexican soldier, perhaps to his misfortune.
19 Foote, *Texas and the Texans*, II: 270–271.
20 Foote, *Texas and the Texans*, II: 271. This action likely contributed to Thompson's bitterness toward Houston, as displayed in later testimony.
21 Foote, *Texas and the Texans*, II: 271.
22 Foote, *Texas and the Texans*, II: 271.

CHAPTER 6: ARRIVING AT BEESON'S–DAY 5, MARCH 20

1 Barker, "San Jacinto Campaign," 334.
2 James W. Winters, "An Account of the Battle of San Jacinto," *The Quarterly of the Texas State Historical Association* 6 (Oct. 1902): 139–140. In 1901, Winters returned to San Jacinto with the Texas Veterans Association and designated important sites on the battlefield as he remembered them. These points were later permanently marked by the Daughters of the Republic of Texas.
3 Dixon and Kemp, *Heroes of San Jacinto*, 357.
4 Foote, *Texas and the Texans*, II: 271. Considering that the guard Karnes' scouts met was under the command of Captain Wyly Martin, it seems likely that his company was already there awaiting Houston's arrival.
5 Lindley, *Biographical Directory of Texas Conventions and Congresses*, 15, 17, 19–20, 134. An *alcalde* might be considered equivalent to a mayor and/or justice of the peace for a municipality.

6 Lindley, *Biographical Directory of Texas Conventions and Congresses*, 134. Martin in fact outranked Houston during the War of 1812.
7 Dixon and Kemp, *Heroes of San Jacinto*, 365.
8 Nicholas D. Labadie, "San Jacinto Campaign," in *The Texas Almanac for 1859* (Galveston: Richardson & Co., 1858), 41.
9 Moore, *Eighteen Minutes*, 100.
10 Nicholas D. Labadie, "Narrative of the Anahuac, or Opening Campaign of the Texas Revolution," in *Texas Almanac for 1859*, pp. 30, 42–43. Labadie was the surgeon of the Mexican garrison at Anahuac.
11 Moore, *Eighteen Minutes*, 100.
12 Ebenezer R. Hale, Sept. 9, 1836, Republic Claims, Audited Claim Number 7604 (TSLA, online: Reel Number 39, Image Numbers 334–335); Moore, *Eighteen Minutes*, 100. Daniel Perry's company eventually merged with Captain William Fisher's company (Velasco Blues).
13 Zuber, *My Eighty Years in Texas*, 43, 57; Thomas W. Cutrer, "Bennett, Joseph L.," *Handbook of Texas Online, Texas State Historical Association*, https://tshaonline.org/handbook/entries/bennett-joseph-l [Accessed Mar. 16, 2021]; Louis W. Kemp, "Veteran Biographies: Joseph L. Bennett," *San Jacinto Museum of History*, https://www.sanjacinto-museum.org/Library/Veteran_Bios/Bio_page/?id=59&army=Texian [Accessed Mar. 6, 2021]. . Bennett later became a lieutenant colonel under Sidney Sherman and fought gallantly at San Jacinto. He wrote to Houston afterwards that he led Sherman's regiment while Sherman "left in great haste for a small island of timber, about three hundred yards distant, in the rear of our left wing, where he secured himself, and remained...until the enemy had all fled." See Williams and Barker, *Writings of Sam Houston*, VII: 322–323. Bennett's claims concerning Sherman may be dubious, but Houston praised his actions in the battle and beyond and promoted him to colonel and commander of a regiment of mounted gunmen. Houston thus had critics, but he earned staunch allies as well.
14 Stephen L. Moore, *Savage Frontier: Rangers, Riflemen, and Indian Wars in Texas* (4 vols.; Denton: University of North Texas Press, 2002–2010), I: 84–85. Stephen Townsend served as sheriff of Colorado County from 1837 to 1838 before eventually settling near Round Top in Fayette County.
15 Zuber, *My Eighty Years in Texas*, 58.
16 Zuber, *My Eighty Years in Texas*, 58. Zuber mentioned a company arriving commanded by a lieutenant with the nickname "Black Hawk." This was likely Henry Teal.
17 Lack, *Diary of Gray*, 122. Teal later contracted measles, which prevented his participation in the Battle of San Jacinto.
18 Hockley to Rusk, Mar. 23, 1836, in Jenkins, *Papers of the Texas Revolution*, V: 167; Zuber, *My Eighty Years in Texas*, 58. Houston and Rusk referred to Dewees' Ford as Mosely's [sic] Crossing after Robert Moseley, who lived on the east bank of the river where Sherman's command was stationed.
19 Barker, "San Jacinto Campaign," 334; Rhoda Hunt, Nov. 22, 1853, Republic Claims, Unpaid and Miscellaneous Claim Number N/A (TSLA, online: Reel Number 252, Image Number 370–371).

20 Hunt, Nov. 22, 1853, Republic Claims, Unpaid and Miscellaneous Claim Number N/A.
21 Joseph W. E. Wallace, July 4, 1874, Republic Claims, Pension Claim Number N/A (TSLA, online: Reel Number 244, Image Numbers 94–97); Houston, Army Order, Mar. 26, 1836, in Jenkins, *Papers of the Texas Revolution*, V: 200. A few days later, Houston mentioned Wallace in one of his written orders. Wallace, however, did not stay with the main army for long but rather was tasked with trying to convince the Coushatta Indians to fight with the Texians against Mexico.
22 Wallace, Nov. 23, 1837, Republic Claims, Audited Claim Number 5135. One wonders whether Houston approved the delivery of whiskey to Sherman's encampment at Dewees'. Perhaps it was for 'medicinal' purposes. Wallace had another store at Matagorda, from which he supplied provisions to the Texas army as well.
23 Houston, Army Orders, Mar. 17, 1836, in Jenkins, *Papers of the Texas Revolution*, V: 122.
24 Hunter, *Narrative of Robert Hancock Hunter*, 11–12.
25 Foote, *Texas and the Texans*, II: 273.
26 Jackson and Wheat, *Almonte's Texas*, 395.
27 Robert E. Davis, ed., *The Diary of William Barrett Travis* (Waco: Texian Press, 1966), 91.
28 Bill Stein, "Beyond Boosterism: Establishing the Age of Columbus," *Nesbitt Memorial Library Journal* 2 (May 1992): 85; John J. Tumlinson, Petition, Dec. 19, 1833, Texas, Colorado County, Deed Records, Book J, 626–629, County Clerk Records, Colorado County Courthouse, Columbus, TX.
29 *William B. Dewees v. Martha Bronson (alias Bostick)*, Sep. 28, 1839, Texas Twenty-Fifth District Court, Civil Records, Case File Number CV63, Case ID Number 33306, Colorado County Courthouse, Columbus, TX. The case in which Wallace gave his testimony was for Dewees to recover costs from Bronson for using his teams to move her house. The implication may be that Bronson requested that her house be moved. Regardless, this seems bizarre.
30 Barker, "San Jacinto Campaign," 334.
31 Austin to James E. B. Austin, Jan. 1, 1823, in Barker, *Austin Papers*, II, Part 1: 565–566.
32 Austin to the Colonists, Aug. 6, 1823, in Barker, *Austin Papers*, II, Part 1: 679–681.
33 Austin to Josiah H. Bell, Aug. 29, 1823, in Barker, *Austin Papers*, II, Part 1: 689–690.
34 William B. Dewees, *Letters from an Early Settler of Texas* (1852; reprint, Waco: Texian Press, 1968), 42. In his publication, Dewees had a habit of inserting himself into important events in Texas. This was likely done for dramatic effect. But whether Dewees accompanied Austin or not, his description is a fair one.
35 Elizabeth Tumlinson, English Field Notes, in Texas General Land Office, *Land Grant Search: Colorado County,* https://s3.glo.texas.gov/glo/history/archives/land-grants/landgrants.cfm?intID=150584 [Accessed Nov. 16, 2021]. Rawson Alley supplied field notes in English of his early surveys. He surveyed virtually all the early land grants along the Colorado from southern Fayette County into Wharton County.
36 Jonathan H. Kuykendall, ed., "Reminiscences of Early Texans, I," *The Quarterly of the Texas State Historical Association* 6 (Jan. 1903): 248.
37 Stephen F. Austin, *Mapa Geographico de la Provincia de Tejas*, 1822, from Texas General Land Office, *Map Store* (Non-GLO Digital Images Collection) https://s3.glo.texas.gov/glo/history/archives/map-store/index. cfm#item/ 94457 [Accessed Mar. 9, 2019].

38 Stephen F. Austin, *A Map of Austin's Colony and Adjacent Country in Texas Drawn Principally from Actual Survey by Stephen F. Austin*, from Texas General Land Office, Map Store (Non-GLO Digital Images Collection) https://s3.glo.texas.gov/glo/history/archives/map-store/index.cfm#item/93353 [Accessed Feb. 20, 2019]. A thorough explanation as to how the name of Montezuma migrated from Atascosito Crossing to where the town of Columbus was eventually situated can be found in Stein, "Beyond Boosterism," 74–75.
39 Ernest W. Winkler, ed., *Manuscript Letters and Documents of Early Texians, 1821–1845* (Austin: Steck Company, 1937), 24–25; Bill Stein, "Consider the Lily: The Ungilded History of Colorado County (Part 1)," *Nesbitt Memorial Library Journal* 6 (Jan. 1996a): 9–10.
40 Bugbee, "Old Three Hundred," 110.
41 Jack Jackson, ed., *Texas by Terán: The Diary Kept by General Manuel de Mier y Terán on His 1828 Inspection of Texas* (Austin: University of Texas Press, 2000), 52–53, 216.
42 Mary Austin Holley, *Texas* (1833; reprint, Austin: Texas State Historical Association, 1990), 200.
43 Census Report, Dec. 31, 1825, in Barker, *Austin Papers*, II, Part 2: 1,244.
44 Jackson, *Texas by Terán*, 52–53, 216.
45 Jean Louis Berlandier, *Journey to Mexico During the Years 1826 to 1834*, trans. Sheila M. Ohlendorf, Josette M. Bigelow, and Mary M. Standifer (2 vols.; Austin: Texas State Historical Association, 1980), II: 314. Camotes are sweet potatoes. .
46 Bugbee, "Old Three Hundred," 108–109.
47 Bugbee, "Old Three Hundred," 108–109; Bill Stein, "Consider the Lily: The Ungilded History of Colorado County (Part 2)," *Nesbitt Memorial Library Journal* 6 (Jan. 1996b): 39.
48 Winkler, *Early Texians*, 28–29; Dan E. Kilgore, *A Ranger Legacy: 150 Years of Service to Texas* (Austin: Madrona Press, 1973), 21–26; Austin, Address to Colonists, Aug. 5, 1823?, in Barker, *Austin Papers*, II, Part 1: 678–679. Later in 1823, Austin would recommend forming a group of men "to act as rangers" to defend against Indians.
49 Bugbee, "Old Three Hundred," 117.
50 *Texas Gazette* (San Felipe de Austin), Mar. 13, 1830.
51 Stein, "Consider the Lily (Part 2)," 44.
52 Davis, *Diary of Travis*, 158–159.
53 Jackson and Wheat, *Almonte's Texas*, 398.
54 Austin to Permanent Council, Oct. 8, 1835, in Barker, *Austin Papers*, III: 166–167. Ironically, in this letter, Austin was trying to arrange for a cannon to be delivered to San Felipe. Houston would suffer a similar plight while part of his army was at Moseley's in March 1836.
55 Thomas Earle, ed., *The Life, Travels, and Opinions of Benjamin Lundy* (New York: Augustus M. Kelley, 1971), 123.
56 Stein, "Consider the Lily (Part 2)," 37.

57 Eugene C. Barker, ed., "Minutes of the Ayuntamiento of San Felipe de Austin, 1828–1832, III," *Southwestern Historical Quarterly* 22 (July 1918): 80–81; Stein, "Consider the Lily (Part 2)," 37. When Austin's Colony was elevated to the status of municipality, governance of many local issues was accorded to a council called an *ayuntamiento*. This council usually consisted of an *alcalde*, two *regidors*, and a *síndico procurador*. This might be loosely equivalent to a mayor, councilmen, and a city attorney.

58 Stein, "Consider the Lily (Part 2)," 37.

59 Stein, "Beyond Boosterism," 85.

60 Petition Asking for a New Municipality to be Called Colorado, n.d. [Dec. 1835], Memorials and Petitions, 1834-1929 (TSLA, online: Images 197–198); Colorado County Historical Survey Committee and Historic Preservation Committee, comp., *Early Settlers and Bits of History of Columbus and Colorado County, 1821–1845* (Columbus, TX: [n.p.], 1973), 26.

61 Stein, "Beyond Boosterism," 83. There is also a thought that the town was named after Columbus, Ohio, though there is no obvious connection to that town. Dewees did spend time in communities in Arkansas and Kentucky that ultimately were named Columbus, but the name did not stick until after Dewees had left that area.

62 Burkhalter, *Gideon Lincecum*, 25–26, 39, 48–49.

63 H.P.N. Gammel, comp., *The Laws of Texas: 1822–1897* (10 vols.; Austin: Gammel Book Company, 1898), I: 757.

64 Baker to Editors and Hockley to Rusk, Mar. 23, 1836, in Jenkins, *Papers of the Texas Revolution*, V: 159, 167; *Telegraph and Texas Register* (San Felipe de Austin), Mar. 24, 1836.

CHAPTER 7: BEESON'S & DEWEES'–DAY 6, MARCH 21

1 Barker, "San Jacinto Campaign," 298.

2 Williams and Barker, *Writings of Sam Houston*, I: 361. Travis was in charge of the regulars and James Bowie commanded the volunteers at the Alamo. When Bowie became ill, Travis became the de facto commander of all forces in the Alamo.

3 Houston to Collinsworth, Mar. 15, 1836, in Jenkins, *Papers of the Texas Revolution*, V: 83.

4 Moore, *Savage Frontier*, I: 65. Lamar left Texas again on business but returned just before the Battle of San Jacinto, in which he firmly cemented himself as a hero of Texas.

5 Kilgore, *Ranger Legacy*, 41.

6 Moore, *Savage Frontier*, I: 108–109.

7 Hockley to Rusk, Mar. 21, 1836, in Jenkins, *Papers of the Texas Revolution*, V: 152.

8 Houston Army Orders, Mar. 21, 1836, in Jenkins, *Papers of the Texas Revolution*, V: 154.

9 Stephen L. Hardin, "The San Jacinto Campaign, The Generalship of Sam Houston," *Sons of DeWitt Colony Texas*, http://www.sonsofdewittcolony.org//adp/archives/feature/hardin.html [Accessed Jan. 13, 2022].

10 Barker, "San Jacinto Campaign," 334–335; Day, *Texas Almanac: 1857–1873*, p. 321.

11 Labadie, "San Jacinto Campaign," 43–44.

12 There was a family of Wrights that lived near where Sherman camped. It is unknown, but certainly possible, that Felix Wright was part of that family and knew the area well. Only a few weeks later, Wright died near the Brazos River, becoming the first casualty of what can be termed the "San Jacinto Campaign," which spans from the time that Houston left Gonzales through the Battle of San Jacinto. Jonathan H. Kuykendall later wrote about the events during this period.

13 Coe was affiliated with Captain William Ware's Company of Washington volunteers, and John Ingram served under Coe. However, Ware was stationed with Sherman at Dewees' Ford. Having just arrived, Ingram may not have been officially posted to a unit when he joined the expedition. Kuykendall wrote that Ingram was part of Captain William Hill's company, but that was not until April 1836.

14 Jonathan H. Kuykendall, ed. "Reminiscences of Early Texan, II," *The Quarterly of the Texas State Historical Association* 6 (Apr. 1903): 320–321, 329.

15 Barker, "San Jacinto Campaign," 298. Houston ordered the men to proceed by foot to the crossing, but then later said they should ride back as fast as possible should the enemy be encountered. Perhaps he intended that they walk their horses there.

16 Davis, *Diary of Travis*, 48; and Mexico to Rawson Alley, July 5, 1824, Colorado County Deed Records, Book A [Transcribed Spanish], 1–5, County Clerk Records, Colorado County Courthouse.

17 William H. Harrison, *Alleyton, Texas: Back Door to the Confederacy* (Austin: Show-Me Type & Print, 1993), 219. Annabell Neal Everett, great granddaughter to Abram and Nancy Millar Alley, recalled a conversation with the latter in which she recounted Abram's displeasure in this matter. Everett is the author's great grandmother.

18 Laura Ann Dick Rau, "Nancy Millar Alley (1817–1893)," in Carrington, *Women in Early Texas*, 15.

19 Louis Houck, *A History of Missouri: from the Earliest Explorations and Settlements until the Admission of the State into the Union* (3 vols.; Chicago: Lakeside Press, 1908), I: 369–370. At this time, though the area was heavily influenced and settled by the French, it was under Spanish control.

20 Houck, *History of Missouri*, I: 373.

21 Harrison, *Alleyton*, 22–27, A1. It can be presumed that Catherine Baker, whom Thomas Alley married, was probably related to Abraham Baker, his partner. It is also probably no coincidence that Thomas Alley named one of his sons after his partner, further suggesting a very closer relationship between the two.

22 Mary Austin to Austin, Apr. 10, 1822, in Barker, *Austin Papers*, II, Part 1: 491–493.

23 Josiah W. Wilbarger, *Indian Depredations in Texas* (1889; reprint, Austin: Eakin Press, 1985), 200–201.

24 Wilbarger, *Indian Depredations*, 200–201; Freytag, *Chronicles of Fayette*, 37; Jonathan H. Kuykendall, ed., "Reminiscences of Early Texans, III," *The Quarterly of the Texas State Historical Association* 7 (July 1903): 47. There are conflicts on when this event occurred. Wilbarger says it occurred in the summer of 1823, whereas Abram Alley, in a recollection edited by Kuykendall, says it happened in the winter of 1822–1823. The date was most likely in February 1823.

25 Sinks, "Reminiscences of Burnam," 15.

26 Constable's Bond, Jan. 26, 1824, in Barker, *Austin's Papers*, II, Part 1: 731–732; Allen G. Hatley, *Texas Constables: A Frontier Heritage* (Lubbock: Texas Tech University Press, 1999), 11–12.
27 James E. B. and Stephen F. Austin to Emily M. Perry, June 15, 1826, in Barker, *Austin's Papers*, II, Part 2: 1,358–1,359.
28 Virginia H. Taylor Houston, "Surveying in Texas," *Southwestern Historical Quarterly* 65 (Oct. 1961): 209; Rawson Alley to Austin, Jan. 29, 1825; Thomas M. Duke to Austin, Jan. 23, 1825; Rawson Alley to Austin, Jan. 29, 1825, in Barker, *Austin's Papers*, II, Part 2: 1,016, 1,023, 1,025.
29 Bugbee, "Old Three Hundred," 110.
30 Election Return, Jan. 10, 1825, in Barker, *Austin's Papers*, II, Part 2, 1014.
31 Eugene C. Barker, ed., "Minutes of the Ayuntamiento of San Felipe de Austin, 1828–1832, I," *Southwestern Historical Quarterly* 21 (Jan. 1918): 302–304.
32 Lamar, Information from A. Rabb in Gulick et al., *Lamar Papers*, IV, Part 1: 216–217.
33 Lamar, Information from A. Rabb, in Gulick et al. *Lamar Papers*, IV, Part 1: 216–217; Mary Crownover Rabb, *Travels and Adventures in Texas in the 1820's* (Waco: W. M. Morrison, 1962), 11–12. This was a dangerous flood. John Rabb, near La Grange, had to evacuate his family when floodwaters covered his floor. He and another man came back to salvage belongings. Separated, his friend spent the night in the top of a tree, while Rabb cut a hole in the roof of his brother's nearby house and spent the night in the attic.
34 Davis, *Diary of Travis*, 44, 48.
35 Bugbee, "Old Three Hundred," 110.
36 Rau, "Nancy Millar Alley," 13. The Millars would likely have settled on Rawson Alley's grant. Nancy's brother Daniel was a veteran of the Battle of San Jacinto but was recorded as "Miller" instead of Millar. See Dixon and Kemp, *Heroes of San Jacinto*, 217.
37 Peña, *With Santa Anna in Texas*, 58.
38 Jackson and Wheat, *Almonte's Texas*, 351.
39 Vicente Filisola, "Representation to the Supreme Government with Notes on His Operations as General-in-Chief of the Army of Texas," in Carlos E. Casteñeda, ed., *The Mexican Side of the Texas Revolution* (Dallas: P. L. Turner Company, 1956), 70.
40 Filisola, "Representation," 170; Antonio López de Santa Anna, "Manifesto Relative to His Operations in the Texas Campaign and His Capture," in Casteñeda, *Mexican Side of the Texas Revolution*, 15–16.
41 De la Peña, *With Santa Anna in Texas*, 65; Filisola, "Representation to the Supreme Government," 169. Filisola reported having only fifty cavalrymen from the Dolores Regiment and made no mention of cavalry from the Tampico Regiment.
42 The Toluca and Matamoros battalions were heavily engaged in the Battle of the Alamo. The Aldama Battalion was held in reserve, as was the Dolores Regiment. The Toluca Battalion was devastated in the Alamo assault.
43 Gregg J. Dimmick, *The Mexican Army in the Texas Revolution, Volume III* (College Station: Texas A&M Press, forthcoming). Dimmick kindly allowed a pre-publication perusal and citation of his manuscript.
44 Jackson And Wheat, *Almonte's Texas*, 394.

45 Austin and Perry, *Connected Map of Austin's Colony*.
46 A line from this proposed site of the Mexican army encampment to Houston's encampment across from Beeson's Crossing would cross the Colorado River five times!
47 Barker, "San Jacinto Campaign," 298–299; Zuber, *My Eighty Years in Texas*, 58.
48 Alan Barber, *David Kokernot: Rogue Soldier of the Texas Revolution* (Sandpoint, ID: Kullyspel Press, 2012), 183. Ratliff Creek was likely named after Elijah Ratliff, who was married to Jane Tumlinson, daughter of John J. and Elizabeth Tumlinson. The creek is almost wholly on the Tumlinson land grant.
49 Jackson and Wheat, *Almonte's Texas*, 395; Stein, "Consider the Lily (Part 2)," 48. Stein's interpretations of Alamo being Skull and San Antoñito being Ratliff seem consistent.
50 Barker, "San Jacinto Campaign," 309.
51 Note that mining not only affected the elevation but also the flow of nearby streams. It is likely that Ratliff Creek originally flowed in a generally east and northeasterly direction, but mining caused the stream to bend first south then back north before reaching the river. Wolfpen Creek has been almost eliminated by mining, in many places looking like nothing more than a ditch. Like Ratliff Creek, mining seems to have deflected it to the south as well.
52 De la Peña, *With Santa Anna in Texas*, 79–80.
53 Dimmick, *Mexican Army in the Texas Revolution*, Vol. III.

CHAPTER 8: BEESON'S & DEWEES'–DAY 7, MARCH 22

1 Barker, "San Jacinto Campaign," 334–335.
2 At this point, no serious attempt was made by the Mexican army to cross the Colorado at Dewees' Ford. At best, there were isolated skirmishes. Baker perhaps exaggerated to stir his fellow Texans into action.
3 Baker's estimate of Mexican forces at the time was probably understated, since there were about 6,000 soldiers in Texas at the time. He, however, overstated the number of Mexicans under General Sesma's command.
4 *Telegraph and Texas Register* (San Felipe de Austin), Mar. 24, 1836.
5 Martin Flores, May 15, 137, Republic Claims, Audited Claim Number 1244 (TSLA, online: Reel Number 32, Image Numbers 66–70); Dixon and Kemp, *Heroes of San Jacinto*, 100–101; Hockley to Rusk, Mar. 23, 1836, in Jenkins, *Papers of the Texas Revolution*, V: 167; Barker, "San Jacinto Campaign," 298. Frederick Lemsky won notoriety as the piper who played "Will You Come to my Bower" during the Battle of San Jacinto.
6 Barker, "San Jacinto Campaign," 298.
7 Hockley to Rusk, Mar. 23, 1836, in Jenkins, *Papers of the Texas Revolution*, V: 167.
8 Austin, *Original Map of Texas by Citizen*, 1829.
9 Labadie, "San Jacinto Campaign," 43.
10 Jackson and Wheat, *Almonte's Texas*, 391.
11 Dimmick, *Sea of Mud*, 287.

12 Labadie, "San Jacinto Campaign," 43. The loss of horses and mules would have been notable to the Mexican army; however, there is no known Mexican account that confirms this incident.
13 Labadie, "San Jacinto Campaign," 44.
14 Barber, *David Kokernot*, 183. Once again, there is inconsistency with spelling of names. Robert Moseley signed his name with an extra 'e' that was often omitted in official documents. Moseley's place was on the east side of the Colorado adjacent to Sherman's encampment. Dewees' cabin was on the west side of the river closer to the Mexican encampment.
15 Barber, *David Kokernot*, 183.
16 Hunter, *Narrative of Robert Hunter*, 12. The mention of a hill here is interesting because the present topography would suggest no such hill exists. However, as previously mentioned, the substantial open-pit sand and gravel mining in the area may have appreciably altered the landscape in the immediate vicinity.
17 Hunter, *Narrative of Hunter*, 12.

CHAPTER 9: BEESON'S & DEWEES'–DAY 8, MARCH 23

1 Houston to Rusk, Mar. 23, 1836, in Jenkins, *Papers of the Texas Revolution*, V: 169.
2 Houston to Rusk, Mar. 26, 29, 1836, in Jenkins, *Papers of the Texas Revolution*, V: 168, 234.
3 Dixon and Kemp, *Heroes of San Jacinto*, 73–74.
4 Williams and Barker, *Writings of Sam Houston*, I: 361.
5 Vigness, *Revolutionary Decades*, 185. Rusk was elected to the cabinet on March 17, 1836.
6 Houston to Rusk, Mar. 23, 1836, in Jenkins, *Papers of the Texas Revolution*, V: 168.
7 In the future, President David G. Burnet would be so frustrated with Houston that he sent Rusk to relieve him of command of the army, but Rusk assessed the situation and left Houston in command.
8 Houston to Rusk, Mar. 23, 1836, in Jenkins, *Papers of the Texas Revolution*, V: 169–170.
9 DeShields, *Tall Men with Long Rifles*, 137.
10 Rosa Kleberg, "Some of My Early Experiences in Texas," *The Quarterly of the Texas State Historical Association* 1 (Apr. 1898): 301. These men were not technically deserters, but rather men who chose not to join the army.
11 *Telegraph and Texas Register* (San Felipe de Austin), Mar. 24, 1836.
12 Stephen. F. Sparks, "Recollections of S. F. Sparks," *The Quarterly of the Texas State Historical Association* 12 (July 1908): 62–63.
13 Lack, *Diary of Gray*, 124–125.
14 Houston to Rusk, Mar. 23, 1836, in Jenkins, *Papers of the Texas Revolution*, V: 169–170. The Texas government began evacuating Washington before daylight on March 17, 1836.

15 Wilson W. Crook III, ed., *Reminiscences of Moses Austin Bryan* (Houston: Houston Archeological Society, 2016), 31. Bryan was only eighteen years of age at the time and a private in Captain Mosely Baker's company. Despite his young age, he had already accompanied Stephen F. Austin to Mexico, working as his secretary. The trip no doubt helped his Spanish. Bryan would interpret during the conference between Houston and Santa Anna after the Battle of San Jacinto.

16 Houston to Rusk, Mar. 23, 1836, in Jenkins, *Papers of the Texas Revolution*, V: 168. Hockley was in the process of writing a letter to Rusk when the recently captured prisoners were brought into camp. Both Hockley and Houston related in separate letters to Rusk information about the capture, but Hockley conveyed more detail. Moses A. Bryan indicated that there were three prisoners captured. It could be that once Houston and Hockley had heard virtually the same account from the first two prisoners, they did not stay for the interrogation of the third.

17 Houston to Rusk, Mar. 23, 1836, in Jenkins, *Papers of the Texas Revolution*, V: 169.
18 Houston to Rusk, Mar. 23, 1836, in Jenkins, *Papers of the Texas Revolution*, V: 167.
19 Houston to Rusk, Mar. 23, 1836, in Jenkins, *Papers of the Texas Revolution*, V: 170–171.
20 William Alley, May 22, 1854, Republic Claims, Unpaid and Miscellaneous Claim Number N/A (TSLA, online: Reel Number 248, Image Numbers 110–111).
21 Moore, *Eighteen Minutes*, 107; Barker, "San Jacinto Campaign," 299.
22 Barker, "San Jacinto Campaign," 299.
23 Houston to Rusk, Mar. 23, 1836, in Jenkins, *Papers of the Texas Revolution*, V: 169.
24 Houston to Rusk, Mar. 23, 1836, in Jenkins, *Papers of the Texas Revolution*, V: 169–170. Fannin was aware that General José de Urrea's cavalry was in the area but may not have had a full appreciation for the proximity of the larger forces. His seemingly lackadaisical attitude was costly.
25 Houston to Rusk, Mar. 23, 1836, in Jenkins, *Papers of the Texas Revolution*, V: 169. Fannin's delay in retreat was in large part due to waiting to hear from Ward and Amos B. King, both of whom he had sent out days beforehand. Ward was captured the previous day near Dimitt's Landing; King and his men became prisoners on March 15, 1836.

CHAPTER 10: BEESON'S & DEWEES'–DAY 9, MARCH 24

1 Houston to Richardson R. Royal, Mar. 24, 1836, in Jenkins, *Papers of the Texas Revolution*, V: 180.
2 Houston to Royal, Mar. 24, 1836, in Jenkins, *Papers of the Texas Revolution*, V: 180.
3 Foote, *Texas and the Texans*, II: 278.
4 Barker, "San Jacinto Campaign," 335.
5 Barker, "San Jacinto Campaign," 299.
6 Zuber, *My Eighty Years in Texas*, 59.
7 De la Peña, *With Santa Anna in Texas*, 66; Jackson and Wheat, *Almonte's Texas*, 392–394.

8. Jackson and Wheat, *Almonte's Texas*, 394–395. Almonte brought back two maps published in 1833 from his 1834 expedition to Texas. One, compiled by Austin, was published by H. S. Tanner in Philadelphia. David H. Burr generated the second map and published it in New York. The Tanner map shows the Old San Antonio Road, the La Bahía Road, and the newest road from Béxar to Gonzales and on to San Felipe. The Burr map depicts two of these but not La Bahía Road. It also shows Montezuma at the site of present-day Columbus. Neither of these two maps shows a road to Burnam's Ferry. Both maps depict the Atascosito Road, established by Spaniards as a primary route through Texas. This ran from La Bahía (Goliad) through Victoria, then northeastward toward what would become San Felipe, thence eastward toward an old military outpost called Atascosito on the Trinity River near what is now Liberty.
9. Austin and Perry, *Connected Map of Austin's Colony*.
10. Jackson and Wheat, *Almonte's Texas*, 395.
11. Barker, "San Jacinto Campaign," 299, 309; Zuber, *My Eighty Years in Texas*, 59–60. Labadie, no fan of Houston's, claimed that when they returned, the Texians had abandoned their camp at Beeson's Crossing.
12. Barker, "San Jacinto Campaign," 299. As noted earlier, Stein determined that the stream sometimes called Alamo was Skull Creek, and the stream San Antoñito was Ratliff Creek. Based on the direction from which Almonte traveled and the position of the creek, this assessment seems logical. Ratliff Creek, at that time, likely flowed in a more east by northeast direction without the loop south shown on modern maps. Gravel mining likely influenced the course of this creek. Maps in the late 19th and early 20th centuries support this supposition.
13. Barker, "Kuykendall's Recollections," 299.
14. Moore, *Eighteen Minutes*, 100, 113.
15. This John A. Wharton is not to be confused with the John A. Wharton that grew up in Texas and became a Confederate general during the Civil War. This Wharton would be responsible for procuring the "Twin Sisters," cannons that would be instrumental in the Battle of San Jacinto. He would become Secretary of War for the Republic of Texas and a representative in the First Congress of Texas. He died of illness in 1838.
16. Dixon and Kemp, *Heroes of San Jacinto*, 51–53. There most certainly was a controversy around Perry's presence. Houston allegedly caught him sending a letter from camp even though he ordered that no correspondence could leave unless he personally reviewed it. The letter slammed Houston for his poor leadership of the military campaign. A few days prior to the Battle of San Jacinto, "he [Perry] was taken by Capt. Karnes and Private Secrest, of the spies, and brought to the general…they believed he had communicated with the enemy." Houston had him placed under guard but allowed him to participate in the battle. Rusk recounted similar events regarding Perry but was less harsh, writing, "Some vague charges were made against Mr. Perry, of an intention to desert, or join the enemy. These charges, I looked upon at the time, as injurious to Mr. Perry. I believe they were unfounded."

CHAPTER 11: BEESON'S & DEWEES'–DAY 10, MARCH 25

1. Daniel Shipman, *Frontier Life, 58 Years in Texas* (1879; reprint, Pasadena, TX: Abbotsford Publishing Company, 1965), 125-126.
2. Jackson and Wheat, *Almonte's Texas*, 395.
3. Jackson and Wheat, *Almonte's Texas*, 395.
4. Zuber, *My Eighty Years in Texas*, 60-61; Zoraster Robinson, Oct. 7, 1874, Republic Claims, Pension Claim Number N/A (TSLA, online: Reel Number 236, Image Number 155-157). Zuber stated that Sesma's cavalry fired "escopetas" at the Texians. Of note is that Zuber's assessment of the date of this incident is different in his book from the affidavit provided on behalf of Zoraster Robinson. More credence is given to his book's date for the incident, since the dates in the affidavit are prior to his company's arrival at Dewees' Ford. It is an indication of how inconsistent recollections can be.
5. Zuber, *My Eighty Years in Texas*, 60-61; Robinson, Oct. 7, 1874, Republic Claims, Pension Claim Number N/A.
6. Houston to Rusk, Mar. 23, 1836, in Jenkins, *Papers of the Texas Revolution*, V: 170.
7. Hockley to Rusk, Mar. 23, 1836, in Jenkins, *Papers of the Texas Revolution*, V: 168.
8. Darrell Debo, *Burnet County History, Family Histories* (2 vols.; Burnet, TX: Eakin Press, 1979), II: 177.
9. Zuber, *My Eighty Years in Texas*, 61.
10. Debo, *Burnet County History*, II, 177; Smithwick, *Evolution of a State*, 104. Peter and William Kerr were evidently not related.
11. Ana Carolina Castillo Crimm, *De León, A Tejano Family History* (Austin: University of Texas Press, 2003), 154-156; Joe Tom Davis, *Legendary Texians* (4 vols.; Austin: Eakin Press, 1986), III: 36; Stephen L. Hardin, "Plácido Benavides: Fighting Tejano Federalist," in *Tejano Leadership in Mexican and Revolutionary Texas*, ed. Jesús F. de la Teja (College Station: Texas A&M University Press), 63-64. Carbajal escaped from Monterrey through the efforts of Plácido Benavides (Fernando de León's brother-in-law), who bribed the guards and assisted him. Twenty-two of his men involved in the expedition, however, were captured. Carbajal eventually found his way back to Victoria.
12. Alex Dunst, "The Navy of the Republic of Texas," *The Quarterly of the Texas State Historical Association* 12 (Jan. 1909): 184-185.
13. Hockley to Rusk, Apr. 1, 1836, in Jenkins, *Papers of the Texas Revolution*, V: 286-287. Evidently, "Carr" is how Kerr pronounced his name, so it was not unusual to see it recorded as such when he was referenced, just as Hockley had in his letter.
14. Houston to Rusk, Apr. 3, 1836, in Jenkins, *Papers of the Texas Revolution*, V: 309-310. The "Beregardo" mentioned by Houston is presumably Anselmo Bergara, who had, with Andres Barcena, brought the first report of the fall of the Alamo to the General in Gonzales. Este is presumably Edward Este, a brother-in-law to President Burnet. He would be involved in the Mier Expedition, during which he would be one of the unfortunate Texans to draw a black bean and be executed by the Mexicans.

CHAPTER 12: MOVING EASTWARD–DAY 11, MARCH 26

1. Houston, "Houston's Speech in the United States Senate," 319.
2. James, *Raven*, 236.
3. Houston Army Order, Mar. 26, 1836, in Jenkins, *Papers of the Texas Revolution*, V: 200. The "Colonel Wallace" mentioned would have been Joseph W. E. Wallace, who lived in the area and provided the army with significant provisions. The "troops from the lower country" would include some sent to guard Mercer's Crossing at Egypt.
4. Barker, "San Jacinto Campaign," 277–278.
5. Zuber, *My Eighty Years in Texas*, 62.
6. Dewees, *Letters from an Early Settler of Texas*, 191–192.
7. Foote, *Texas and the Texans*, II: 280–281; Zuber, *My Eighty Years in Texas*, 62. Zuber stated that a small picket guard at a ford upriver from the Dewees encampment was not called in at the time of retreat. If true, this would have been an oversight by Sherman rather than Houston.
8. Louis W. Kemp, "Veteran Biographies: Moses Lapham," *San Jacinto Museum of History*, https://www.sanjacinto-museum.org/Library/Veteran_Bios/Bio_page/?id=487&army=Texian [Accessed July 21, 2021].
9. Joe B. Frantz, ed., "Moses Lapham: His Life and Some Selected Correspondence, I," *Southwestern Historical Quarterly* 54 (Jan. 1951): 326; Kemp, "Veteran Biographies: Moses Lapham."
10. Frantz, "Lapham, Life and Correspondence, I," 326. Lapham would volunteer to go with Deaf Smith and others to destroy Vince's Bridge prior to the Battle of San Jacinto.
11. Wisehart, *Sam Houston*, 196; Coleman, *Houston Displayed*, 13.
12. Jackson and Wheat, *Almonte's Texas*, 395; Dewees, *Letters from an Early Settler of Texas*, 192.
13. Wisehart, *Sam Houston*, 196; Jackson and Wheat, *Almonte's Texas*, 395. Almonte noted that the Texians reconnoitered his position late in the afternoon of March 26, 1836.
14. Shipman, *Frontier Life*, 126; Hunter, *Narrative of Hunter*, 12.
15. Shipman, *Frontier Life*, 128; Zuber, *My Eighty Years in Texas*, 62–63; Barker, "San Jacinto Campaign," 300.
16. Dewees, *Letters from an Early Settler of Texas*, 192.
17. Zuber, *My Eighty Years in Texas*, 62–63.
18. Barker, "San Jacinto Campaign," 299.
19. Zuber, *My Eighty Years in Texas*, 62–63; Barker, "San Jacinto Campaign," 299–300. Kuykendall's account claims that no fires were lit during the night.
20. Houston to Rusk, Mar. 23, 1836, in Jenkins, *Papers of the Texas Revolution*, V: 168. George W. Poe arrived at Houston's camp at Beeson's Crossing on March 24, 1836, according to Hockley's letter to Rusk.
21. Moore, *Eighteen Minutes*, 123; Louis W. Kemp, "Veteran Biographies: John Forbes," *San Jacinto Museum of History*, https://www.sanjacinto-museum.org/Library/Veteran_Bios/Bio_page/?id=308&army= Texian [Accessed July 16, 2021].

22 Moore, *Eighteen Minutes*, 124–125; Kemp, "Veteran Biographies: Forbes."
23 Kemp, "Veteran Biographies: Forbes."
24 Kemp, "Veteran Biographies: Forbes."
25 Shipman, *Frontier Life*, 128.
26 Dixon and Kemp, *Heroes of San Jacinto*, 345.
27 Madison G. Whitaker, Oct. 12, 1870, Republic Claims, Pension Claim Number N/A (TSLA, online: Reel Number 245, Image Numbers 207–208). Leander Smith was elected captain on Mar. 13, 1836, while on the march.
28 Dixon and Kemp, *Heroes of San Jacinto*, 345.
29 Asa Hoxey, Apr. 1, 1837, Republic Claims, Audited Claim Number 831 (TSLA, online: Reel Number 48, Image Number 158).
30 Hoxey, Apr. 1, 1837, Republic Claims, Audited Claim Number 831; Dixon and Kemp, *Heroes of San Jacinto*, 345.
31 Louis W. Kemp, "Veteran Biographies: Moses Lapham," *San Jacinto Museum of History*, http://www.sanjacinto-museum.org/Library/Veteran_Bios/Bio_page/?id=487&army=Texian [Accessed July 21, 2021]. Lapham clearly meant that the Texian army retreated from the Colorado upon learning of Fannin's defeat.
32 "Compendium of the History of Texas," 57.
33 Rabb, *Travels and Adventures*, 14.
34 Barker, "San Jacinto Campaign," 277–278.
35 "Compendium of the History of Texas," 57.
36 "Compendium of the History of Texas," 57. There is no reason to believe that Mexican cavalry fleeing from Sesma's camp would join Urrea. Instead, they would likely have fled toward San Antonio and met Tolsa, who was on the way to reinforce Sesma. The premise that a victory by Houston could have saved Fannin and his men is flawed from several different angles and was promulgated only to cast Houston in a negative light.
37 Barker, "San Jacinto Campaign," 278–279.
38 Foote, *Texas and the Texans*, II, 276. To be sure, Foote also put forth the other perspective of retreat being the best course of action.
39 Coleman, *Houston Displayed*, 13.
40 Louis W. Kemp, "Veteran Biographies: Jesse Billingsley," *San Jacinto Museum of History*, https://www.sanjacinto-museum.org/Library/Veteran_Bios/Bio_page/?id=59&army=Texian [Accessed Sept. 12, 2021].
41 Barker, "San Jacinto Campaign," 300, 309.
42 Leone R. Weyand and Houston Wade, *An Early History of Fayette County* (La Grange, TX: La Grange Journal Plant, 1936), 135. To celebrate the centennial of Texas Independence, Weyand and Wade co-authored a thorough account of the history of Fayette County. It was in a footnote regarding Houston's decision to retreat that the authors made their pronouncement; however, they may have been a bit presumptuous to speak on behalf of the entire citizenship of Fayette County.
43 "Compendium of the History of Texas," 58.
44 Foote, *Texas and the Texans*, II: 279–280.

45 William R. Newman, Nov. 10, 1870, Republic Claims, Pension Claim Number N/A (TSLA, online: Reel Number 231, Image Numbers 322–325).
46 Rabb, *Travels and Adventures*, 15.
47 Dewees, *Letters from an Early Settler of Texas*, 192.
48 Labadie, "San Jacinto Campaign," 44; Dixon and Kemp, *Heroes of San Jacinto*, 213.
49 Barker, "San Jacinto Campaign," 245–246.
50 Bancroft, *History of the North Mexican States and Texas*, II: 244. As recorded by Bancroft, several participants gave estimates of manpower at the time. These include Anson Jones (1,570), Ben F. Smith (1,360), Amasa Turner (1,468), James Tarlton (1,800), Robert J. Calder (1,400); Benjamin C. Franklin (1,400+), and William J. Heard (1,500 to 1,600). Aside from Tarlton's figure, which seems high, the rest are within an expected range.
51 Sharp to -----, Mar. 27, 1836, in Jenkins, *Papers of the Texas Revolution*, V: 209–210.
52 Yoakum, *History of Texas*, I: 106.
53 Houston Army Orders, Mar. 17, 1836, in Jenkins, *Papers of the Texas Revolution*, V: 122.
54 Houston to Royall, Mar. 24, 1836, in Jenkins, *Papers of the Texas Revolution*, V: 180.
55 Houston, "Houston's Speech in the United States Senate," 319.
56 Houston, "Houston's Speech in the United States Senate," 319.
57 Jackson and Wheat, *Almonte's Texas*, 395.
58 Robert J. Calder, "Recollections of the Texas Campaign of 1836," in *The Texas Almanac for 1861* (Galveston: Richardson & Company, 1860), 63.
59 Calder, "Recollections of the Texas Campaign of 1836," 63.
60 Santa Anna, "Manifesto," 15–16.
61 Filisola, "Representation," 170; Santa Anna, "Manifesto," 15–16.
62 Dimmick, *Mexican Army in the Texas Revolution, Vol III*. With Tolsa's reinforcements, Sesma estimated Mexican forces at 1,400 and Texian forces at 1,200. Considering the rate that reinforcements had been arriving, this is a good estimate. The sides were almost equal in numbers at that point, though the Mexicans had artillery that the Texians lacked.
63 Dimmick, *Mexican Army in the Texas Revolution. Vol. III*.
64 Dimmick, *Mexican Army in the Texas Revolution, Vol. III*. Filisola was Santa Anna's second-in-command.
65 As mentioned earlier, Colonel Almonte, on his prior trip to Texas, brought back the Tanner and Burr maps. These, along with other early maps, would have shown the location of the Atascosito Crossing.
66 Jackson and Wheat, *Almonte's Texas*, 395–396.

CHAPTER 13: TOWARD THE BRAZOS

1 Labadie, "San Jacinto Campaign," 44.
2 Shipman, *Frontier Life*, 127–128. This evidently is the same James Wilson that served in Captain William Ware's company at San Jacinto. Presumably he found some suitable shoes prior to the battle.
3 Shipman, *Frontier Life*, 128.

4   Barker, "San Jacinto Campaign," 300.
5   Zuber, *My Eighty Years in Texas*, 64.
6   Barker, "San Jacinto Campaign," 300; Zuber, *My Eighty Years in Texas*, 64. Zuber claims Houston ordered them to take the left flank, while Kuykendall recalls them taking the right flank.
7   Labadie, "San Jacinto Campaign," 44; Zuber, *My Eighty Years in Texas*, 60–64; "Bullinger's Creek," *The Handbook of Texas Online*, Texas State Historical Association, https://www.tshaonline.org/handbook/entries/ bullingers-creek [Accessed Sept. 30, 2021]. Zuber mistakenly referred to Arroyo Dulce as Aqua Dulce. It has also been called Palmetto Creek and is now called Bullinger's Creek. Austin considered this an important creek for water since it was a spring, independent of the Brazos. Both Williams and Austin had homesteads on this creek.
8   Ruth G. Nichols, "Samuel May Williams," *Southwestern Historical Quarterly* 56 (Oct. 1952): 194–195; Gammel, *Laws of Texas*, I: 15.
9   Matthew Ellenberger, "Illuminating the Lesser Lights: Notes on the Life of Albert Clinton Horton," *Southwestern Historical Quarterly* 88 (Apr. 1985): 369–370.
10 Moore, *Eighteen Minutes*, 127.
11 Bill Walraven, "Baylor, John Walker," *Handbook of Texas Online*, Texas State Historical Association https://www.tshaonline.org/handbook/entries/baylor-john-walker [Accessed Sept. 30, 2021]; Amelia Williams, "A Critical Study of the Siege of the Alamo and of the Personnel of its Defenders, Chapter 5," *Southwestern Historical Quarterly* 37 (Apr. 1934): 308–309. Not including other adventures and skirmishes, Baylor may have the distinction of being involved in more battles of the Texas Revolution than anyone. He fought in the Battle of Goliad and Battle of Concepción. He was a courier out of the Alamo just prior to the battle there and was scouting during the Battle of Coleto Creek. He also participated in the Battle of San Jacinto.
12 Moore. *Eighteen Minutes*, 132.
13 Jackson and Wheat, *Almonte's Texas*, 397.
14 Harbert Davenport, "The Men of Goliad: Dedicatory Address at the Unveiling of the Monument Erected by the Texas Centennial Commission at the Grave of Fannin's Men," *Southwestern Historical Quarterly* 43 (July 1939): 23; Claude Elliott, "Georgia and the Texas Revolution," *Georgia Historical Quarterly* 28 (Dec. 1944): 194. Samuel G. Hardaway's mother was in her mid-40's, but his father was 80.
15 Jewel Davis Scarborough, "The Georgia Battalion in the Texas Revolution: A Critical Study," *Southwestern Historical Quarterly* 63 (Apr. 1960): 513; Foote, *Texas and the Texans*, II: 255. Velasco was the location of Fannin's family plantation.
16 Davenport, "Men of Goliad," 23; Robert S. Davis Jr., "Georgia Battalion in the Texas Revolution," *Central Georgia Genealogical Society Quarterly* 7 (Sept. 1985): 66. Uriah Bullock was assigned to command the company, but he was too sick to leave Velasco and never led it in the field.
17 Davenport, "Men of Goliad," 23.
18 Foote, *Texas and the Texans*, II: 256; *Georgia Messenger* (Macon), June 9, 1836.

19 Andrew Boyle, "Reminiscences of the Texas Revolution," *The Quarterly of the Texas State Historical Association* 13 (Apr. 1910): 286; Davenport, "Men of Goliad," 23; Information Derived from J. W. Andrews, 185?, in Gulick et al., *Lamar Papers*, IV, Part 2: 237–240; John J. Linn, *Reminiscences of Fifty Years in Texas* (1883; reprint, Austin: State House Press, 1986), 199.

20 Foote, *Texas and the Texans*, II: 256; *Georgia Messenger* (Macon), June 9, 1836; José de Urrea, "Diary of the Military Operations of the Division Which Under the Command of General José Urrea Campaigned in Texas," in Castañeda, ed., *Mexican Side of the Texas Revolution*, 220.

21 Urrea, "Diary of Military Operations," 220.

22 Information Derived from J. W. Andrews, 237–240.

23 Foote, *Texas and the Texans*, II: 256; *Georgia Messenger* (Macon), June 9, 1836.

24 Foote, *Texas and the Texans*, II: 256–257; *Georgia Messenger* (Macon), June 9, 1836.

25 Foote, *Texas and the Texans*, II: 257; *Georgia Messenger* (Macon), June 9, 1836.

26 Foote, *Texas and the Texans*, II: 257; *Georgia Messenger* (Macon), June 9, 1836. The Mexican campsite Hardaway references would likely have been where the main body of Sesma's army had camped.

27 Foote, *Texas and the Texans*, II, 257–258; *Georgia Messenger* (Macon), June 9, 1836. The two Texians identified by Hardaway would have likely been Daniel Shipman, who was part of Austin's Old Three Hundred, and Moses Lapham, who had arrived in Texas in 1831. There is much greater uncertainty as to the two Tennesseans. There were several Johnsons who served in the army. One possibility, known to have been from Tennessee, was David Johnson, who served in Captain Kokernot's mounted volunteers. There is no record of anybody named Cawmack. Perhaps he mistook Karnes, who was from Tennessee, for that name. One intriguing possibility is that the person in question was Karnes' brother-in-law, whose last name was Carmack. However, it is unknown whether he ever traveled to Texas, even temporarily.

28 Foote, *Texas and the Texans*, II: 258; *Georgia Messenger* (Macon), June 9, 1836. By this time, the bulk of the Texian army would have moved north to Groce's Landing. Hardaway found Moseley Baker's company still situated at San Felipe.

29 Louis W. Kemp, "Veteran Biographies: Moseley Baker," *San Jacinto Museum of History*, https://www. sanjacinto-museum.org/Library/Veteran_Bios/Bio_page/?id=29&army=Texian [Accessed Sept. 30, 2021].

30 William Alley, May 22, 1854, Republic Claims, Unpaid and Miscellaneous Claim Number N/A.

31 William Alley, April 21, 1854, Republic Claims, Unpaid and Miscellaneous Claim Number N/A (TSLA, online: Reel Number 248, Image Number 117).

32 William Alley, May 22, 1854, Republic Claims, Unpaid and Miscellaneous Claim Number N/A. Unless he was talking about Moseley Baker's company, Ramsey must have meant the Texian encampment on the west side of the Brazos.

33 William Alley, May 22, 1854, Republic Claims, Unpaid and Miscellaneous Claim Number N/A. William Alley claimed that his estimate of hogs and cattle he supplied to the army was conservative. He ultimately claimed compensation for $7,750 (250 hogs at 0/head and 350 cattle at 5/head). Supporting affidavits were received from his brother Abraham Alley, and neighbors Leander and Abel Beeson, Martin Ramsey, Daniel Millar, and Kidder Walker.

34 William Alley, May 22, 1854, Republic Claims, Unpaid and Miscellaneous Claim Number N/A. William Alley had a cousin with the same name who lived on the Lavaca River who evidently helped him drive the cattle to San Felipe and who had only days earlier joined Captain Wyly Martin's company.

35 Baker, "San Jacinto Campaign," 279. Old Fort was located at present-day Richmond.

36 Jackson and Wheat, *Almonte's Texas*, 396–398.

37 Jackson and Wheat, *Almonte's Texas*, 397–398.

38 Jackson and Wheat, *Almonte's Texas*, 398. Almonte recorded that it was about 2.5 leagues (6.5 miles) from Atascosito to Beeson's Crossing and then another 1.5 leagues (3.9 miles) to Moseley's or Dewees'. He further noted that it was another league (2.6 miles) to the Colorado. A look at the map suggests his estimate of distances was too great. From the Atascosito Crossing to Beeson's along the river would be about three miles or so. From Beeson's to the ford at Dewees' would be about 4.5 miles. Moseley's house was on the east bank of the Colorado and likely set back a mile or so from the river. Almonte noted that the road from Moseley's to the river was "bad and miry," understandable considering the recent rain and rapid rise of the river. It was on this poor road that Sesma's command camped on the night of April 4, 1836.

39 Santa Anna, "Manifesto," 15–16.

40 Jackson and Wheat, *Almonte's Texas*, 398–399.

41 Filisola, "Representation," 170. Santa Anna countermanded his order to Urrea to move to San Felipe, confident that he had the force he needed. Gaona was substantially delayed coming from Mina, having gotten lost.

42 Dimmick, *Mexican Army in the Texas Revolution, Vol. III*; Filisola, "Representation," 170.

43 Dimmick, *Sea of Mud*, 16, 172–173.

CHAPTER 14: AFTERMATH

1 Dewees, *Letters from an Early Settler of Texas*, 201.

2 Elizabeth Beeson, "Miscellaneous Letters: 1. Elizabeth Beeson to David G. Burnet, April 10, 1836," *Nesbitt Memorial Library Journal* I (Sept. 1997): 182. Spring Creek is the present-day boundary between Harris and Montgomery counties and extends westward into Waller County.

3 For whatever reason, some authors write that the Beesons did in fact operate a boarding house or inn at Harrisburg. The letter to Burnet may have precipitated that idea, but the timing of the letter would make that idea seem implausible.

4 Barber, *David Kokernot*, 183; Dewees, *Letters from an Early Settler of Texas*, 193, 201.

5 Dewees, *Letters from an Early Settler of Texas*, 201. Dewees never related who had accompanied him back to the Colorado. One could assume with some confidence that someone from the Beeson family, possibly Collins or Abel Beeson, neither of whom were serving in the army, was with him.
6 Dewees, *Letters from an Early Settler of Texas*, 210–211.
7 Dimmick, *Sea of Mud*, 319–322.

CONCLUSION

1 Houston to Royall, Mar. 24, 1836, in Jenkins, *Papers of the Texas Revolution*, V: 180.
2 Foote, *Texas and the Texans*, II: 278.
3 Barker, "San Jacinto Campaign," 279; Labadie, "San Jacinto Campaign," 44.
4 "Compendium of the History of Texas," 59.

BIOGRAPHICAL APPENDIX

1 Karnes' friend, Texian hero Deaf Smith, died soon after Texan independence, in November 1837.
2 Dixon and Kemp, *Heroes of San Jacinto*, 307.
3 Barker, "San Jacinto Campaign," 263.
4 Reuben M. Potter, "Escape of Karnes and Teal from Matamoros," *The Quarterly of the Texas State Historical Association* 4 (Oct. 1900): 74–75.
5 Potter, "Escape of Karnes and Teal from Matamoros," 75–77.
6 Potter, "Escape of Karnes and Teal from Matamoros," 77–81; Moore, *Savage Frontier*, I: 153.
7 Anna Muckleroy, "The Indian Policy of the Republic of Texas," *Southwestern Historical Quarterly* 26 (July 1922): 19–20.
8 James T. DeShields, *Border Wars of Texas* (Waco: Texian Press, 1976), 245.
9 John H. Brown, *Indian Wars and Pioneers of Texas* (Austin: L. E. Daniell, 1880), 50–51.
10 Moore, *Savage Frontier*, II: 231–232.
11 Moore, *Savage Frontier*, III: 120–122; Gammel, *Laws of Texas*, II: 15–20, 29–30.
12 Moore, *Savage Frontier*, II: 288–289.
13 Moore, *Savage Frontier*, II: 333; Difficulties with the Tonkaway [sic] and Comanche Indians in Bexar and Vicinity, 1836–41, and between Austin and the Falls of the Brazos, 1840; Hays's Expeditions against Laredo, 1840, in Gulick et al., *Lamar Papers*, IV, Part 1: 231–232.
14 Moore, *Savage Frontier*, II: 335–336.
15 A. Sidney Johnston, "Instructions to Lieutenant-Colonel William S. Fisher, Relative to a Talk with the Comanches, January 30, 1840," Texas Legislature, *Appendix to the Journals of the House of Representatives, Fifth Congress of the Republic of Texas* (Austin: Austin city Gazette, 1841), Document E, 134–135.
16 Moore, *Savage Frontier*, III: 4, 10–11; DeShields, *Border Wars of Texas*, 311–312; Johnston, "Instructions to Fisher."

17 Hugh McLeod, "Letter from Col. Hugh McLeod, Communicating the Defeat of the Comanches at San Antonio, March 20, 1840," *Appendix to the Journals of the House of Representatives: Fifth Congress*, Document F, 136–139.
18 M. B. Lamar Address to Harrisburg Volunteers, Mar. 1839, in Gulick at al., *Lamar Papers*, II: 510–511.
19 *Brazos Courier* (Brazoria), Sep. 1, 1856.
20 Potter, "Escape of Karnes and Teal from Matamoros," 81–82.
21 Norman C. Krischke, *A Visit to the Holman Valley: 9 Dec 1844–29 Feb 1996, Over 150 Years of the Holman Valley* (Schulenburg, TX: N. C. Krischke, 1996), 1. Evidently, Jesse Burnam was content with his oldest daughter's engagement, but he wanted the couple to delay their marriage until Mary turned 18.
22 Jesse Austin Holman, "Recollections and Legendry of My Maternal Grandfather and His Family," Feb. 5, 1921, Burnham [Burnam] Family Papers (Fayette Public Library, Museum & Archive, La Grange, TX; original in the Dolph Briscoe Center for American History, The University of Texas at Austin). Jesse's wife Temperance died of cholera in 1833.
23 Krischke, *Visit to the Holman Valley*, 1; Willey, *Capt. Jesse Burnam*, 70.
24 Burnam-Ross Marriage Record, Aug. 1, 1837, Colorado County, Marriage Records, Book B, p. 2, County Clerk Records, Colorado County Courthouse; Colorado County Historical Survey Committee and Historic Preservation Committee, *Early Settlers and Bits*, 35.
25 Burnam-Zumwalt Marriage Record, Aug. 1, 1837, Colorado County, Marriage Records, Book B, p. 3, County Clerk Records, Colorado County Courthouse. More dates attributed to the marriage of William Owen Burnam and Caroline Zumwalt are 1836; May 25, 1837; Aug. 1, 1837; Aug. 1, 1838, 1840, and others.
26 Townsend-Burnam Marriage Record, Aug. 1, 1837, Burnam-Ross Marriage Record, Aug. 1, 1837, Burnam-Zumwalt Marriage Record, Aug. 1, 1837, Colorado County, Marriage Records, Book B, pp. 2–3; Colorado County Historical Survey Committee and Historic Preservation Committee, *Early Settlers and Bits*, 35.
27 Brown, *History of Texas from 1685 to 1892*, II: 103–104; Willey, *Capt. Jesse Burnam*, 50.
28 Gideon Lincecum Burnam, "Biography of Jesse Burnam," Aug. 1, 1882, Burnham [Burnam]/Freytag Papers (Fayette Library, Museum & Archives; originally published in *The Alamo, A Monthly Magazine for Everybody* 1 (Aug. 1882).
29 Freytag, *Chronicles of Fayette*, 57–60.
30 Brown, *Indian Wars and Pioneers of Texas*, 83–84.
31 Lindley, *Biographical Directory of the Texas Conventions and Congresses*, 59.
32 Frances T. Ingmire, comp., *Fayette County, Texas Marriage Records, 1838–1870* (St. Louis: Frances T. Ingmire, 1980), 1.
33 Jesse Burnam to George Holman, June 29, 1846, Texas, Fayette County, Deed Records, Book D, pp. 292–293, County Clerk Records, Fayette County Courthouse, La Grange, TX; Krischke, *Visit to the Holman Valley*, 5; Holman, "Recollections and Legendry of My Maternal Grandfather and His Family."
34 "Notes and Fragments: Early Courts of Fayette County," *The Quarterly of the Texas State Historical Association* 7 (July 1903), 81–83.

35 Mark Abolaifia-Rosenweig, *Monument Hill State Historic Site: The Dawson and Mier Expeditions and Their Place in Texas History* (Schulenburg, TX: Fayette County Historical Commission, n.d.), 8–10; Holman, "Recollections and Legendry of My Maternal Grandfather and His Family;" George Holman evidently had trouble corralling his mule and was therefore in a later group to arrive at the battle site, thus likely saving his life.

36 Krischke, *Visit to the Holman Valley*, 1.

37 Jesse Burnam to John Holman, Dec. 9, 1844, Fayette County, Deed Records, Book C, p. 412; Krischke, *Visit to the Holman Valley*, 5.

38 Krischke, *Visit to the Holman Valley*, 5.

39 Krischke, *Visit to the Holman Valley*, 1.

40 Gifford White, ed., *The 1840 Census of the Republic of Texas* (Austin: Pemberton Press, 1966), 26.

41 Holman, "Recollections and Legendry of My Maternal Grandfather and His Family;" Jesse Burnam to George Holman, Dec. 31, 1853, Fayette County, Deed Records, Book J, pp. 436–437.

42 Tula Townsend Wyatt, *The Seven Townsend Brothers of Texas, 1826–1838* (Austin: Aus-Tex Duplicators, 1974), 276; Holman, "Recollections and Legendry of My Maternal Grandfather and His Family;" W. S. Townsend Estate, Jan. 22, 1848 (Case #153), Burnam Family Papers; Townsend Estate, Feb. 2, 1848, Fayette County, Probate Records, Book A, pp. 283–284, County Clerk Records, Fayette County Courthouse.

43 Townsend Guardianship, Jan. 2, 1850, Fayette County, County Court Minutes, Book B, pp. 29–30, County Clerk Records, Fayette County Courthouse.

44 Holman, "Recollections and Legendry of My Maternal Grandfather and His Family;" Robert J. Burnam to Jesse B. Holman, June 3, 1853, Colorado County, Deed Records, Book I, p. 350.

45 Willey, *Capt. Jesse Burnam*, 54–55. John Townsend was a son of William and Mary Burnam Townsend and one of Jesse's wards.

46 Holman, "Recollections and Legendry of My Maternal Grandfather and His Family."

47 Smithwick, *Evolution of a State*, 312.

48 Miller, *Bounty and Donation Land Grants of Texas*, 144.

49 Willey, *Capt. Jesse Burnam*, 56–57.

50 Smithwick, *Evolution of a State*, 319.

51 Willey, *Capt. Jesse Burnam*, 56–57; Betty McNabb, "Life on the Double Horn in 1864," *Highlander* (Marble Falls), July 22, 1976.

52 Smithwick, *Evolution of a State*, 312.

53 Willey, *Capt. Jesse Burnam*, 58–60; W. L. Burnam, "Vivid Recollections of Eighty Years in Burnet County," *Burnet Bulletin*, June 30, 1938.

54 Willey, *Capt. Jesse Burnam*, 63.

55 Willey, *Capt. Jesse Burnam*, 65; Krischke, *Visit to the Holman Valley*, 6, 10–12.

56 Holman, "Recollections and Legendry of My Maternal Grandfather and His Family;" United States Department of War, Compiled Service Records of Confederate Soldiers Who Served in Organizations from Texas (Record Group 109, National Archives, Washington, DC): Twenty-First Texas Cavalry (J. Bennett Burnham and J. H. Alexander).
57 Debo, *Burnet County History*, II: 40; Willey, *Capt. Jesse Burnam*, 65.
58 Willey, *Capt. Jesse Burnam*, 63–64; McNabb, "Life on the Double Horn in 1864."
59 Willey, *Capt. Jesse Burnam*, 65. Note that in 1864, Jesse Burnam was 72 years old.
60 Jesse Burnam, Property Destroyed in 1836.
61 Jesse Burnam, Jan. 3, 1871, Republic Claims, Pension Claim Number N/A (TSLA, online: Reel Number 206, Image Numbers 365–397).
62 *Burnet Bulletin*, Oct. 12, 1881, Barry Caraway, trans., "Captain Burnam's 90th Birthday," *Burnet County TXGenWeb*, https://txgenwebcounties.org/burnet/BurnamBio.html [Accessed Nov. 1, 2021].
63 Holman, "Recollections and Legendry of My Maternal Grandfather and His Family."
64 "Details for Burnam's Ferry (Historical Marker–Atlas Number 5089000575)" and "Details for Captain Jesse Burnam (Historical Marker–Atlas Number 5507017813)," Texas Historical Commission, *Texas Historic Sites Atlas*, https://atlas.thc.texas.gov/ [Accessed Jan. 18, 2022].
65 Zuber, *My Eighty Years in Texas*, 51–52.
66 Fayette County History Book Committee, *Fayette County, Texas Heritage*, I: 34. Fayette was carved from parts of Colorado County to the south and Bastrop County to the north. Lafayette's castle in France was named Chateau de la Grange-Bléneau, which accounts for the name La Grange.
67 *Matagorda Bulletin*, Dec. 6, 1837; *Telegraph and Texas Register* (Houston), Nov. 4, 1837.
68 Fayette County History Book Committee, *Fayette County, Texas Heritage*, I: 60.
69 Weyand and Wade, *Early History of Fayette County*, 102.
70 Fayette County History Book Committee, *Fayette County, Texas Heritage*, I, 37.
71 Brown, *Indian Wars and Pioneers of Texas*, 75.
72 Brown, *Indian Wars and Pioneers of Texas*, 74–75.
73 Weyand and Wade, *Early History of Fayette County*, 79–80.
74 Brown, *Indian Wars and Pioneers of Texas*, 79.
75 J. S. Lester to Lamar, July 16, 1840, in Gulick et al., *Lamar Papers*, III: 419–421.
76 J. H. Kerr to Moore, Aug. 9, 1840, in Gulick et al., *Lamar Papers*, III: 428–429. Linnville was located just northwest of present-day Port Lavaca on the coast.
77 Brown, *Indian Wars and Pioneers of Texas*, 82.
78 Brown, *History of Texas from 1685 to 1892*, II: 182–183.
79 *Texas Sentinel* (Austin), Nov. 14, 1840.
80 Weyand and Wade, *Early History of Fayette County*, 145; Joseph M. Nance, *Attack and Counterattack: The Texas-Mexican Frontier, 1842* (Austin: University of Texas Press, 1964), 25–26, 36.
81 Nance, *Attack and Counterattack*, 26–28; Yoakum, *History of Texas*, I: 349. During the incursion by Vásquez, Goliad and Refugio were also captured along with San Antonio.

82 Yoakum, *History of Texas*, I: 450.
83 *Telegraph and Texas Register* (Houston), Aug. 17, 24, 1842.
84 Zenas N. Morrell, *Flowers and Fruits from the Wilderness: Thirty-Six Years in Texas and Two Winters in Honduras* (1872; Waco: Baylor University Press, 1976), 169; George R. Nielsen, "Mathew Caldwell," *Southwestern Historical Quarterly* 64 (Apr. 1961): 497; Joseph M. Nance, ed., "Notes and Documents, Brigadier General Adrian Woll's Report of His Expedition into Texas in 1842," *Southwestern Historical Quarterly* 58 (Apr. 1955): 545.
85 Weyand and Wade, *Early History of Fayette County*, 155-158.
86 Abolaifia-Rosenweig, *Monument Hill State Historic Site*, 8-9.
87 Nielsen, "Mathew Caldwell," 498.
88 Nielsen, "Mathew Caldwell," 498-499.
89 Rena Maverick Green, ed., *Memoirs of Mary A. Maverick, A Journal of Early Texas* (1921; San Antonio: Maverick Publishing Company, 2006), 75.
90 John H. Jenkins, ed., *Recollections of Early Texas, the Memoirs of John Holland Jenkins*, 6th ed. (Austin: University of Texas Press, 2008), 99-101.
91 Morrell, *Flowers and Fruits*, 178-179.
92 Charles W. Corkran, "John Henry Moore, 1800-1880," (M.A. Thesis, University of Texas, 1964), 294-295.
93 *Weekly State Gazette* (Austin), Oct. 12, 1878; Barkley Thompson, "'You Assassin!'-Intrigue in Old Fayette County; The Murder of Captain Ira Griffin Killough," *Journal of the West* 57 (Fall 2018): 74.
94 *Weekly State Gazette* (Austin), Oct. 12, 1878; *Weekly Democratic Statesman* (Austin), Oct. 10, 1878; *Galveston Daily News*, Oct. 4, 1878; *Denison Daily Herald*, Oct. 16, 1878; *Daily Banner* (Brenham), Oct. 11, 1878; *La Grange Journal*, Sep. 29, 1881.
95 *Galveston Daily News*, Feb. 26, 1879. Twenty years later, Sayers would become the governor of Texas.
96 Thompson, "You Assassin!" 77-78.
97 *Daily Banner* (Brenham), July 13, 1879.
98 Thompson, "You Assassin!" 77; *Daily Banner* (Brenham), Sept. 30, 1879. The Brenham newspaper credited the *Colorado Citizen* (Columbus) for its report.
99 *La Grange Journal*, Dec. 15, 1880.
100 *La Grange Journal*, Dec. 22, 1880; John H. Moore Estate, Jan. 20, 1880, Fayette County, Probate Records, Book K, pp. 509-510. Richard and Eliza Moore Cook both died in 1877.
101 *La Grange Journal*, Sept. 29, 1881.
102 "Details for Battle of Gonzales (Historical Marker-Atlas Number 5177002221)," "Details for Colonel John H. Moore House-Atlas Number 5149003460)," and "Details for John Henry Moore (Historical Marker-Atlas Number 5149003462)," Texas Historical Commission, *Texas Historic Sites Atlas*.
103 Dewees, Letters from an Early Settler of Texas, 192.
104 Dewees, *Letters from an Early Settler of Texas*, 193.
105 Elizabeth Beeson, "Miscellaneous Letters: 1. Elizabeth Beeson to David G. Burnet, April 10, 1836," *Nesbitt Memorial Library Journal* 7 (Sept. 1997): 182.

106 Dewees, *Letters from an Early Settler of Texas*, 201.
107 *Telegraph and Texas Register* (Columbia), Oct. 25, 1836.
108 *Telegraph and Texas Register* (Columbia), Oct. 4, 1836; Dewees, *Letters from an Early Settler of Texas*, 213–214.
109 *Telegraph and Texas Register* (Columbia), Mar. 14, 1837; B. Beeson Estate, Feb. 27, 1837, C. Beeson Estate, Feb. 27, 1837, Colorado County, Probate Records, Book A [Transcribed], p. 1, County Clerk Records, Colorado County Courthouse; Berry & Perry v. Dewees & Beeson, Nov. 12, 1856, Twenty-Fifth District Court, Civil Records, Case File Number CV1101, Case ID Number 20653. This seemingly innocent appointment of Leander Beeson and William Dewees as executor of Collins Beeson's estate would be challenged decades later. Mary Ann Beeson Perry and her nephew, John Berry (Nepsey's son), sued Dewees and Leander Beeson, claiming that land awarded to Collins in Henderson County had not been divided among the heirs. The suit continued for over a decade and a half after Leander's death.
110 Berry Estate, Feb. 27, 1837, Colorado County, Probate Records, Book A [Transcribed], p. 1.
111 J. Berry Guardianship, Feb. 1850, Colorado County, Probate Records, Book C [Transcribed], p. 227.
112 Benjamin Beeson, Dec. 24, 1836, Republic Claims, Audited Claim Number 187 (TSLA, online: Reel Number 6, Image Numbers 772–773).
113 Beeson Guardianship, Feb. 27, 1837, Colorado County, Probate Records, Book A [Transcribed], p. 1.
114 Bill Stein, "Consider the Lily: The Ungilded History of Colorado County (Part 3)," *Nesbitt Memorial Library Journal* 6 (May 1996): 73.
115 Republic of Texas v Leander Beeson, et al, Dec. 15, 1837, Twenty-Fifth District Court, Criminal Records, Case File Number R6, Case Number 15166, Colorado County Courthouse; Stein, "Consider the Lily (Part 3)," 73.
116 Republic of Texas v Abel Beeson, Nov. 14, 1839, Twenty-Fifth District Court, Criminal Records, Case File Number R80, Case Number 15182.
117 Gammel, *Laws of Texas*, II: 1,110; Beeson-Gibberson Marriage Record, Jan. 10, 1842, Baxter-Pace Marriage Record, Jan. 23, 1842, Colorado County, Marriage Records, Book B, pp. 29, 40.
118 Republic of Texas v. Leander Beeson, Sept. 5, 1844, Twenty-Fifth District Court, Criminal Records, Case File Number R327, Case Number 15092.
119 State of Texas v. Leander Beeson, Oct. 1848, Twenty-Fifth District Court, Criminal Records, Case File Number 568, Case ID Number 10904.
120 State of Texas v. Gideon Townsend, Nov. 4, 1850, Twenty-Fifth District Court, Criminal Records, Case File Number 600, Case ID Number 11787; Wyatt, *Seven Townsend Brothers*, 100, 131.
121 State of Texas v. Leander Beeson, Oct. 30, 1851, Twenty-Fifth District Court, Criminal Records, Case File Number 718, Case ID Number 12734.
122 State of Texas v. L. Beeson, J. Berry, and A. Shannon, Oct. 23, 1854, Twenty-Fifth District Court, Criminal Records, Case File Number 147, Case ID Number 3338.
123 L. Beeson Estate, Jan. 25, 1858, Colorado County, Probate Records, Book D, p. 559.

124 Perry-Sapp Marriage Record, Nov. 16, 1853, Colorado County, Marriage Records, Book C, p. 55; George W. Breeding and Bill Stein, comps., "Index to 1860 Census," https://www.columbustexaslibrary.net/local-history-and-genealogy-material/links-to-colorado-county-censuses/index-to-1860-census [Accessed Oct. 14, 2021]. The 1860 census shows Lenora Sapp, only child of Basil and Mary Ann Sapp, living in the household of George and Mary Ann Perry.

125 "Details for Beason's (Beeson's) Crossing (Historical Marker–Atlas Number 5089000347)" and "Details for Benjamin Beason's Crossing of the Colorado River (Historical Marker–Atlas Number 5089000368)," Texas Historical Commission, *Texas Historic Sites Atlas.* Somehow the Beeson name morphed into a different spelling with the letter 'a' in it. Despite the present-day memorials, Benjamin Beeson and his sons signed their name with the double 'e'.

126 Dewees, *Letters from an Early Settler of Texas,* 201, 210–211.

127 *Telegraph and Texas Register* (Houston), May 2, 1837. In this first ad, Dewees is listed as proprietor along with Thomas Thatcher and Robert Brotherton. Evidently, this partnership was not fully affirmed and the latter two were subsequently replaced with Joseph W. E. Wallace in future ads.

128 Colorado County, County Court Minutes, Book A, pp. 20–22, County Clerk Records, Colorado County Courthouse.

129 Andrew F. Muir, ed., *Texas in 1837: An Anonymous Contemporary Narrative* (Austin: University of Texas Press, 1958), 80–81.

130 Ferdinand Roemer, *Texas with Particular Reference to German Immigration and the Physical Appearance of the Country* (San Antonio: Standard Printing Company, 1935), 81; Friedrich W. von Wrede, *Sketches of Life in The United States of North America and Texas,* comp. Emil Drescher, trans. Chester W. Geue (Waco: Texian Press, 1973), 94.

131 Bronson-Bostick Marriage Record, Oct. 4, 1837, Colorado County, Marriage Records, Book B, p. 4.

132 "Known Elected and Appointed Officials," *Nesbitt Memorial Library,* https://www.columbustexas library.net/ local-history-and-genealogy-material/public-records/public-records-from-early-colorado-county-history/known-elected-and-appointed-officials [Accessed Jan. 2, 2022]; Colorado County, County Court Minutes, Book A, pp. i–viii.

133 Colorado County, County Court Minutes, Book A, p. 64. In October 1841, the county court paid Dewees $7 per month so they could use his "Billiard Room" on the town square for a temporary courthouse. The agreement was canceled the following April.

134 Republic of Texas v. Leander Beeson, et al., Dec. 15, 1837, Twenty-Fifth District Court, Criminal Files, Case File Number R6, Case Number 15166, State of Texas v. Leander Beeson, Oct. 30, 1851, Twenty-Fifth District Court, Criminal Records, Case File Number 718, Case ID Number 12734. The district court records indicate Dewees was a primary defendant. Though clearly part of the mob, he appeared peripheral to the main incident. It may well be that only Leander Beeson and Spencer Townsend were ultimately defendants in the trial and the charge against Dewees was not pursued.

135 Stein, "Consider the Lily (Part 3)," 71–72.
136 Republic of Texas v. Colin De Bland, Sep. 11, 1838, Twenty-Fifth District Court, Criminal Records, Case File Number R16, Case Number 15026.
137 Republic of Texas v. L. J. Bryan Rhine, Sep. 5, 1844, Twenty-Fifth District Court, Criminal Records, Case File Number R339, Case ID Number 15114.
138 State of Texas v. William B. Dewees, Randolph Foster, Ira A. Harris, Don Turner, Amos Besch, Don F. Payne, and Cook, Feb. 26, 1866, Twenty-Fifth District Court, Criminal Records, Case File Number 582, Case ID Number 11286. Ira A. Harris was the husband of Dilue Rose Harris, well known for her documentation of early Texas life.
139 *Texas Monument* (La Grange), Aug. 31, 1853.
140 *Texas Presbyterian* (Victoria), Mar. 13, 1847.
141 Dewees-Besch Marriage Record, Mar. 7, 1847, Colorado County, Marriage Records, Book B, p. 87; Archibald McNeil, Dorothy Albrecht and Bill Stein, comps., "Index to 1850 Census," https://www.columbustexaslibrary.net/local-history-and-geneology-materials/links-to-colorado-county-censuses/index-to-1850-census [Accessed Oct. 18, 2021].
142 Dewees Estate, June 1, Sept. 28, 1847, Colorado County, Probate Records, Book C [Transcribed], pp. 58, 70.
143 Lydia G. Dewees to W. B. Dewees, Jan. 1, 1847, Colorado County, Deed Records, Book F, pp. 52–53.
144 McNeil, Albrecht, and Stein, "Index to 1850 Census."
145 Bill Stein, "Consider the Lily: The Ungilded History of Colorado County (Part 4)," *Nesbitt Memorial Library Journal* 6 (Sept. 1996): 133–134; William B. Dewees, "Letter from William B. Dewees to his Mother," *Nesbitt Memorial Library Journal* 1 (Sept. 1991): 315–316.
146 *Texas Monument* (La Grange), Feb. 9, 1853.
147 Dewees, *Letters from an Early Settler of Texas*, 42.
148 Brown, Indian Wars and Pioneers of Texas, 79.
149 Dewees, "Letter from William B. Dewees to his Mother," 315–316.
150 *Colorado Citizen* (Columbus), March 5, 19, 1859.
151 Colorado County, County Court Minutes, Book I, p. 71.
152 State of Texas v. William B. Dewees, Feb. 29, 1868, Twenty-Fifth District Court, Criminal Records, Case File Number 740, Case ID Number 12869; E. M. Wheelock, *Reports of Cases Argued and Decided in the Supreme Court of the State of Texas, Volume 32: Tyler and Austin Sessions, 1869, and the Greater Part of the Galveston Session, 1870* (Galveston: Richardson, Belo & Company, 1871), 570–572.
153 Bill Stein, "Consider the Lily: The Ungilded History of Colorado County (Part 8)," *Nesbitt Memorial Library Journal* 10 (Jan. 2000): 62.
154 *Colorado Citizen* (Columbus), Apr. 18, 1878.
155 "Details for William B. DeWees (Historical Marker–Atlas Number 5089001193)," Texas Historical Commission, *Texas Historic Sites Atlas*.
156 Rau, "Nancy Millar Alley," 16.
157 Harrison, *Alleyton*, 23.

158 Betts Estate, Mar. 27, 1837, and Millar Guardianship, Mar. 27, 1837, Colorado County, Probate Records, Book A (Transcribed), p. 2. Elizabeth Payne Millar's husband had died in October 1831. She later married Jacob Betts.
159 Rau, "Nancy Millar Alley," 16.
160 McNeil, Albrecht, and Stein, "Index to 1850 Census."
161 Rau, "Nancy Millar Alley," 15–16. Abram Alley's simple brand was the capital letter "A."
162 "Known Elected and Appointed Officials," *Nesbitt Memorial Library*.
163 Harrison, *Alleyton*, 7.
164 Harrison, *Alleyton*, 7; Rau, "Nancy Millar Alley," 16–17.
165 Colorado County Historical Commission, *Historic Homes of Colorado County: 1832–1915* (Columbus, TX: A to Z Printing & Graphic Design, 2006), 4.
166 Harrison, *Alleyton*, 6.
167 Harrison, *Alleyton*, 6–9; S. G. Reed, *A History of Texas Railroads* (Houston: St. Clair Publishing, 1941), 54–61. Part of the agreement was that Alley would raise $800 toward the purchase of an engine.
168 Harrison, *Alleyton*, 41.
169 "Details for Abram Alley Log Cabin (Historical Marker–Atlas Number 5089008827)," "Details for Alleyton (Historical Maker–Atlas Number 5089000129)," and "Details for Alleyton Cemetery (Historical Marker–Atlas Number 5507016466)," Texas Historical Commission, *Texas Historic Sites Atlas*.
170 Williamson Daniels, Aug. 9, 1838, Republic Claims, Audited Claim Number 8059 (TSLA, online: Reel Number 24, Image Numbers 44–52); Daughters of the Republic of Texas, *Muster Rolls of the Texas Revolution* (Austin: Daughters of the Republic of Texas, 1986), 70.
171 Williamson Daniels, Texas General Land Office, *Land Grant Search: Lavaca County*, https://s3.glo.texas.gov/glo/history/archives/land-grants/landgrants.cfm?intID=170583 [Accessed Jan. 13, 2022].
172 Petition Asking for a New Municipality to be Called Colorado, n.d., Texas Memorials and Petitions, 1834–1929 (TSLA, online: Images 197–198); Colorado County Historical Survey Committee and Historic Preservation Committee, *Early Settlers and Bits of History of Columbus and Colorado County*, 26.
173 Harrison, *Alleyton*, 187; Williamson Daniels, Sept. 26, 1853, Republic Claims, Public Debt Claim Number 2439 (TSLA, online: Reel Number 147, Image Numbers 627–711).
174 Hockley to Rusk, Apr. 1, 1836, in Jenkins, *Papers of the Texas Revolution*, V: 286–287.
175 Houston to Rusk, Apr. 3, 1836, in Jenkins, *Papers of the Texas Revolution*, V: 309–310.
176 Debo, *Burnet County History*, II: 177.
177 Debo, *Burnet County History*, II, 177; Harriet Smither, ed., *House Journal, Fourth Congress of the Republic of Texas, 1839–1840* (3 vols.; Austin: Von Boeckmann-Jones Co., 1840), II: 28, 123.
178 Miller, *Bounty and Donation Land Grants of Texas*, 393.
179 Smithwick, *Evolution of a State*, 105; Smither, *House Journal*, II: 123.
180 Debo, *Burnet County History*, II: 178.
181 Debo, *Burnet County History*, II: 178.

182 Debo, *Burnet County History*, II: 178–179.
183 Debo, *Burnet County History*, II: 179; "Details for Peter Kerr (Historical Marker-Atlas Number 5053009723)," *Texas Historical Commission, Texas Historic Sites Atlas*.
184 *Southern Recorder* (Milledgeville, GA), June 14, 1836; *Georgia Messenger* (Macon), June 9, 1836.
185 James P. Trezevant, Texas General Land Office, *Land Grant Search, County: N/A*, https://s3.glo.texas.gov/glo/history/archives/land-grants/landgrants.cfm?intID=491007 [Accessed Nov. 2, 2021]; James P. Trezevant, Nov. 23, 1836, Republic Claims, Audited Claim Number 1581 (TSLA, online: Reel Number 106, Image Numbers 376–379).
186 M. K. Moses, Oct. 26, 1836, Republic Claims, Audited Claim Number 1278 (TSLA, online: Reel Number 75, Image Numbers 671–674).
187 Joseph Andrews, Dec. 1, 1837, Republic Claim, Audited Claim Unnumbered 01 (TSLA, online: Reel Number 3, Image Numbers 59–62). Joseph Andrews did provide a written account of the fighting at Refugio and his subsequent escape and capture. He did not mention the Battle of San Jacinto.
188 John Minton, Oct. 1, 1870, Republic Claims, Pension Claim Number N/A (TSLA, online: Reel Number 230, Image Number 79); Robert W. Trezevant, "Biographical Sketches: James Peter Trezevant (1815–1860), Mary Ann Elizabeth Williams (nee Hicks) (1807–1893)," *The Georgia Battalion Project*, http://georgiabattalion.com/biographical-sketches/james-peter-trezevant-1815-1860mary-ann-elizabeth-williams-nee-hicks-1807-1893/ [Accessed Nov. 8, 2021].
189 Samuel G. Hardaway, June 12, 1874, Republic Claims, Pension Claim Number N/A (TSLA, online: Reel Number 219, Image Number 184); Samuel G. Hardaway, Apr. 30, 1836, Republic Claims, Audited Claim Unnumbered 01 (TSLA, online: Reel Number 41, Image Numbers 16–19); *Georgia Messenger* (Macon), June 9, 1836.
190 *Georgia Messenger* (Macon), June 9, 1836.
191 *Georgia Messenger* (Macon), June 9, 1836.
192 Scarborough, "Georgia Battalion in the Texas Revolution," 515–517.
193 Miller, *Bounty and Donation Land Grants of Texas*, 323; Samuel G. Hardaway, Texas General Land Office, *Land Grant Search: Goliad County*, https://s3.glo.texas.gov/glo/history/archives/land-grants/landgrants. cfm?intID=158642 [Accessed Nov. 2, 2021]. Miller's work mistakenly sites Hardaway's service as ending Sept. 30, 1836, instead of Apr. 30, 1836.
194 Robert W. Trezevant, "Biographical Sketches: Samuel George Hardaway (1820–1873)," *The Georgia Battalion Project*, http://georgiabattalion.com/biographical-sketches/samuel-george-hardaway-1820-1873/ [Accessed Nov. 8, 2021].

BIBLIOGRAPHY

PRIMARY SOURCES

UNPUBLISHED PAPERS

Burnham [Burnam] Family Papers. Fayette Public Library, Museum & Archive, La Grange, TX.

Burnham [Burnam]/Freytag Papers. Fayette Public Library, Museum & Archive, La Grange, TX.

UNPUBLISHED GOVERNMENT DOCUMENTS

Texas. Twenty-Fifth District Court. Civil Records. Colorado County Courthouse, Columbus, TX.

———. ———. Criminal Records. Colorado County Courthouse, Columbus, TX.

———. Colorado County. County Court Minutes. Book A. County Clerk Records. Colorado County Courthouse, Columbus, TX.

———. ———. County Court Minutes. Book I. County Clerk Records. Colorado County Courthouse, Columbus, TX.

———. ———. Deed Records. Book A [Transcribed Spanish]. County Clerk Records. Colorado County Courthouse, Columbus, TX.

———. ———. Deed Records. Book F. County Clerk Records. Colorado County Courthouse, Columbus, TX.

———. ———. Deed Records. Book I. County Clerk Records. Colorado County Courthouse, Columbus, TX.

———. ———. Deed Records. Book J. County Clerk Records. Colorado County Courthouse, Columbus, TX.

———. ———. Marriage Records. Book B. County Clerk Records. Colorado County Courthouse, Columbus, TX.

———. ———. Marriage Records. Book C. County Clerk Records. Colorado County Courthouse, Columbus, TX.

———. ———. Probate Records. Book A [Transcribed]. County Clerk Records. Colorado County Courthouse, Columbus, TX.

———. ———. Probate Records. Book C [Transcribed]. County Clerk Records. Colorado County Courthouse, Columbus, TX.

———. ———. Probate Records. Book D. County Clerk Records. Colorado County Courthouse, Columbus, TX.

———. Comptroller. Republic Claims. Texas State Library and Archives, Austin, TX [online].

———. Fayette County. Deed Records. Book C. County Clerk Records. Fayette County Courthouse, La Grange, TX.

———. ———. Deed Records. Book D. County Clerk Records. Fayette County Courthouse, La Grange, TX.

———. ———. Deed Records. Book J. County Clerk Records. Fayette County Courthouse, La Grange, TX.

———. ———. Probate Records. Book A. County Clerk Records. Fayette County Courthouse, La Grange, TX.

———. ———. Probate Records. Book B. County Clerk Records. Fayette County Courthouse, La Grange, TX.

———. ———. Probate Records. Book K. County Clerk Records. Fayette County Courthouse, La Grange, TX.

———. Legislature. Memorials & Petitions, 1834–1929. Texas State Library and Archives, Austin, TX.

United States. Department of War. Compiled Service Records of Confederate Soldiers Who Served in Organizations from Texas. Record Group 109. National Archives, Washington, DC.

PUBLISHED PAPERS

Alsbury, Samuel E., editor. "The Private Journal of Juan Nepomuceno Almonte." *Southwestern Historical Quarterly* 48 (July 1944), 10–32.

An Old Soldier. "First Breaking Out of the Texas Revolution at Gonzales." *The Texas Almanac of 1860* (Galveston: Richardson & Company, 1859).

Barker, Eugene C., editor. *The Austin Papers*. 3 volumes. Washington, DC: Government Printing Office, 1920–1926; Austin: University of Texas Press, 1927.

———. "Minutes of the Ayuntamiento of San Felipe de Austin, 1828–1832, I." *Southwestern Historical Quarterly* 21 (January 1918), 299–326.

———. "Minutes of the Ayuntamiento of San Felipe de Austin, 1828–1832, III." *Southwestern Historical Quarterly* 22 (July 1918), 78–95.

_____. "The San Jacinto Campaign." *The Quarterly of the Texas State Historical Association* 4 (April 1901), 237–343.

Beeson, Elizabeth. "Miscellaneous Letters: 1. Elizabeth Beeson to David G. Burnet, April 10, 1836." *Nesbitt Memorial Library Journal* 7 (September 1997), 182.

Berlandier, Jean Louis. *Journey to Mexico During the Years 1826 to 1834*. Translated by Sheila M. Ohlendorf, Josette M. Bigelow, and Mark M. Standifer. 2 volumes. Austin: Texas State Historical Association, 1980.

Boyle, Andrew A. "Reminiscences of the Texas Revolution." *The Quarterly of the Texas State Historical Association* 13 (April 1910), 285–291.

Bradford, A. L., and T. N. Campbell, editors. "Notes and Documents: Journal of Lincecum's Travels in Texas, 1835." *Southwestern Historical Quarterly* 53 (October 1949), 180–201.

Burke's Texas Almanac and Immigrant's Handbook for 1883. Houston: J. Burke, 1883.

Calder, Robert J. "Recollections of the Texas Campaign of 1836." *The Texas Almanac for 1861* (Galveston: Richardson & Company, 1860).

Casteñeda, Carlos E., editor. *The Mexican Side of the Texas Revolution*. Dallas: P. L. Turner Company, 1956.

Coleman, Robert M. *Houston Displayed, or Who Won the Battle of San Jacinto?* Austin: Brick Row Book Shop, 1964.

"Compendium of the History of Texas." *The Texas Almanac of 1860* (Galveston: Richardson & Company, 1859).

Crook, Wilson W. III, editor. *Reminiscences of Moses Austin Bryan*. Houston: Houston Archeological Society, 2016.

Davenport, Harbert. "The Men of Goliad: Dedicatory Address at the Unveiling of the Monument Erected by the Texas Centennial Commission at the Grave of Fannin's Men." *Southwestern Historical Quarterly* 43 (July 1939), 1–41.

Davis, Robert E., editor. *The Diary of William Barrett Travis*. Waco: Texian Press, 1966.

Day, James M., compiler. *The Texas Almanac: 1857–1873: A Compendium of Texas History*. Waco: Texian Press, 1967.

De la Peña, José Enrique. *With Santa Anna in Texas: A Personal Narrative of the Revolution*. Translated by Carmen Perry. College Station: Texas A&M University Press, 1975.

De la Teja, Jesús F., editor. *A Revolution Remembered: The Memoirs and Selected Correspondence of Juan N. Seguín*. Austin: Texas State Historical Association, 2002.

Dewees, William B. "Letter from William B. Dewees to his Mother." *Nesbitt Memorial Library Journal* 1 (September 1991), 313–316.

_____. *Letters from an Early Settler of Texas*. 1852; reprint, Waco: Texian Press, 1968.

Franz, Joe B., editor. "Moses Lapham: His Life and Selected Correspondence, I." *Southwestern Historical Quarterly* 54 (January 1951), 324–332.

Freytag, Walter P., editor. *Chronicles of Fayette: The Reminiscences of Julia Lee Sinks.* Schulenburg, TX: Schulenburg Printing & Office Supplies, 1975.

Green, Rena Maverick, ed. *Memoirs of Mary A. Maverick, A Journal of Early Texas.* 1921; San Antonio: Maverick Publishing Company, 2006.

Gulick, Jr., Charles Adams, Winnie Allen, Katherine Elliott and Harriet Smither, editors. *The Papers of Mirabeau Buonaparte Lamar.* 6 volumes. 1921–1927; reprint, Austin: Pemberton Press, 1968.

Hansen, Todd, editor. *The Alamo Reader: A Study in History.* Mechanicsburg, PA: Stackpole Books, 2003.

Holley, Mary Austin. *Texas.* 1836; Austin: Texas State Historical Association, 1990.

Horton, Alexander. "Life of A. Horton and Early Settlement of San Augustine County." *The Quarterly of the Texas State Historical Association* 14 (April 1911), 305–314.

Hunter, Robert H. *Narrative of Robert Hancock Hunter.* Austin: Encino Press, 1966.

Jackson, Jack, editor, and John Wheat, translator. *Almonte's Texas: Juan N. Almonte's 1834 Inspection, Secret Report, and Role in the 1836 Campaign.* Austin: Texas State Historical Association, 2003.

———. *Texas by Terán: The Diary Kept by General Manuel de Mier y Terán on His 1828 Inspection of Texas.* Austin: University of Texas Press, 2000.

Jenkins, John H., editor. *The Papers of the Texas Revolution, 1835–1836.* 10 volumes. Austin: Presidial Press, 1973.

———, editor. *Recollections of Early Texas, the Memoirs of John Holland Jenkins.* 6th Edition. Austin: University of Texas Press, 2008.

Kleberg, Rosa. "Some of My Early Experiences in Texas." *The Quarterly of the Texas State Historical Association* 1 (April 1898), 297–302.

Kuykendall, Jonathan H., editor. "Reminiscences of Early Texans, I." *The Quarterly of the Texas State Historical Association* 6 (January 1903), 236–253.

———. "Reminiscences of Early Texans, II." *The Quarterly of the Texas State Historical Association* 6 (April 1903), 311–330.

———. "Reminiscences of Early Texans, III." *The Quarterly of the Texas State Historical Association* 7 (July 1903), 29–64.

Labadie, Nicholas B. "Narrative of the Anahuac, or Opening, Campaign of the Texas Revolution." *The Texas Almanac of 1859.* Galveston: Richardson & Company, 1858.

———. "San Jacinto Campaign." *The Texas Almanac of 1859.* Galveston: Richardson & Company, 1858.

Lack, Paul D., editor. *The Diary of William Fairfax Gray: from Virginia to Texas, 1835–1837.* Dallas: DeGolyer Library & William P. Clements Center for Southwest Studies, 1997.

Linn, John J. *Reminiscences of Fifty Years in Texas.* 1883; reprint, Austin: State House Press, 1986.

Morrell, Zenas N. *Flowers and Fruits from the Wilderness.* 1872; reprint, Waco: Baylor University Press, 1976.

Muir, Andrew F., editor. *Texas in 1837: An Anonymous Contemporary Narrative.* Austin: University of Texas Press, 1958.

Nance, Joseph M., editor. "Notes and Documents, Brigadier General Adrian Woll's Report of His Expedition into Texas in 1842." *Southwestern Historical Quarterly* 58 (April 1955), 523–552.

"Notes and Fragments: Early Courts of Fayette County." *The Quarterly of the Texas State Historical Association* 7 (July 1903), 81–84.

Rabb, Mary Crownover. *Travels and Adventures in Texas in the 1820's Being the Reminiscences of Mary Crownover Rabb.* Waco: W. M. Morrison, 1962.

Roemer, Ferdinand. *Texas with Particular Reference to German Immigration and the Physical Appearance of the Country.* Translated by Oswald Mueller. San Antonio: Standard Printing Company, 1935.

Shipman, Daniel. *Frontier Life, 58 Years in Texas.* 1879; reprint, Pasadena, TX: Abbotsford Publishing Company, 1965.

Sinks, Julia Lee, editor. "Reminiscences of Capt. Jesse Burnam." *The Quarterly of the Texas State Historical Association* 5 (July 1901), 12–18.

Smithwick, Noah. *The Evolution of a State or Recollections of Old Texas Days.* Austin: University of Texas Press, 1983.

Sparks, Stephen F. "Recollections of S. F. Sparks." *The Quarterly of the Texas State Historical Association* 12 (July 1908), 61–79.

Von Wrede, Friedrich W. *Sketches of Life in The United States of North America and Texas.* Compiled by Emil Drescher. Translated by Chester W. Geue. Waco: Texian Press, 1973.

Williams, Amelia W. and Eugene C. Barker, editors. *The Writings of Sam Houston, 1813–1836.* 8 volumes. Austin: University of Texas Press, 1938–1942.

Winkler, Ernest W., editor. *Manuscript Letters and Documents of Early Texians, 1821–1845.* Austin: Steck Company, 1937.

Winters, James W. "An Account of the Battle of San Jacinto." *The Quarterly of the Texas State Historical Association* 6 (October 1902), 139–144.

Zuber, William P. "The Escape of Rose from the Alamo." *The Quarterly of the Texas State Historical Association* 5 (July 1901), 1–11.

———. *My Eighty Years in Texas*. Edited by Janis Boyle Mayfield. Austin: University of Texas Press, 1971.

———. "Notes and Fragments: Capt. Jesse Burnam's Name." *The Quarterly of the Texas State Historical Association* 5 (October 1901), 164.

———. "Notes and Fragments: Last Messenger from the Alamo." *The Quarterly of the Texas State Historical Association* 5 (January 1902), 263–265.

PUBLISHED GOVERNMENT DOCUMENTS

Daughters of the Republic of Texas. *Muster Rolls of the Texas Revolution*. Austin: Daughters of the Republic of Texas, 1986.

Gammel, H.P.N., editor. *The Laws of Texas: 1822–1897*. 2 volumes. Austin: Gammel Book Company, 1898.

Ingmire, Frances T., compiler. *Fayette County, Texas Marriage Records 1838–1870*. St. Louis: Frances T. Ingmire, 1980.

Smither, Harriet, editor. *Journals of the Congress of the Fourth Congress of the Republic of Texas, 1839–1840*. Austin: Von Boeckmann-Jones Company, 1930.

Texas Legislature. *Appendix to the Journal of the House of Representatives, Fifth Congress of the Republic of Texas, 1839–1840*. Austin: Austin City Gazette, 1841.

Wheelock, E. M. *Reports of Cases Argued and Decided in the Supreme Court of the State of Texas, During the Tyler and Austin Sessions, 1869, and the Greater Part of the Galveston Session, 1870*. Galveston: Richardson, Belo & Company, 1871.

White, Gifford, editor. *The 1840 Census of the Republic of Texas*. Austin: Pemberton Press, 1966.

NEWSPAPERS [ALL TEXAS UNLESS OTHERWISE INDICATED]

Brazos Courier (Brazoria)
Burnet Bulletin
Colorado Citizen (Columbus)
Daily Banner (Brenham)
Denison Daily Herald
Galveston Daily News
Georgia Messenger (Macon, GA)
Highlander (Marble Falls)
La Grange Journal
Matagorda Bulletin
Southern Recorder (Milledgeville, GA)
Telegraph and Texas Register (San Felipe de Austin/Columbia/Houston)
Texas Gazette (San Felipe de Austin)
Texas Monument (La Grange)
Texas Presbyterian (Victoria)
Texas Sentinel (Austin)
Weekly State Gazette (Austin)
Weekly Democratic Statesman (Austin)

SECONDARY SOURCES

ARTICLES AND CHAPTERS

Baker, James K. "The Lavaca River Trench and Lost Cannon." *Journal of South Texas* 22 (Fall 2005), 145–154.

Brasher, James E. "A Pivotal Battle Never Fought." *Texas Gun Collector* (Fall 2018), 27–33.

Bugbee, Lester G. "The Old Three Hundred." *The Quarterly of the Texas State Historical Association* 1 (October 1897), 108–117.

Davis, Robert S. Jr. "Georgia Battalion in the Texas Revolution." *Central Georgia Genealogical Society Quarterly* 7 (September 1985), 64–68.

Dunst, Alex. "The Navy of the Republic of Texas." *The Quarterly of the Texas State Historical Association* 12 (January 1909), 165–203.

Ellenberger, Matthew. "Illuminating the Lesser Lights: Notes on the Life of Albert Clinton Horton." *Southwestern Historical Quarterly* 88 (April 1985), 363–386.

Elliott, Claude. "Georgia and the Texas Revolution." *Georgia Historical Quarterly* 28 (December 1944), 190–212.

Hardin, Stephen L. 'Plácido Benavides: Fighting Tejano Federalist," in *Tejano Leadership in Mexican and Revolutionary Texas*, edited by Jesús F. de la Teja. College Station: Texas A&M University Press, 2010.

Houston, Virginia H. Taylor. "Surveying in Texas." *Southwestern Historical Quarterly* 65 (October 1961), 204–233.

Muckleroy, Anna. "The Indian Policy of the Republic of Texas." *Southwestern Historical Quarterly* 26 (July 1922), 1–29.

Nichols, Ruth G. "Samuel May Williams." *Southwestern Historical Quarterly* 56 (October 1952), 189–210.

Nielsen, George R. "Mathew Caldwell." *Southwestern Historical Quarterly* 64 (April 1961), 427–574.

Potter, Reuben M. "Escape of Karnes and Teal from Matamoros." *The Quarterly of the Texas State Historical Association* 4 (October 1900), 71–84.

Rather, Ethel Z. "De Witt's Colony." *The Quarterly of the Texas State Historical Association* 8 (October 1904), 95–192.

Scarborough, Jewel Davis. "The Georgia Battalion in the Texas Revolution: A Critical Study." *Southwestern Historical Quarterly* 63 (April 1960), 511–532.

Smith, W. Roy. "The Quarrel Between Governor Smith and the Council of the Provisional Government of the Republic." *The Quarterly of the Texas State Historical Association* 5 (April 1902), 269–346.

Stein, Bill. "Beyond Boosterism: Establishing the Age of Columbus." *Nesbitt Memorial Library Journal* 2 (May 1992), 71–90.

———. "Consider the Lily: The Ungilded History of Colorado County (Part 1)." *Nesbitt Memorial Library Journal* 6 (January 1996a), 3–34.

———. "Consider the Lily: The Ungilded History of Colorado County (Part 2)." *Nesbitt Memorial Library Journal* 6 (January 1996b), 35–51.

———. "Consider the Lily: The Ungilded History of Colorado County (Part 3)." *Nesbitt Memorial Library Journal* 6 (May 1996), 63–94.

———. "Consider the Lily: The Ungilded History of Colorado County (Part 4)." *Nesbitt Memorial Library Journal* 6 (September 1996), 115–149.

———. "Consider the Lily: The Ungilded History of Colorado County (Part 8)." *Nesbitt Memorial Library Journal* 10 (January 2000), 3–62.

Thompson, Barkley. "'You Assassin!'—Intrigue in Old Fayette County; The Murder of Captain Ira Griffin Killough." *Journal of the West* 57 (Fall 2018), 72–81.

Williams, Amelia. "A Critical Study of the Siege of the Alamo and of the Personnel of its Defenders, Chapter 1." *Southwestern Historical Quarterly* 36 (April 1933), 251–287.

———. "A Critical Study of the Siege of the Alamo and of the Personnel of its Defenders, Chapter 4." *Southwestern Historical Quarterly* 37 (January 1934), 157–184.

———. "A Critical Study of the Siege of the Alamo and of the Personnel of its Defenders, Chapter 5." *Southwestern Historical Quarterly* 37 (April 1934), 237–312.

BOOKS

Abolaifia-Rosenweig, Mark. *Monument Hill State Historic Site: The Dawson and Mier Expeditions and Their Place in Texas History*. Schulenburg, TX: Fayette County Historical Commission, n.d.

Bancroft, Hubert H. *History of the North Mexican States and Texas*. 2 volumes. San Francisco: History Company, 1889.

Barber, Alan. *David Kokernot: Rogue Soldier of the Texas Revolution*. Sandpoint, ID: Kullyspel Press, 2012.

Brown, John H. *History of Texas from 1685 to 1892*. 2 volumes. St. Louis: L. E. Daniell, Publisher, 1893.

———. *Indian Wars and Pioneers of Texas*. Austin: L. E. Daniell, 1880.

Burkhalter, Lois W. *Gideon Lincecum 1793–1874*. Austin: University of Texas Press, 1965.

Carrington, Evelyn M., editor. *Women in Early Texas*. Austin: Jenkins Publishing Company, The Pemberton Press, 1975.

Colorado County Historical Commission. *Historic Homes of Colorado County: 1832–1915.* Columbus, TX: A to Z Printing & Graphic Design, 2006.

Colorado County Historical Survey Committee. *Early Settlers and Bits of History of Columbus and Colorado County, 1821–1845.* Columbus, TX: n.p., 1973.

Cravens, Jonathan N. *James Harper Starr: Financier of the Republic of Texas.* Austin: Daughters of the Republic of Texas, 1950.

Crimm, Ana Carolina Castillo. *De León, A Tejano Family History.* Austin: University of Texas Press, 2003.

Davis, Joe Tom. *Historic Towns of Texas, Volume 2: Columbus, Gonzales, Jefferson.* Austin: Eakin Press, 1996.

_____. *Legendary Texians.* 4 volumes. Austin, Eakin Press, 1986.

Debo, Darrell. *Burnet County History, Family Histories.* 2 volumes. Burnet, TX: Eakin Press, 1979.

DeShields, James T. *Border Wars of Texas.* Waco, TX: Texian Press, 1976.

_____. *Tall Men with Long Rifles.* San Antonio: Naylor Company, 1971.

Dimmick, Gregg J. *The Mexican Army in the Texas Revolution, Volume 3.* College Station: Texas A&M Press, forthcoming.

_____. *Sea of Mud: The Retreat of the Mexican Army After San Jacinto.* Austin: Texas State Historical Association, 2004.

Dixon, Sam H., and Louis W. Kemp. *The Heroes of San Jacinto.* Houston: Anson Jones Press, 1932.

Earle, Thomas, editor. *The Life, Travels and Opinions of Benjamin Lundy.* New York: Augustus M. Kelley, 1971.

Fayette County History Book Committee. *Fayette County, Texas Heritage.* 2 volumes. Raleigh, NC: Curtis Media, 1996.

Foote, Henry S. *Texas and the Texans or Advance of the Anglo-Americans to the South-West.* 2 volumes. Austin: Steck Company, 1935.

Greaser, Galen D., Douglas J. Howard, and Michael T. Moore. *Austin's Colony 1821–1836: In Commemoration of the Two Hundredth Birthday of Stephen F. Austin.* Austin: Texas General Land Office, 1993.

Guertin, Iris R. *Navidad Country.* Sugar Land, TX: CreateSpace Independent Publishing Platform, 2009.

Haile, Bartee. *Unforgettable Texans.* Charleston, SC: History Press, 2017.

Haley, James L. *Sam Houston.* Norman: University of Oklahoma Press, 2002.

Hardin, Stephen L. *Texian Iliad: A Military History of the Texas Revolution.* Austin: University of Texas Press, 1996.

Harrison, William H. *Alleyton, Texas: "Back Door to the Confederacy."* Austin: Show-Me Type & Print, 1993.

Hatley, Allen G. *Texas Constables: A Frontier Heritage.* Lubbock: Texas Tech University Press, 1999.

Houck, Louis. *A History of Missouri: From the Earliest Explorations and Settlements until the Admission of the State into the Union.* 3 volumes. Chicago: Lakeside Press, 1908.

James, Marquis. *The Raven: A Biography of Sam Houston.* Indianapolis: Bobbs-Merrill Company, 1929.

Jordan, Terry G. *Texas Log Buildings, A Folk Architecture.* Austin: University of Texas Press, 1978.

Kilgore, D. E. *A Ranger Legacy: 150 Years of Service to Texas.* Austin: Madrona Press, 1973.

Krischke, Norman C. *A Visit to the Holman Valley: 9 Dec 1844–29 Feb 1996, Over 150 Years of the Holman Valley.* Schulenburg, TX: N. C. Krischke, 1996.

Lindley, Ernest R. compiler. *Biographical Directory of the Texas Conventions and Congresses, 1832–1845.* Austin: Book Exchange, 1941.

Lord, Walter. *A Time to Stand.* New York: Harper & Brothers, 1961.

Miller, Thomas L. *Bounty and Donation Land Grants of Texas, 1835–1888.* Austin: University of Texas Press, 1967.

Moore, Stephen L. *Savage Frontier: Rangers, Riflemen, and Indian Wars in Texas.* 4 volumes. Denton: University of North Texas Press, 2002–2010.

———. *Eighteen Minutes: The Battle of San Jacinto and the Texas Independence Campaign.* Dallas: Republic of Texas Press, 2004.

Nance, Joseph M. *Attack and Counterattack: The Texas-Mexican Frontier, 1842.* Austin: University of Texas Press, 1964.

Reed, S. G. *A History of Texas Railroads.* Houston: St. Clair Publishing, 1941.

Vigness, David M. *The Revolutionary Decades, The Saga of Texas: 1810–1836.* Austin: Steck-Vaughn Company, 1965.

Weyand, Leone R. and Houston Wade. *An Early History of Fayette County.* La Grange, TX: La Grange Journal Plant, 1936.

Wilbarger, J. W. *Indian Depredations in Texas.* 1889; Austin: Eakin Press, 1985.

Willey, Ethel M. *Capt. Jesse Burnam, A Texas Pioneer.* Waco: Davis Brothers Publishing Company, 1997.

Wisehart, M. K. *Sam Houston, American Giant.* New York: Van Rees Press, 1962.

Woodrick, James V. *Lost Texas Cannons: From the Snippets of Texas History Series.* Sugar Land, TX: CreateSpace Independent Publishing Platform, 2016.

Wortham, Louis J. *A History of Texas: From Wilderness to Commonwealth.* 5 volumes. Fort Worth, TX: Wortham-Molyneaux Company, 1924.

Wyatt, Tula Townsend. *The Seven Townsend Brothers of Texas, 1826–1838.* Austin: Aus-Tex Duplicators, 1974.

Yoakum, Henderson. *History of Texas: From Its First Settlement in 1685 to Its Annexation to the United States in 1846.* 2 volumes. 1855; Austin: Steck-Vaughn Company, 1961.

THESIS

Corkran, Charles W. "John Henry Moore, 1800–1880." M.A. Thesis. University of Texas, 1964.

WEBSITES

Baker, Moseley. "Letter from Gonzales to the Standing Committee of San Felipe, March 8, 1836." Texas State Library and Archives Commission. *Texans' Fight for Independence Exhibit.* https://www.tsl.texas.gov/sites/default/files/public/tslac/exec/documents/struggles1_2015001_24.pdf.

Breeding, George W., and Bill Stein, compilers. "Index to 1860 Census." https://www. columbustexaslibrary.net/local-history-and-genealogy-material/links-to-colorado-county-censuses/index-to-1860-census.

Caraway, Barry, transcriber. "Captain Burnam's 90th Birthday." *Burnet County TXGenWeb.* https://txgenwebcounties.org/burnet/BurnamBio.html.

Hardin, Stephen L. "The San Jacinto Campaign, The Generalship of Sam Houston." http://www.sonsofdewittcolony.org//adp/archives/feature/hardin.html.

Kemp, Louis W. "Veteran Biographies." *San Jacinto Museum of History.* https://www.sanjacinto-museum.org/Library/Veteran_Bios/.

McNeill, Archibald, Dorothy Albrecht, and Bill Stein, compilers. "Index to 1850 Census." https://www.columbustexaslibrary.net/local-history-and-genealogy-material/links-to-colorado-county-censuses/index-to-1850-census.

"Known Elected and Appointed Officials." *Nesbitt Memorial Library.* https://www.columbus texaslibrary.net/local-history-and-genealogy-material/ public-records/public-records-from-early-colorado-county-history/known-elected-and-appointed-officials.

Texas General Land Office. *Land Grant Search.* https://s3.glo.texas.gov/glo/history/archives/land-grants/index.cfm.

———. *Map Store.* https://s3.glo.texas.gov/glo/history/archives/map-store/index.cfm#search.

Texas Historical Commission. *Texas Historic Sites Atlas.* https://atlas.thc.texas.gov/.

Texas State Historical Association. *New Handbook of Texas.* https://www.tshaonline.org/ handbook.

Trezevant, Robert W. "Biographical Sketches." *The Georgia Battalion Project.* https://georgiabattalion.com/biographical-sketches/.

INDEX

A

Adams, Thomas J., 175
Agua Dulce, Battle of (1836), xi
Alabama Red Rovers, 175
Alamo, Siege of (1836), xi
   Albert Martin at, 53
   Antonio López de Santa Anna's reaction to, 102, 168
   Joaquín Ramírez y Sesma at, 102–103
   John W. Baylor at, 175
   John W. Smith at, 24
   Sam Houston receives news of results of, 2, 4
   Sam Houston's reaction to, 9, 12, 24–25, 39, 44, 195–196
   Texian army's organization during, 95
   Texian army's reaction to, xii, 12, 29, 158
   Washington-on-the-Brazos's reaction to, 127
Albany, Texas, 257
Alexander, Jerome, Jr., 216
Alexander, Jerome, Sr., 213
Alley, Abraham ("Abram"), 99, 101–102, 246–248
   as Colorado County Board of Land Commissioners president, 247, 250
   house of, pictured, 249
   Texas arrival of, 100
   in Texas Revolution's immediate aftermath, 194
   Thomas Alley's death and, 100–101
Alley, Cynthia, 250–251
Alley, John, 100
Alley, Nancy Millar, 101, 246–247, 247–248
   house of, pictured, 249
Alley, Rawson, 85, 99–102, 250
Alley, Thomas, 100–101
Alley, William (son of Abram), 248
Alley, William A. (brother of Abram), 100, 101, 185–186, 248, 250
   as Texian army supplier, 130, 185
Alley family, 99–102
   biographical sketch of, 246–251
Alleyton, Texas, 248, 250
Almonte, Juan N.:
   Ben as cook for, 4
   on captured Texians, 176
   Colorado River approached and crossed by, 23, 82, 89, 107, 135, 137, 141, 169–170, 187–188
   journal of, 135, 137, 138, 141, 169–170, 176
   pictured, 136
   on Sam Houston's scorched earth policy, 26
Andrade, Juan José, 102
Andrews, Joseph, 181, 255
   on Goliad retreat, 178, 180
Arnold, Hayden, 158
Arroyo Dulce, 174
Arroyo Hondo, 228
Arroyo Seco, 205, 207

Atascosito Crossing, 86, 101, 155
  Alley house moved from, 248, 249
  Mexican army crosses at, 152, 169–170, 183, 188–189, 193–194, 240, 246
  Texian army at, 98–99, 115–116, 151, 156, 172
Atascosito Road, 21, 85–86, 97-98, 115, 118, 137, 169
Austin, Moses, 99–100
Austin, Stephen F.:
  Alley family and, 100, 101
  Colorado River settlements and, 83, 85
  maps commissioned by, 20–23, 65, 85, 116
  as military commander, ix–x, 60–61
  Samuel May Williams appointed as secretary of state by, 174
  San Felipe de Austin founded by, 98
  on single (unmarried) colonizers, 87–88
  on Texan independence, ix, 76
  Tumlinson family and, 89
Austin, William T., 15, 133–134, 166, 198

B

Baker, Abraham, 100
Baker, Catherine, 100
Baker, Moseley:
  call to arms (March 22, 1836) by, 93, 113–114
  command of, 2, 158, 185, 251, 254
  criticism of Sam Houston by, 20, 23, 158–159, 160, 186–187, 200
  Franklin J. Starr's furlough and, 52
  Samuel G. Hardaway's arrival noted by, 185
  on Texian army in Gonzales, 5
Barcena, Andres, 2, 145
Bastrop, Baron de, 83, 85
Bastrop, Texas, 127, 228, 247
  See also Mina, Texas
Bastrop County, Texas, 223, 251

Baylor, John Walker, 175
Baylor, Robert, 175
Beason's Park (Columbus, Texas), 90, 201, 239
Beeson, Abel, 186, 234, 238
  death of, 239
  Naham Mixon and, 236, 237
Beeson, Benjamin, 86–87, 191
  biographical sketch of, 232–239
  Columbus's founding and, 91
  death of, 234
  legacy of, 239
  in Texas Revolution's immediate aftermath, 194
Beeson, Collins, 238
  death of, 233–234, 238
Beeson, Elizabeth ("Betsy"), 86–87, 232
  fate of, 234, 236
  letter to David G. Burnet, 192, 233
Beeson, Leander, 186, 233–234
  death of, 238–239
  gambling and, 238
  legal problems of, 236–238, 241, 242
  in Texian army, 233, 236
Beeson, Lydia, 88, 163
  death of, 238, 243
  on civilians with Texian army, 232–233
Beeson, Mary Ann, 234, 238
Beeson, Nepsey. See Berry, Nepsy Beeson
Beeson's Crossing, 19, 20, 52, 75
  earliest depiction of, 21
  Manuel de Mier y Terán on, 87
  Jean Louis Berlandier on, 87
  origins of, 86–87
  Samuel G. Hardaway near, 183
  site pictured, 84
  smokehouse of, 121–122
  Texian army at, 65–66, 71, 73, 75–76, 78, 79–80, 121–122, 126, 130, 137, 151-152, 156, 197, 201, 239
Ben (free Black man), 4

Bennett, Joseph L., 41, 79
   command of, 52–54, 65, 78–79
Bergara, Anselmo, 2, 145, 147
Berlandier, Jean Louis, 87
Berry, John F., 238
Berry, Nepsey Beeson, 238, 243
Besch, Amos, 242
Besch, Angelica, 243
Betts, Elizabeth Millar, 246
Béxar, Siege of (1835), x, 1, 30, 61
   Almeron Dickinson at, 4
   Henry W. Karnes at, 48
   John H. and William O. Burnam at, 30
   John Ingram at, 99
   Joseph L. Bennett at, 79
   Peyton Splane at, 16
   William M. Logan at, 78
   William Ware at, 76
Big Hill (near Moulton, Texas), 12–13
Billingsley, Jesse:
   command of, 2, 175
   on Sam Houston's decision to abandon the Colorado River, 161
   in Adrián Woll raid (1842), 229
Bird, John, 12
   command of, 12, 16, 82, 97, 116, 118, 121
Blockhouses:
   at Burnam's Ferry, 31–32
   at Fort Parker, pictured, 57
   at Moore's Fort, 56–58
Boom, Garret E., 175
Borden, Gail, 21
Borden, John, 21
Borden, Thomas, 21
   on Texian army's retreat from Beeson's Crossing, 151–152
Bostick, Martha Hill, 82
Bravo (Mexican warship), 147
Brazos Courier, 210

Brazos River:
   Beeson family crossing of, 233
   Peter Kerr at, 251
   Stephen F. Austin homestead on, 85
   Texian army at, 164, 186
   Texian civilians cross, 191
   Texian troops recruited from area around, 16
   Thomas J. Rabb falls sick on, 163
   William T. Austin sent to acquire supplies at mouth of, 15, 134
   See also San Felipe de Austin, Texas
Brenan, William, 176
Brown, John Henry:
   on William B. Dewees, 244
Bryan, Moses Austin, 128
Buckner, Aylett C., 100
Buffalo Bayou, Brazos, and Colorado (BBB&C) Railroad Company, 248
Buffalo Hump (Comanche leader), 222
Bullock, Uriah:
   command of, 177, 181
Burleson, Edward, 8, 130
   Franklin J. Starr's furlough approved by, 52
   furlough requested by, 163
   Jesse Burnam invoiced by, 39
   resignation of, 209
Burnam, Amanda, 213, 214
   death of, 216
Burnam, Emily, 215
Burnam, Jesse, 31–32, 36
   biographical sketch of, 211–219
   Columbus's founding and, 92
   death and burial of, 218–219
   Gideon Lincecum on, 33
   leadership of, 202
   legacy, 219
   pictured, 34
   after Texas Revolution, 194
   See also Burnam's Ferry

Burnam, Jesse Bennett, 216
Burnam, John Hickerson, 30, 40, 211
Burnam, Mary, 211, 212, 214–215
Burnam, Minerva, 211
Burnam, Nancy (daughter of Jesse), 31, 213, 214
Burnam, Nancy (wife of Jesse), 211, 212, 216
Burnam, Robert J., 215, 216
Burnam, William O., 30, 40, 211, 216
Burnam Station, 214
Burnam's Ferry:
    blockhouses at, 56
    destruction of, 39–41, 64, 197, 217–218
    famous visitors at, 32–33
    pictured, 37
    Sam Houston's decision to go to, 19–26, 109
    after Texas Revolution, 212–214
    Texian army at, 27, 36–38, 39–41, 63, 197, 201
Burnet, David G., 139
    Elizabeth Beeson's letter to (April 10, 1836), 192, 233
    Sam Houston ordered replaced by, 200
    Sam Houston's official report to, 203–204
    warned of Mexican army's approach, 192
Burnet, Texas, 252
Burnet County, Texas:
    Jesse Burnam's relocation to, 215–216
    Peter Kerr and, 252, 253–254

C

Calavira Creek. See Skull Creek
Calder, Robert J., 167, 168
    command of, 49, 83, 97, 134, 138
    on potential battle, 134

Caldwell, Mathew, 222
    in Adrían Woll raid (1842), 225, 227–229
Caldwell County, Texas, 239
Callahan, Joseph, 257
Carbajal, José María Jesús de, 145, 147
Carothers, W. S., 253–254
Carrasco, José María, 224–225
Casteñeda, Francisco, 60
Castro (Lipan Apache leader), 220–221, 223
Chance, Joseph B., 61
Chriesman, Horatio, 24
Civil War:
    Alleyton during, 248
    Burnam family in, 216–217
    Moore family in, 229
    Samuel G. Hardaway in, 258
    William B. Dewees in, 245
Clear Creek, 26
Coe, Phillip:
    command of, 98
Coleman, Robert M:
    pictured, 7
    on Sam Houston's decision to abandon the Colorado River, 161
    on Sam Houston's leadership abilities, 6
Cole's Settlement, Texas, 156, 158
Coleto Creek, Battle of (1836), 130–131, 179–180
    Antonio López de Santa Anna's confidence after, 188
    Sam Houston informed of, 144–147, 166, 174–175, 251
    Texian army's reaction, 158
Collinsworth, James T.:
    letters to, 19–20, 21, 38, 43, 44, 48, 124
    Sam Houston and, 124
Colorado Municipality, 92
Colorado Citizen:
    on David Hunt, 231

William B. Dewees encouraged to run for Congress by, 244–245
Colorado College, 247
Colorado County, Texas:
Abram Alley as official in, 247, 250
Jesse Burnam's land ownership in, 214
William A. Alley as official in, 248
William B. Dewees as treasurer of, 245
Williamson Daniels as official of, 250–251
Colorado River:
battle expected on, 52, 133–134, 137, 149, 165–166, 198, 199
Mexican army arrival at, 110–111, 137
Mexican army crossing of, 152, 169–170, 183, 187–189, 193–194, 240, 246
strategic value of, 98, 126, 142, 167–168
Texian army crossing of, 36–37, 61, 63
Texian army retreat from, 149–170
Columbia, Texas, 150, 155, 156, 212, 255
Columbus, Texas, 21, 22, 67, 75, 81, 82, 101, 231, 233, 236, 245, 247
Alley house moved to (1976), 248
Atascosito Road crosses Colorado River near, 85
Beason's Park in, 239
Beeson's Crossing misidentified as early site of, 239
founding of, 21, 91, 92, 93, 239, 240, 246, 248
Mexican army near, 106, 107, 118, 119, 128, 201
Texian army near, 81, 128, 155, 170, 201, 207
William B. Dewees and, 240–241
Comanches:
expedition against (1840), 212
Henry W. Karnes and, 205–210
Jesse Burnam and, 212
John H. Moore and, 220–224, 228, 229
Sam Houston's peace with (1843), 229
Tonkawa horse raids against, 59
William B. Dewees and, 244
See also Buffalo Hump and Plum Creek (1840)
Cook, James, 88
Cook, Richard V., 232
Cooke, William, 209
Cos, Martín Perfecto de, x, 26
Consultation of 1835:
Jesse Burnam at, 36
Wyly Martin at, 76
Convention of 1832:
Jesse Burnam at, 32
Wyly Martin at, 76
Convention of 1833:
Jesse Burnam at, 32
Wyly Martin at, 76
Council House Fight (1840), 209–210, 221
Creek Nation, 255–256
Crier, Andrew, 41, 64
Crier, John:
Columbus's founding and, 92
Texian army at home of, 41, 63–64, 66, 201
Crier Creek, 41
Cummins, Eliza, 54, 56
Cummins, James, 54, 90, 211
Cummins Creek named after, 66
elected as Colorado District *alcalde*, 101
Stephen F. Austin on home of, 85
Cummins Creek, 66, 201
pictured, 67

D

Daniels, Williamson, 250–251
Mexican army encamped at house, 103
Texian army encamped at house, 13, 15, 16, 21, 24, 53, 71, 103
Dawson, Nicholas M., 213, 223
in Ráfael Vásquez raid (1842), 224
in Adrián Woll raid (1842), 227–228

314 | 11 DAYS on the COLORADO

Dawson Massacre (1842), 213
Dean, William, 237
De Bland, Colin, 241–242
De León, Fernando, 144, 145, 147
De León, Martín, 145
Dewees, Emily, 243
Dewees, Lydia Beeson. *See* Beeson, Lydia
Dewees, William B., 82, 83, 85, 88, 90, 92–93, 232–233, 236–237
   as Beeson family executor, 234
   biographical sketch of, 239–246
   Columbus's founding and, 92, 239
   furlough, 163
   legacy, 246
   on Texas Revolution aftermath, 193–194
   Texian army's withdrawal and, 191–192
   Letters of an Early Settler of Texas, 244
   Life on a Frontier or Adventures of Will Dewees, 244
Dewees' Ford, 64, 75, 106
   destruction of, 120–121
   origins of, 88–93
   pictured, 81, 143
   Texian army at, 65, 78–79, 80, 96, 114, 120, 124, 126, 128, 130, 134, 137–138, 142, 150, 159, 168
   Texian army retreat from, 151, 152–153, 156, 158
Dickinson, Almeron, 4
Dickinson, Angelina, 4
   pictured, 3
Dickinson, Susanna, 4
   pictured, 3
Double Horn, Texas, 215, 218–219

E

Eagle Lake, 155
Eastland, William M., 121, 219

F

Faires, Richard O.:
   on John H. Moore, 231–232
Fannin, James W., 13, 196
   at Burnam's Ferry, 33
   leadership ability, 8–9
   Sam Houston and, 8, 25, 41, 43, 130
   surrender of, 130–131, 133, 144–147, 150, 158, 166, 174–175, 198, 251
Fayette County, Texas:
   founding, 219
   growth, 215
   Jesse Burnam's property in, 214
   oldest structure in (purportedly), 56, 58
   Rutersville College in, 247
Filisola, Vicente, 169, 203
   Colorado River crossed by, 189
   on Mexican camp followers, 43
   replaced by José de Urrea, 204
   retreat to Mexico, 193–194, 240
   San Antonio de Béxar, 102
Fisher, William S., 155, 156, 172, 209
Flores, José, 2
Flores, Martin, 114
Foote, Henry S.:
   on Sam Houston's decision to abandon the Colorado River, 160
Forbes, John, 153, 155–156, 158, 166
   command of, 172
Fort Croghan, 252, 254
Fort Houston, 96
Fort Parker:
   blockhouse at, pictured, 57
Franklin, Benjamin C., 49, 71
Franks, Louis B., 206
Fredericksburg, 208
Frontier Regiment, 206

G

Gambling:
  Leander Beason and, 238
  William B. Dewees and, 242
Gaona, Antonio, 102, 160, 199
  on Mexican army pillaging, 38
  ordered to reinforce Antonio López de Santa Anna, 188
Georgia Battalion, 129, 176–177, 257
  monuments erected to, 257
Giberson, Rebecca, 237
Gilleland, James, 99
Goliad County, Texas, 257–258
Goliad Massacre (1836), xi, 33, 41, 102, 130, 155, 160, 165, 168, 174-185, 200
  See also Coleto Creek, Battle of (1836), and Fannin, James W.
Gonzales, Battle of (1835), ix, 1, 36
  Almeron Dickinson in, 4
  Jesse Billingsley in, 229
  John H. Moore in, 55, 59–61, 202, 224, 229, 232
  John Ingram at, 99
  Peyton Splane in, 16
  Joseph W. E. Wallace in, 59–60, 82, 92
Gonzales, Texas:
  destruction of, 10, 12, 26, 38
  Indian depredations near, 207
  Mexican army in, 102
  Sam Houston on, 96
  Sam Houston's route from Washington-on-the-Brazos to, 23–24
  Texian army in, 2, 4–9, 195–196
Gonzales-San Felipe Road, 21, 25, 54, 105, 197
  Texian army at, 24, 49, 64, 68
Gray, Thomas, 54
Gray, William F., 127
Groce, Jared, 186
Groce's Landing:
  Texian army at, 164, 186–187

Guadalupe River, 180, 233
  cannons sunk in, 8
  Mexican army's crossing of, 104, 135
  Comanche depredations (1840), 222
  during Ráfael Vásquez raid (1842), 225

H

Hale, Ebenezer, 78
Hamilton, Andrew J., 245
Hamilton, John, 252
Hamilton, Texas, 252
Hamilton Creek, 252
Handy, Robert E., 4, 48, 49, 68
Hannah Elizabeth (ship), 147
Hardaway, Samuel G., 176–178, 180–185, 202, 254–258
  pictured, 182
Hardin, Benjamin F., 78
Harmon, Clark, 49, 71
Harper, Benjamin, 78
Harris, Ira A., 242
Harrisburg, Texas:
  Betsy Beeson seeks to open a boarding house in, 192, 233
  Buffalo Bayou, Brazos, and Colorado (BBB&C) Railroad line from, 248
  Mexican army burns, 192
  Texas Congress meets at, 212
Hays, John C. ("Jack"):
  Comanches and, 206, 208
  during Ráfael Vásquez raid (1842), 224, 225
  during Adrián Woll raid (1842), 228–229
Hazen, Nathanial C., 176
Heard, William J. E., 29, 162–163
  as Colorado County chief justice, 240–241
  on Texian army's retreat, 9, 151
Hill, William W., 2

Hockley, George W., 93
　Andres Barcena and Anselmo Bergara's arrests and, 2
　on Atascosito Crossing, 115
　Burnam's Ferry destruction and, 217–218
　on Dewees' Ford, 80
　on Henry W. Karnes, 49, 96–97
　on Joaquín Ramírez y Sesma, 110
　on Mexican army's threat, 144
　on Peter Kerr, 147, 251
　pictured, 125
　Sam Houston and, 123–124
　on Texian army morale, 45
　on Texian army supplies, 129

Holman, George T., 212–213, 214

Holman, Jesse A., 218

Holman, Jesse B., 215

Holman, John T., 212–214, 216

Holman, Texas, 27, 214
　Jesse Burnam historical marker in, 219

Holman Valley plantation, 214

Horton, Albert C., 174–175

Houston, Sam:
　Abram Alley and, 247
　on civilian refugees crossing the Colorado River, 37
　criticism of, 6, 151, 158–162, 195, 200, 217
　decision to abandon Colorado River of, 149–150, 168, 199
　on furloughs, 52
　George W. Hockley and, 123–124
　Indian policy of, 221, 229
　James Collinsworth and, 124
　on James W. Fannin's surrender, 131
　Jonathan H. Kuykendall on, 174
　leadership abilities of, 6
　on logistics, 167
　on Matamoros Expedition (1835–36), x
　on Mexican army, 43, 44, 144
　pictured, 125, 146
　on reconnaissance, 48
　Antonio Lopez de Santa Anna's letter to (1836), 4
　scorched earth policy of, 10, 12, 26, 37, 39–41, 64, 103, 120–121, 196–197, 217–218
　as Texian commander-in-chief, xi–xii, 1–2, 6, 24, 95, 123, 126, 129, 149, 166, 195–200, 244
　Thomas J. Rusk and, 124
　on Washington-on-the-Brazos's abandonment, 128
　William B. Dewees and, 244
　William P. Zuber on, 172, 174

Hoxey, Asa, 156, 158

Hunt, David, 230–232

Hunt, John, 230

Hunt, Rhoda, 80

Hunter, Henry H., 216

Hunter, Robert H., 82, 121

Huston, Felix, 222

I

Independence, Texas. See Cole's Settlement, Texas

Indians:
　Henry W. Karnes and, 205–209
　Jesse Burnam and, 212, 216–217
　John H. Moore and, 57, 59, 220–224, 229
　Mirabeau B. Lamar's policy toward, 206, 221, 223
　Sam Houston and, 221, 229
　See also specific groups.

Ingram, John, 98–99

J

Joe (enslaved Black man), 4
　pictured, 3

Johnson, Herschel V., 257

Johnston, Albert S., 208–209

Jones, Anson, 138
Jones, David J., 176

K

Karankawas, 58, 100
Karnes, Henry W., 115
   biographical sketch of, 203–211
   imprisonment of, 204–205
   Indians and, 205–209
   legacy, 210–211
   pictured, 117
   reconnaissance by, 4, 47–49, 63, 68–73, 96, 97, 104, 116, 121, 137, 138, 141–142, 167, 197, 201, 203
   reliability of, 202
   Sam Houston on, 203–204
   Texian army's retreat from Beeson's Crossing and, 152
Kemp, Thomas, 176
Kennard, William, 54
Kerr, Andrew, 253
Kerr, J. H., 222
Kerr, Peter:
   arrest of, 145–147, 202, 251
   biographical sketch of, 251–254
   James W. Fanin's surrender related to Sam Houston by, 144–147, 166, 174, 198, 251
   legacy, 254
   pictured, 146
Kerr, William, 145
Killough, Ira G., 230–231, 232
Kimball, Amanetta Cara, 243–244
King, Amon B., 177–178
Kleberg, Rosa, 126
Kokernot, David, 107, 120, 192
Kornegay, David, 64
Kuykendall, Jonathan H.:
   at Atascosito Crossing, 115
   on Colorado River as battle location, 134
   on March 19 encampment location, 65–66
   on Mexican army's threat to Gonzales, 5
   on position of Mexican army, 106–107, 138
   reconnaissance by, 98
   on Sam Houston's decision to abandon the Colorado River, 161, 174
Kuykendall, Robert H., 85, 100

L

Labadie, Nicholas D., 78
   on Mexican army's position, 107
   on reconnaissance, 116
   on Sam Houston's decision to abandon the Colorado River, 161
La Bahía Road, 13, 24, 52, 85, 97, 219
   Burnam's Ferry erroneously placed on, 20, 32
   civilian refugees on, 53
   on maps, 20–21
   Mexican army on, 135
   Moore's Fort on, 54, 55, 78–79
   Texian army on, 24, 156, 158
Lacey, William, 92
La Grange, Texas, 85
   Burnam family in, 215
   founding and growth of, 219–220, 221
   historical markers in, 58, 219, 232
   John Holman in, 213
   See also Moore's Fort
La Grange Journal, 231
Lamar, Mirabeau B., 96, 203
   Indian policy of, 206, 209, 221, 223
   Santa Fe Expedition and, 210
Land speculation:
   by William B. Dewees, 241

Lapham, Moses, 151–152, 183
  on Sam Houston's decision to abandon Colorado River, 158
Lavaca River, 13, 15, 54, 250
Lawrence, David, 98
Lemsky, Frederick, 114
Lester, James S., 59
  on Indians, 221–222
  La Grange's founding and, 219, 221
Liberty Volunteers, 78, 97
Lincecum, Gideon:
  as Burnam's Ferry visitor, 32–33
  Columbus's naming and, 92
  on Jesse Burnam, 33
  pictured, 35
Lipan Apaches, 220, 223
Llano River valley, 208
Lockhart, Matilda, 209
Lockhart, Texas, 222
Logan, William M., 78, 97
Lundy, Benjamin, 90

M

Mabbitt, Leonard H.:
  command of, 250
Marble Falls, Texas:
  historical marker to Jesse Burnam near, 219
Martin, Albert, 53
Martin, Wyly, 76
  command of, 71, 76, 78, 82, 110–111, 186, 187
  on Sam Houston's decision to abandon San Felipe de Austin, 186–187, 200
Matamoros, Tamaulipas, x, 147, 204–205
Mayfield, James, 228
McClure, Bartlett D.:
  Texian army at plantation of, 10–12, 24, 38
McClure, Sarah, 11, 38
McIntire, Thomas, 78
McLeod, Hugh, 209
McNutt, Robert:
  command of, 15, 98, 130
Menefee, William, 92
Mercer, Eli, 29–30
Mercer, Elijah, 29–30
Mercer's Crossing (Egypt, Texas), 163
Mexican army, 102–105
  Antonio López de Santa Anna takes field command of, x–xi, 1
  artillery of, xi, 5, 48, 71, 83, 111, 121, 128–129, 141, 187, 227
  camp followers of, 43–44
  Colorado River crossed by, 152, 169–170, 183, 187–189
  foraging by, 128
  George W. Hockley on, 144
  morale in, 189, 194
  pillaging by, 37
  reinforcement of, 134–135, 137, 167–168, 198–199
  Sam Houston on, 43–44, 144
  threat to Texian army of, 5, 27, 29, 166–167 reconnaissance missions, 187–188
Mexican Constitution of 1824, ix, 36
Mier y Terán, Manuel de:
  on Beeson's Crossing, 87
Mier Expedition (1842–43), 229
Milam, Benjamin R., 48
Millar, Nancy. See Alley, Nancy Millar
Mina, Texas, 2, 54, 85, 102
  Mexican army in, 188
  See also Bastrop, Texas
Mission Concepción (San Antonio, Texas), 207
Mixon, Naham, 236–237, 241
Montezuma, Texas, 85–86

Moore, Armstead A., 56
Moore, John H., 54, 56, 57, 59
   affidavit for Jesse Burnam's pension
      from, 218
   at Battle of Gonzales (1835),
      59–60, 202, 229
   biographical sketch of, 219–232
   in Civil War, 229
   Comanche expedition (1840) led by,
      212, 223
   death of, 231
   legacy, 232
   pictured, 55
   in Texas Revolution aftermath, 194
   in Texian army, 59–61
   See also Moore's Fort
Moore, Tabitha, 56, 230–231
Moore, William B., 56
Moore's Fort, 13, 24, 41, 54, 79
   pictured, 57
   William Zuber on, 56
Morales, Juan, 102
Moseley, Robert, 82, 89, 90
   Columbus's founding and, 91
Moseley's Crossing, 64, 93, 120
   Mexican army at, 188
   pictured, 81
   See also Dewees' Ford
Moses, M. K., 181, 183, 255
Moulton, Texas, 12–13
Murphree, David, 49, 69, 71
Murphy, Daniel, 176

N

Nacogdoches Volunteers, 96, 156, 158
Nalle, Temperance, 31, 32
Navidad River:
   Burnam family at, 217
   Holman family at, 213, 214, 215
   Mexican army at, 103, 105

roads near, 23, 135
   Texian army at, 16, 21, 25, 49, 68–69, 197,
      201, 207
Neill, James C., 2
Nelson, James, 29

O

Oakland, Texas, 213, 214
   Texian army near, 16
Old Fort, 187
   Mexican army's march toward, 189
Opelousas Road, 97
Owen, James, 49, 71, 73

P

Patton, William, 82
   Burnam's Ferry's destruction and,
      39–40, 217–218
   command of, 49, 65, 76, 79, 175
Peach Creek:
   Texian army encamped on, 9, 10–12, 13,
      24, 37, 197
Pease, Elisa M, 257
Peffer, H. K., 253, 254
Peña, José de la:
   on Joaquín Ramírez y Sesma, 108, 110
   on Mexican camp followers, 43–44;
Pennsylvania (schooner), 176
Perry, Daniel:
   command of, 78, 138
Perry, George, 238
Perry, James F., 21, 27
   on Mexican army's threat, 29
Perry, James H., 139
Plum Creek, Battle of (1840), 222–223, 244
Poe, George W., 153
Prairie Point, Texas, 213
   See also Oakland, Texas

R

Rabb, John, 59

Rabb, Mary Crownover:
    on Sam Houston's decision to abandon the Colorado River, 158

Rabb, Thomas J., 163, 223
    command of, 2, 29–30, 121, 162, 175, 186
    on Sam Houston's decision to abandon the Colorado River, 158, 164
    in Ráfael Vásquez raid (1842), 224

Rabb, William, 99

Ramírez y Sesma, Joaquín, 82, 250
    Colorado River crossed by, 152, 168–170, 188
    command of, 12, 71, 102–107, 110, 118, 128, 134, 144, 166–167, 181, 183
    criticism of, 103, 108, 110, 197
    pictured, 104
    on scorched earth policy, 103

Ramsey, Martin D., 130, 186

Ratliff Creek:
    Mexican army on, 107, 138.
    See also San Antoñito Stream

Rhodes, John, 15, 21

Rhyne, L. J. Bryan, 242

Robinson, James, 144

Robinson, Joel, 218

Robinson, John G., 212

Rocky Creek, 135
    Texian army at, 15, 27, 68, 69

Rogers, Thomas, 85–86

Rolluson, Eliza McCoy, 250

Rolluson, Thomas, 250

Roman, Richard, 155, 156
    command of, 172

Ross, James (father of James T.), 41, 58, 59

Ross, James T. (son of James), 66

Royal, Richardson R., 133

Runaway Scrape, 126–127
    Alley family in, 102, 246
    historians' treatment of, xii, 200
    Moore homestead survives, 58
    Rabb family in, 163
    Rosa Kleberg on, 126
    start of, 10

Rusk, Thomas J., 156
    dispatched to command Texian army, 200
    importance to Texian army of, 126
    letters to, 45, 49, 80, 96–97, 110, 115, 123, 124, 126, 128, 129, 130–131, 144, 147, 204, 251
    Sam Houston and, 124

Rutersville College, 240, 247

S

Sadler, William, 96
    command of, 96, 116

Salado Creek, Battle of (1842), 213, 225, 227

San Antonio de Béxar, Texas:
    Antonio López de Santa Anna's departure from, 188–189
    Henry W. Karnes in, 207–208, 210
    Mexican raids against (1842), 224–229
    See also Alamo, Siege of (1836), Béxar, Siege of (1835)

San Antonio Road, 85, 97, 102

San Antoñito Stream, 107, 169
    See also Ratliff Creek

San Bernard River, 76, 89, 155, 172

San Felipe de Austin, Texas, 20
    founding of, 98
    Mexican army at, 189
    as Antonio López de Santa Anna's target, 102, 168
    Texian army at, 185–186, 200
    Texian civilians cross Brazos River at, 191, 233

San Jacinto, Battle of (1836), 168, 176
193, 195, 199, 255
   Dewees and Beeson families get news of, 233
   Garret E. Boom at, 175
   Henry W. Karnes at, 203–204
   James H. Perry at, 139
   John H. Burnam at, 40
   John W. Baylor at, 175
   Juan N. Almonte's journal found after, 138
   Leander Beeson at, 236
   Moseley Baker on the unnecessariness of, 160
   Moses Lapham at, 151
   Peter Kerr at, 251
   Robert M. Coleman at, 6
   Samuel G. Hardaway at, 254
   Thomas J. Adams at, 175
   Thomas J. Rabb at, 163
   William O. Burnam at, 40
   Sea of Mud, 194

San Jacinto River, 193, 233

San Patricio, Battle of (1836), xi, 102

Sandy Branch Creek, 153

Santa Anna, Antonio López de:
   letter to Sam Houston (1836), 4
   as Mexican commander, x–xi, 1, 102, 168
   departure from San Antonio de Béxar, 188–189
   Tejano opposition to, 145, 147

Santa Fe Expedition (1841), 210

Sapp, Basil, 238

Sayers, Joseph D., 230

Searight, Gilbert A., 253, 254

Secrest, Washington, 49, 68–69, 71
   pictured, 51

Seguín, Juan N., 115–116
   Bostick homestead moved by, 82–83
   Colorado River crossing and, 38
   Comanches and, 206

Shackleford, Jack:
   command of, 175

Shain, Charles, 176

Sharp, John:
   on Gonzales's destruction, 10
   sent to Velasco to reassure civilians, 133–134, 164, 198
   pictured, 70
   reconnaissance by, 49, 69–71
   on Texian retreat from Colorado River, 164–165

Sherman, Sidney, 8
   Buffalo Bayou, Brazos, and Colorado (BBB&C) Railroad extension to Alleyton and, 248
   as Dewees' Ford commanding officer, 76, 80, 96, 134, 137–138, 142, 150
   at Gonzales, 2
   Mexican foragers captured by, 128
   Texian retreat from Dewees' Ford and, 152–153, 159, 171, 172

Shields, Mary, 213

Shipman, Daniel, 183, 185

Skull Creek, 100, 116
   expedition against Karankawas on (1823), 58
   Mexican army on, 107

Smith, Benjamin F.:
   reconnaissance by, 97, 115–116, 120, 121
   as Sam Houston's adjutant general, 83, 139
   on Sam Houston's decision to abandon Colorado River, 161
   Texian supplies, 63–64

Smith, Erastus ("Deaf"):
   pictured, 50
   reconnaissance by, 4, 47, 48, 49, 68–69, 71, 152, 203

Smith, Henry, 196

Smith, John W., 24

Smith, Leander, 156
Smith, William H., 97, 115
    on Sam Houston's scorched earth policy, 26, 27, 217–218
Smithwick, Noah:
    on Jesse Burnam's settlement, 32
    on Peter Kerr, 252–253
Somervell, Alexander, 8
    on Mexican army's threat, 27, 29
Splane, Peyton, 16, 65
    command of, 16, 65, 83, 97
Spring Creek, 192–193
Steel, Maxwell, 233–234
Stouffer, Henry, 152

T

Tarlton, James:
    on Sam Houston's decision to abandon the Colorado River, 158
Tawakonis:
    John Tumlinson killed by, 88
Teal, Henry:
    command of, 79, 114, 130
    prisoner exchange expedition of, 204–205
Telegraph and Texas Register:
    Beeson family notices printed in, 233, 234
    Columbus advertised in, 240
    John H. Moore's death erroneously reported in, 225
    Moseley Baker call to arms (1836) published in, 93, 113–114
    on Runaway Scrape, 127
Texas Almanac of 1860:
    on Sam Houston's retreat from the Colorado River, 159–160, 162
Texas annexation, 212
Texas Congress, 206, 219
    Jesse Burnam in, 212
    William B. Dewees encouraged to run for, 244–245
    Williamson Daniels in, 250
Texas Monument, 244
Texian army:
    artillery of, 8, 15, 48, 129, 166, 198
    civilian refugees and, 13, 16, 37
    Colorado River crossed by, 36–37, 61, 63
    desertion from, 29, 43, 52, 95, 126, 162
    discipline in, 8, 15, 23, 44–45, 96, 114, 229
    furloughs from, 52, 150–151, 162–163
    at Gonzales, 2, 4–9, 195–196
    guard duty in, 53–54
    impressment into, 126
    logistics of, 63–64, 83, 129–130, 167, 185–186
    morale in, 43, 45
    organization of, 8, 95
    reinforcements for, 78–79, 95, 138–139, 153, 155–156, 158, 163–164, 166–167, 174–185, 197
    Sam Houston as commander-in-chief of, x, xi–xii, 6, 95, 123, 126, 149, 166, 195–200, 244
    Sam Houston named commander-in-chief of, x, 1–2, 24
    veterans pensions of, 218, 258
    reconnaissance missions, 4, 47–49, 68–73, 96–97, 116–120, 137–138, 141–142, 167, 197, 201
Thompson, William W. W., 24–25
    on Burnam's Ferry's destruction, 39–40
    homestead destroyed, 71
    Texian army at homestead of, 16, 25, 26, 64, 69, 71, 201
Tolsa, Eugenio:
    command of, 102, 134–135, 137, 138, 141, 167, 168, 169–170, 189, 198
Tonkawas:
    Henry W. Karnes and, 205
    John H. Moore and, 58, 59, 220
Townsend, Gideon, 237–238

Townsend, Moses, 237, 241
Townsend, Sabrina, 59
Townsend, Stephen, 236–237
    command of, 79
Townsend, William S., 211, 212, 214–215, 237
Travis, William B., 24, 175
    as Burnam's Ferry visitor, 33
    as cavalry officer, 61
    Franklin J. Starr as law partner of, 52
    Rawson Alley and, 101
    Robert Moseley and, 89
Trezevant, James P., 181, 255:
    pictured, 182
Trinity River, 193
    Beeson family at, 233
    Dewees family at, 239
Tumlinson, Elizabeth, 88–89
Tumlinson, John J., 85–86, 88–89
Tumlinson, John J., Jr., 90
Turner, Amasa, 155
    command of, 155–156, 172
Twin Sisters (cannons), 244

U

Urrea, José de, 160, 181, 199
    at Battle of Coleto Creek (1836), 144, 175, 180
    cavalry of, 177, 178
    Colorado River arrival of, 178
    Georgia Battalion surrenders to, 180
    on Gulf Coast, xi, 102, 104, 129, 166, 188
    ordered to reinforce Antonio López de Santa Anna, 188
    prisoner exchange and, 204
    reputation of, 103
    Vicente Filisola replaced by, 204

V

Vásquez, Ráfael:
    raid against San Antonio (1842) led by, 224–225, 250
Velasco, Texas:
    Georgia Battalion at, 176–177
    John A. Wharton commands at, 139, 198
    John Forbes dispatched to, 153, 155, 166
    John Sharp ordered to, 133–134, 164
    Sam Houston orders artillery and munitions from, 15, 133–134, 166, 198
    William T. Austin dispatched to, 198
Velasco, Treaties of (1836), 204
Velasco Blues, 155–156, 172
Victoria, Texas:
    Comanche attack against (1840), 222
    James W. Fannin ordered to fall back to, 8
    José de Urrea ordered to, 102
    Mexican occupation of, 129
    Peter Kerr in, 145
    Stephen G. Hardaway at, 181
    William Ward expedition toward, 178, 180

W

Wacos:
    Beeson family and, 86
    John Tumlinson killed by, 88
Wadsworth, William A. O.:
    command of, 181
Wallace, Joseph W. E., 149
    in Battle of Gonzales (1835), 59–60, 80, 82
    on Bostick home move, 82–83
    store of, 80, 82
Ware, William:
    command of, 65, 76

War of 1812:
: Jesse Burnam in, 31
: Wyly Martin in, 76

Washington Guards, 61

Washington-on-the-Brazos, Texas:
: abandonment of, 124, 127–128
: recruits from, 139
: Sam Houston's call to arms at, 25
: Sam Houston's route to Gonzales from, 23–24

Weimar, Texas, 26–27

Wharton, John A., 15, 134, 139, 153, 166, 198

White, B. J., 129

Wilbarger and La Bahía Road, 24

Williams, Samuel May, 174

Williamson, Robert M. ("Three-legged Willie"), 58, 247
: at Battle of Gonzales (1835), 59–60
: as Washington Guards officer, 61

Wilson, Jim, 171–172

Wilson, William, 207, 208

Winfield, Edward, 130

Wolfpen Creek, 116, 169

Woll, Adrián, 102, 110
: pictured, 226
: raid against San Antonio (1842), 225–229, 250
: reconnaissance by, 137
: at Atascosito Crossing, 189

Wood, William, 82

Woods, Zadock, 56, 90

Wright, Felix, 98

Wright, James, 82

Z

Zuber, William P., 52–54
: on civilian refugees, 53
: on Colorado River as battle location, 134
: on guard duty, 53–54
: on John Crier's homestead being destroyed, 64
: on March 19 encampment location, 65
: on Mexican army's position, 107
: on Moore's Fort, 56, 58
: recruitment of, 79
: on Sam Houston, 172, 174
: on Texian army's retreat from Colorado River, 153
: on transit from Moore's Fort to Burnam's Ferry, 41

Zumwalt, Caroline, 211